FRESHWATER AQUARIUM MODELS

Recipes for Creating Beautiful Aquariums That Thrive

JOHN TULLOCK

D1088298

BICENTENNIAL
1807
WILEY
2007
BICENTENNIAL

Wiley Publishing, Inc.

Howell Book House
Published by Wiley Publishing, Inc., Hoboken, New Jersey

For general information on our other products and services or to obtain technical support please contact our Customer Care Department within the U.S. at (800) 762-2974, outside the U.S. at (317) 572-3993 or fax (317) 572-4002.

Wiley also publishes its books in a variety of electronic formats. Some content that appears in print may not be available in electronic books. For more information about Wiley products, please visit our web site at www.wiley.com.

Library of Congress Cataloging-in-Publication Data:
Tullock, John H., 1951–
Freshwater aquarium models: recipes for creating beautiful aquariums that thrive / John Tullock; [photography: Aaron Norman]
      p. cm.
    Includes bibliographical references and index.
    ISBN-13: 978-0-470-04425-4 (pbk.: alk. paper)
    ISBN-10: 0-470-04425-X (alk. paper)
    1. Aquariums. 2. Aquarium fishes. 3. Aquarium plants. I. Title.
    SF457.3.T86 2007
    639.34—dc22

                                                                2006025098
                                                                CIP

Printed in the United States of America

10   9   8   7   6   5   4   3   2   1

Book design by Elizabeth Brooks
Cover design by José Almaguer
Book production by Wiley Publishing, Inc. Composition Services

TABLE OF CONTENTS

PART I:
Aquarium Basics

PART II:
Aquarium Mechanics

PART III:
Freshwater Aquarium Model Designs

PART IV:
The Appendixes

AQUARIUM BASICS

THE ALLURE OF AQUARIUMS

After forty years and hundreds of individual tanks, I am not bored with aquarium keeping. I get the same thrill from opening the plastic bag and releasing a colorful fish into my tank as I did when I was a teenager. I will never be able to say I've kept them all, of course, even if I live to be a hundred. Thousands of species of tropical fish have been discovered, and countless others swim anonymously in waters not yet explored. The world's smallest fish, for example, was discovered in 2005 in a peat bog in Sumatra. *Paedocypris progenetica*, about the size of a fingernail clipping when fully mature, ranks not only as the tiniest fish, but also as the tiniest vertebrate of any sort. Researchers have discovered hundreds of other new species in Sumatra's bogs. Though not as tiny as *Paedocypris progenetica*, they all generally remain under six inches in length. "Any of them might be perfect for an aquarium!" I found myself thinking as I listened to the story on NPR. So the fun continues. Aquarium keeping can truly provide a lifetime of enjoyment.

In fact, research has demonstrated that there are many benefits to owning an aquarium.

- Almost everyone agrees that watching fish lowers stress.

- One study found that patients whose dentists had aquariums in their waiting rooms were less anxious about their impending treatments than patients with little more to look at than old magazines.

- Watching the movements of fish helps infants learn to focus on objects and strengthens their eye muscles, according to another study.

- Still another investigation found that patients are more likely to follow the doctor's orders later if they have the opportunity for a little fish watching in the waiting room.

- People say that owning an aquarium gives them a much needed sense of control in an often chaotic world.

Here is a complete miniature ecosystem with each element in harmony, enclosed in glass and obediently following rules laid down eons ago, all of it subject to the whims and desires of its owner. Seldom do we enjoy such absolute power in our daily experience.

However, the overwhelming majority of aquarium owners simply find themselves attracted to the natural beauty of the underwater scene. The aquarium in this context becomes a living work of art, complementing the interior décor of the home. It makes a statement about the owner's lifestyle, forges a connection to nature that is often absent from urban life and, sometimes, boasts of success. Residences these days may be graced by installations of a size and level of sophistication that in years past was found only in museums and public aquariums. One company that specializes in custom aquariums recently introduced a "basic" system at around $15,000. I once visited the office of a business in Connecticut that was spending $20,000 a month just to *maintain* several very large aquariums.

Not all of us are positioned to invest thousands for professional installation and maintenance of an aquarium, of course. The majority of tank owners are do-it-yourselfers. Of course, doing it all on your own means you have to devote the time to researching how to create an aquarium habitat as well as devote the time to maintaining the aquarium. But if you check the classified ads in your local supermarket shopper, chances are, you'll find an aquarium for sale, possibly several.

Why do so many people invest the considerable time and expense to set up an aquarium, only to abandon it after a few months? Often, aquariums merely succumb to the exigencies of ordinary life. A new job requires a move, and the tank comes down. It languishes in the garage because no one ever gets around to setting it up again. Undoubtedly, some would-be aquarists quit simply because the aquarium did not meet their original expectations. Maybe they wanted to relax beside tropical waters teeming with colorful life, and could not afford a trip to Cozumel. Maybe in a stressful world they sought calm and quiet, watching the fish swim to and fro. Maybe they wanted to feel closer to nature. For whatever reason, though, the aquarium failed to deliver.

Most aquarium owners are not "hobbyists." Aquarium hobbyists devote much time to the pursuit of their passion:

- They read aquarium magazines, buy books about fish and aquariums, and make the rounds of the local fish shops about once a month.
- They often hold strong opinions about a certain species or technique.
- Many specialize in one or a few types of fish.
- Frequently they plan to breed fish and rear the offspring.
- Most of them know the pH requirements of their favorite aquarium fish like they know the names of their kids.

The majority of aquarium tanks sitting in America's cozy family rooms belong to people who are not pursuing a passion, eager to understand every aspect of the operation of their aquarium, the needs of its inhabitants, and the options for enhancing the experience. Their interest in owning an aquarium stems from the simple desire to incorporate the color, movement, and "naturalness" of tropical fish and plants into their everyday lives.

The basic premise of this book is that the aquarium's primary function is decorative, as opposed to, say, breeding a certain species of fish. So, if you are an aquarium do-it-yourselfer, or are thinking about becoming one, then this book is for you. Following my recommendations will improve your chances of having a successful aquarium that will enhance the appearance of your home and provide years of relaxation and entertainment, without the necessity of becoming an expert in the chemistry of water or the biology of tropical fish.

When I owned a retail aquarium store, one of the things I did to improve my customers' chances of success was to offer them free classes. One Tuesday evening each month I'd give a presentation on some aspect of water chemistry, or a particular family of fishes, or the pros and cons of different types of filters. After these sessions, we poured free coffee and chatted with whomever wanted to talk about fish. People often told me they appreciated the information, but could I please just tell them what fish they should keep? It took quite a while for the realization to dawn on me that the majority of casual aquarists were not really interested in becoming what I thought of as a hobbyist. They were not "fish nuts" like me; they saw an aquarium not as a preoccupation for their weekends, but rather more as art, something to enhance the look and feel of their personal space. And they wanted it plug and play. Never mind all the water chemistry, just tell me what to do and how often to do it. As I helped more and more people design aquariums that looked good and were easy to maintain, I learned what works and what doesn't. Much of that experience has been incorporated here.

Only one chapter covers the basic skills for setting up and maintaining a home aquarium. I cover all the important bases without getting bogged down in too much biology and chemistry. Chapter 2 explains the essential elements of good aquarium design. The next chapter follows up with practical techniques for creating a natural-appearing scene within the aquarium's limited space. The following chapter, "Nuts and Bolts," will interest anyone thinking of a built-in aquarium. Suggestions for designing for ease of maintenance will also interest those planning free-standing installations. And everyone should pay attention to the information about safety found in this chapter.

I devote the remainder of the book to recipes for aquariums of all sizes, depicting a variety of particular biotopes. A *biotope* is a small geographic area, such as part of a stream, with characteristic kinds of life, in this case fish and aquatic plants. Commercial hatcheries produce vast numbers of aquarium fish. Although these fish spend their entire lives in captivity, they nevertheless thrive best in conditions similar to those found in their native biotope. Each model design, therefore, relies on fish, plants, and other elements from one biotope. One model design for a small tank, for example, combines Southeast Asian *Rasbora* species with the *Cryptocoryne* plants also found there. Is your heart set on a particular fish? You should be able to place it in its perfect habitat by using the cross reference I provide in the back of the book.

While most of the advice and suggestions are directed at the casual aquarium owner, seasoned hobbyists will find suggestions for new horizons to explore. I encourage you to improve upon my ideas with insights of your own.

Whether you are pursuing a passion or simply decorating the den, aquarium keeping should above all be a pleasure, not a chore. Choose a model that fits your space and your budget. Plan carefully. Understand what your miniature biotope needs to thrive, and be sure you can provide for those needs. You will have an aquarium you'll show with pride to family and friends. Most importantly, you will have an aquarium you can watch with pleasure every day as the lives of its inhabitants are played out in color and movement.

Aquarists with as much experience as I will undoubtedly find much to criticize about the possible aquariums I have outlined here. I welcome those critiques and suggestions for improvement. The perfect tank has yet to be devised. All the ideas I have shared are ones that I have either put to use myself, or thought about in detail at some point during my long love affair with aquariums. Even so, no design on paper will ever be precisely expressed in the real world. Often when I am arranging an aquascape, the shape of a rock or piece of wood provides inspiration, and the completed aquarium looks very different from the one I had sketched on graph paper. Frequently, the need for a bit of field engineering arises, when the driftwood that looked so perfect in the shop needs to be trimmed, or when sand must be added to accommodate an unexpectedly large mass of plant roots. For me, these little challenges provide part of the enjoyment of the hobby. I like tinkering with things. I like letting the aquascape evolve naturally from the materials available to me at the time. If none of this sounds like fun, you can always have the dealer install the aquarium and aquascape it for you. Many will do this for a reasonable fee. I have tried to give instructions that will help with visualizing the final look of the tank. The visualization process is the key. If you can see it in your mind's eye, you can shape the aquascape toward that vision.

As you come up with aquascapes of your own, please keep in mind my Five Rules for a Successful Aquarium:

1. Keep it simple.
2. Keep it roomy.
3. Keep it stable.
4. Keep it clean.
5. Keep it natural.

I have repeated this advice many times for many audiences. Adhering to these five basic principles nearly guarantees your success with any sort of aquarium.

The aquarium model designs in this book range from the funky to the majestic. You could spin endless variations on each of the themes I have presented in these chapters. I hope you will look at all the model designs as mere guidelines from which you will develop your own specific plans.

I wish for you the most beautiful aquarium in the world, an aquarium you, not I, dream up.

CHAPTER 1

CARING FOR AN AQUARIUM

Caring for an aquarium need not be a terrible chore, and anyone can learn how an aquarium works. Even if you consider yourself a rank amateur, you should have a good grasp of the basics by the end of this chapter. I'll cover basic aquarist skills you will need to develop in order to take proper care of your tank.

Water

Water is the most obvious component of any aquarium system. Aquarists of long experience sometimes make much ado about the chemistry of their aquarium water. Its degree of acidity or lack thereof, the concentration of dissolved minerals, the presence of disinfecting agents in municipal supplies, any or all of these can become the stuff of vigorous debate. From a practical standpoint, however, you will need to make do with whatever comes out of your tap unless you are prepared for a major effort. Commercial preparations for altering the two important water parameters, pH and hardness, abound, but using them to bring tap water in line with desired aquarium conditions becomes a never-ending proposition. Finding out the present condition of your tap water and choosing an aquarium habitat accordingly makes more sense. For example, suppose your water is hard and slightly alkaline. It will be great, as is, for the livebearing fishes of Central America such as swordtails and platies (*Xiphophorus* sp.). On the other hand, discus require soft, acidic water, and may not do as well for you unless you alter the tap water accordingly. Determining your water conditions involves no more than a phone call or a check of your utility company's Web site. Simply search the site or call and ask for information regarding the pH and hardness. With luck, your water will already test within a range that is acceptable to most common tropical fish species, that is, at or just above or below neutral in pH (6.5–7.5) and moderately hard (160–220 ppm).

Water Hardness

Throughout this book, water hardness preferences for fish and plant species will be given in parts per million of calcium carbonate (ppm $CaCO_3$), because many utility companies use this unit of measure. Various other units will be found in the aquarium literature, in particular, German degrees of hardness (dKH, dGH). Knowing the relationships among the commonly given units permits simple conversion among them.

50 ppm $CaCO_3$ is the same amount of hardness as:

2.8 dKH when hardness is expressed as German degrees, dGH, or KH;

2.92 grains per gallon (gr/gal $CaCO_3$) if this somewhat outdated English unit is used;

1 milliequivalent per liter (meq/L) when hardness is expressed as *alkalinity*.

No standard applies to general descriptive terms for water hardness often given in aquarium books. Here is my interpretation:

very soft means water with <75 ppm $CaCO_3$

soft means water with 80–150 ppm $CaCO_3$

moderately hard means water with 160–220 ppm $CaCO_3$

hard means water with 230–360 ppm $CaCO_3$

very hard means water with >360 ppm $CaCO_3$

Your local dealer may do nothing to alter tap water conditions, as this represents an ongoing operating expense. A quick check of the fish that look particularly vibrant in the dealer's tanks may provide clues to choices that will thrive in your local water. If your dealer does make the effort to adjust tap water conditions to meet the demands of certain species, ask for advice on how to do this most cost effectively at home.

The most common and popular tropical fish tolerate a range of water conditions. No doubt, this is one reason for their popularity. Some species, unfortunately, do not adapt so readily to captivity unless their demands for a particular kind of water are met. When this is the case, I include specific recommendations for water conditions. If you choose to create one of these habitats, be prepared to supply sufficient water of the appropriate kind, which may mean altering your tap water.

Altering water to suit tropical fish can be done at home, though the effort requires regular repetition. For example, if you need softer water, you can simply dilute tap water appropriately with distilled water from the grocery store. To reduce the hardness from 200 ppm to 100 ppm, you would mix equal parts of tap water and distilled water. If you have need for more than a few gallons of purified water at a time, you may find it more convenient to install a deionization tank or reverse osmosis unit. Removing something from water is always harder than adding something to it, hence the need to install special equipment to reduce hardness. Lowering the hardness of significant quantities of water imposes a considerable additional expense. For example, a reverse osmosis unit requires regular maintenance and replacement of filter media. Most units waste several gallons of water for each gallon of product. These costs add up.

Increasing the hardness, on the other hand, is easy. Simply add a measured quantity of the appropriate mineral salts. Commercial products abound for this purpose. Many contain common household chemicals, such as baking soda or Epsom salt. The cost per gallon of water treated is small, since these chemicals are cheap. Among aquarium fish, African cichlids in particular benefit from water treated to increase its hardness. No tap water is likely to be as hard and alkaline as these fish prefer. Similarly, fish from estuarine habitats, where seawater mixes with fresh water, do best with added salt. In this case, synthetic seawater mix, sold dry in plastic bags, serves the purpose well. Aquarium stores that stock saltwater fish will have one or more brands on hand. Additions of commercial hardness increasers or seawater mix will typically raise the pH to an alkaline (8.0–8.3) range. Therefore, you seldom need a second additive for pH maintenance.

Lowering the pH can be tricky. Because hard water may be difficult to adjust, beginning with soft water gives the best results. Distilled water or water from a deionization tank or reverse osmosis unit should have a pH close to neutral (7.0). To provide the slightly acidic (6.5) to strongly acidic (5.0) water that some fish insist upon necessitates adding acid. For this purpose, sodium phosphate often appears in a little bottle on the shelves of aquarium shops. Adjusting the pH by adding acid in chemical form is easily overdone, however, because a little of the chemical goes a long way. The added sodium probably does not do plants or fish much good, either, unless they come from an estuarine environment. A more natural method of pH reduction involves passing the water through a small amount of horticultural peat, or introducing commercial additives derived from peat. Organic acids leached from the peat reduce the pH gradually over a period of weeks. The mixture of organic compounds from the peat also confers a buffering effect. (*Buffering* refers to the ability of the aquarium to remain stable with regard to pH over a long period of time.) With time and regular maintenance, under peat filtration the aquarium water remains stable at the target range of pH ± 6.0. Some of the most exquisite small species require such soft, peaty water. Pencilfish (characins in the genera *Nannobrycon* and *Nannostomus*) provide but one example. I consider the brownish color imparted by the peat, giving the water the appearance of weak tea, a desirable, natural effect. If you insist on diamond-clear water, you may want to avoid species demanding soft, acidic water. You can also try removing the color by passing the water over activated carbon. This may thwart your pH control efforts, however, and will require experimentation with different brands of carbon. Then there is the matter of replacing the carbon regularly. I say stick with the natural look.

The necessity for chlorine removal, usually accomplished by adding a small amount of a product containing sodium thiosulfate, is (gasp!) questionable. The use of dechlorinator in aquarium water strikes me as somewhat like carving pumpkins for Halloween. We do it because of tradition, not because it serves any real purpose. Changing 50 percent of the water in my outdoor pond, for example, using replacement water straight from the garden hose and without any dechlorinator added, has never harmed my goldfish. Admittedly, goldfish durability is the stuff of legend, but many aquarium books would have you thinking fish will be dying left and right from the least whiff of chlorine. Were I betting, my money would lie with the following proposition: More fish die from lack of water changes than failure to use dechlorinator when a water change is finally carried out. I seldom use dechlorinator. If you feel more comfortable doing so, go ahead.

The bottom line for water quality: use what you have. Choose species of fish and plants that are naturally adapted to the water conditions found at the sink. Otherwise, prepare to invest time and money to correct those conditions for the needs of your fish. My personal preference is to select the tank's inhabitants with great care, putting the effort into designing a beautiful, natural aquarium that will not require more maintenance than I can comfortably handle.

Physical and Chemical Cycles

Every aquarium book devotes several pages to a discussion of the important physical and chemical cycles that govern the health of the closed aquarium system. All of this discussion can be summarized in four sentences:

- Without a biological filter, an aquarium requires water changes so frequently as to be impractical.
- Life in an aquarium cannot exist without exchange of oxygen and carbon dioxide at the surface.
- A proper initial design and regular maintenance takes care of both these requirements.
- The number of fish an aquarium can adequately support depends on factors beyond basic life support.

Biological Filtration

Fish excrete their wastes directly into the water. Under natural conditions fish population density, considering the total volume of water in a stream or lake, is much lower than that of even the largest aquarium. Dilution, therefore, immediately counters fish waste pollution in natural waters. Additionally, in a short time natural processes degrade the wastes into simple compounds that can be taken up by plants, or utilized in some other ecological process.

When we establish an aquarium system we harness these same natural processes to keep the water sufficiently unpolluted to promote the survival of our fish display. The totality of these processes as they occur in an aquarium is *biological filtration*. Biological filtration is the detoxification of wastes by beneficial bacteria known as *nitrifiers* or nitrifying bacteria. Coating every available surface that lies in contact with oxygenated water, these organisms chemically convert ammonia (the primary component of fish waste) into nitrate (a relatively harmless compound taken up by plants). Biological filtration, or *biofiltration*, readily develops in the aquarium. All that is required is an ammonia source (fish) and the right kinds of bacteria. The latter are automatically transferred along with fish or plants or any other item taken from natural waters or from a previously established aquarium (the dealer's inventory system, for example). Within a month, nitrifying bacteria will have colonized the aquarium system sufficiently to process a moderate amount of waste. This gradual development of biofiltration capacity prompts the widely offered recommendation always to stock the aquarium slowly, over a period of several months. Within six months to a year, the population of beneficial nitrifying bacteria will have matured completely and biofiltration will be adequate to permit fish to be stocked at full capacity indefinitely.

Though biofiltration is a totally natural process, most aquariums are outfitted with some kind of filtration system. If nothing else, a recirculating pump, such as the one in my outdoor pond, oxygenates the water and creates a modest current that causes debris to collect near the pump intake where it may be easily removed. Most filtration equipment is considerably more elaborate. Designed to maximize biofiltration capacity, aquarium filtration equipment may employ a variety of techniques to increase the surface area available for colonization by nitrifiers. The bacteria refuse to carry out the desired chemical transformations when they float freely; they need to be stuck to a solid surface. Thus we have rotating bio-wheel devices, wet-dry systems, and fluidized bed technology. All these filtration methods provide extremely efficient biofiltration, converting all the ammonia generated within the tank to nitrate in a short period of time. Aquarium system design sometimes focuses on biofiltration to the exclusion of other important factors, because the aquarist is often seen as trying to squeeze the maximum number of fish into the minimum number of gallons. Although you can buy a highly efficient filter system and have the tank teeming with fish, doing it that way invites disaster, nearly guarantees it, eventually, in fact, because you will have exceeded what I like to call the *true* carrying capacity of the system.

Carrying Capacity

We can debate all day about carrying capacity; that is, how many fish of what size a particular aquarium can support. If by *support* we simply mean "adequately detoxify the ammonia waste produced" we can bump up the number of fish to high population densities indeed. Consider how many fish might be packed into a dealer's inventory system, for a case in point. Fifty fish in a twenty-gallon tank would not be considered unusual. For the home aquarium display, on the other hand, biofiltration is not the whole story. We must think about the long-term success of an aquarium whose residents will be there for the rest of their lives. Fish and plants need what I like to call *ecological space*. A given species may need swimming room, or a minimum number of companions of its species, or a certain level of water movement, to really thrive. The ability of the aquarium to provide for these needs as well as waste removal is a measure of the true carrying capacity. Taking into account not only waste removal, but also the need for ample oxygen, swimming room, and benign social interactions, ecological space must be allotted in the process of designing the aquarium. Care must be taken not to exceed the true carrying capacity of the system. One test of carrying capacity being met appropriately has to do with fish spawning in a community tank.

For how many kinds of fish do you see in the aquarium literature advice to spawn them in a tank set up especially for the purpose? The answer is "most of them." Yet, fish successfully spawn in the wild, often when surrounded by numerous individuals of other species. Recently, I visited a public aquarium and observed *Cichlasoma nicaraguense* and *Cichlasoma labiatum* both tending healthy, free-swimming broods of young in a giant community tank. In the home aquarium, either of these would be considered far too aggressive to be housed with other species. Provided with a volume of space that roughly corresponds to the size of a natural territory, however, the fish remain preoccupied with their young and only show aggression when a tank mate strays too close. I have observed this same phenomenon in Everglades National Park. All along the Mahogany Hummock trail through the park, introduced cichlids, especially the Oscar, *Astronotus ocellatus*, inhabit the sluggish, blackwater slough traversed by the trail. When spawning, each fish hollows out a depression in the sandy bottom, and drives away anything approaching within about a meter of this spot. So do the math. If the aquarium tank provides less than a circular territory of about a meter in radius, an Oscar large enough to raise a family will sooner or later decide that the entire space should be rid of potential competitors. A smaller tank will not provide enough true carrying capacity for one Oscar and several other fish to live peaceably together indefinitely. On the other hand, even a large Oscar will survive (though likely not exhibit any inclination to breed) in a thirty-gallon tank with a suitably efficient biological filter.

Gas Exchange

Other physiochemical factors affect the carrying capacity of an aquarium. Gas exchange is crucial. The water must continuously contain sufficient oxygen for the fish to breathe (and for both fish and plants at night) and must be continuously rid of carbon dioxide. While plants absorb carbon dioxide during daylight periods, at night this may not be enough to prevent the accumulation of CO_2. Carbon dioxide dissolves in water to produce carbonic acid, which drives down the pH and can inhibit critical respiratory processes in the fish. In sufficient concentration, CO_2 is lethal. Merely agitating the water at the surface facilitates most, if not all, needed gas exchange. Surface agitation can be provided by a simple airstone bubbling in the tank. All filtration systems require water movement, and this usually creates plenty of surface action. Problems sometimes do occur when accumulated debris clogs the filter and causes it to slow down, and the resulting change in flow rate goes unnoticed. However, the most common reason for poor gas exchange is too little surface area for the volume of water in the tank. A tall, narrow tank has considerably less surface area per gallon than a shallow, broad one. Consider the following comparison between two commercially available sizes of tanks:

> ## Filter Numbers
>
> Filter throughput should be three to five times the total tank capacity per hour. For example, a 100-gallon tank needs 300–500 gallons per hour of turnover. Pumps capable of delivering such flow rates will necessarily create water currents. The higher turnover rate might be chosen for a riverine habitat, while the lower flow rate would be more appropriate for a lake-inspired habitat design.

A fifty-gallon "breeder" tank (36 x 18 x 18 in.) has 4.5 square feet of surface, or a ratio of 0.09 square feet per gallon. A seventy-seven-gallon "show" tank (48 x 12 x 24) has only 4.0 square feet of surface, or 0.05 square feet per gallon. The ratio of surface area to water volume is roughly half that of the fifty-gallon tank. The surface to volume ratio determines how quickly oxygen can be replenished from the atmosphere as it is depleted from the water by fish. The difference can be overcome only by using a pump to circulate water within the aquarium, bringing low-oxygen water from the bottom to the surface and carrying oxygenated water in the opposite direction. Much more turnover will be required to maintain the oxygen content of the water in the larger tank, as compared to the smaller one.

Gas exchange must be taken into account in developing an aquarium design. A tall tank may be dramatic in appearance, but it needs to be correspondingly broad (most aquarium shop owners would say "deep") to provide adequate surface area. One company advertises a "picture" aquarium that hangs on the wall. Such tanks are necessarily quite slender in profile, and offer minimal surface area per gallon. This creates sufficient husbandry challenges that the company offers a list of recommended species that are hardy enough to cope with the suboptimal environment the aquarium provides.

Oxygen enters the aquarium, and carbon dioxide escapes it, via the water surface, but water must also circulate within the tank so that oxygen remains constantly available to the fish. Similarly, carbon dioxide must not accumulate. Plants can account for significant oxygen production during the daylight hours, during which time they also remove carbon dioxide. At night, surface exchange must be relied upon. Creating water movement is a secondary benefit of all available filter designs. If the turnover rate meets the standards suggested above, water movement should facilitate adequate gas exchange.

Water Changes

Regardless of its design, every aquarium needs regular partial water changes. I suggest removing 10 percent of the water weekly and replacing it with freshly drawn water. Depending upon your schedule, you might elect to change 20 percent every two weeks or 40 percent monthly, but the aquarium will look better and the fish will appear more vibrant with more frequent, smaller changes.

Lighting

Aquarium lighting should show off the underwater scene to its best advantage and provide energy for photosynthesis by aquatic plants. If the design relies solely on plastic plants, a single fluorescent lamp positioned over the tank may be enough unless the tank is quite deep. Even in an all-plastic ecosystem, more light will always make the tank appear inviting, and will foster the growth of filamentous algae upon which many fish feed. Sometimes, unconventional lighting (by which I mean anything in addition to, or other than, the standard fluorescent strip across the top of the tank) can be used to produce striking effects. For example, a spotlight shining in can direct the eye toward a particular underwater feature, in much the same way that stage lighting directs the attention of the audience.

On the other hand, if you're using aquatic plants, you may need to think more about your lighting choices. Aquatic plants reach their greatest abundance and diversity in clear, shallow waters, such as the spring runs for which west-central Florida is famous. Under such conditions, sunlight penetrates well. Even under the most favorable circumstances, however, the amount of available light under water will only be a fraction of that shining on the surface. Reflection, absorption with increasing depth, and shading by vegetation all limit light availability in natural bodies of water. Even so, enough light for photosynthesis can reach the bottom to support dense plant growth, because sunlight is quite intense. Few home aquariums rely on sunlight as the main light source and most make do with artificial lighting. Choosing an artificial lighting system for a particular aquarium design requires knowledge of the available types of lighting equipment and their respective capabilities. (Check out Appendix B for more information.)

Several factors conspire to limit the efficiency of aquarium lighting. For example, the reflector housing the lamps cannot be 100 percent perfect, and therefore not

> ## Knowing Light Lingo
>
> The amount of light energy emanating from a source is measured in units known as *lumens*. The light intensity, or irradiance, over a given area is measured in *lux* or lumens per square meter. Over a cornfield in Iowa in the middle of summer, the midday sun may provide irradiance of 100,000 lux or more. You'll be lucky to find an aquarium lighting system that can deliver 10 percent of this amount to the plants in the tank underneath it.

all light emitted will reach the water surface. Reflection from the water surface itself reduces light penetration, too. Further, as the tank becomes taller, the amount of light reaching the bottom decreases dramatically due to the Inverse Square Law of optics. Light intensity decreases in proportion to the square of the distance between the source and the object illuminated. In practical terms, this means the same light fixture over a tank 12 inches in height will deliver only one-fourth as much light to the bottom if the height of the tank is increased to 24 inches. Double the distance and illumination decreases fourfold. Further, the greater height of the water column means more absorption by the water itself. This again reduces the effective light intensity.

The implications for aquarium lighting design are straightforward. For aquariums up to about twelve inches in height two fluorescent lamps of the maximum length that can be accommodated across the length of the tank should be used. For deeper tanks up to four feet long, use four fluorescent lamps of the maximum possible length. For larger tanks, use one to several metal halide lamps to provide extremely bright light. Although I suggest here choosing lamps by length, in actual practice it is the wattage that matters. The higher the wattage, the brighter the lamp. For example, a lamp four feet long consumes 40 watts of electricity and produces about 3,000 lumens. Data on the lumen output of various types of lamps can be found on lighting manufacturers' Web sites. Appendix B provides lighting recommendations for all the standard types of aquarium tanks. The recommended lighting should allow you to grow a handsome underwater garden in every aquarium you design.

I have included special lighting recommendations for some of the model designs given later in the book.

The Needs of Aquarium Plants

You cannot grow aquarium plants without sufficient light, but unless the water conditions are also correct, you will end up growing only algae, even if you have the best lighting system on the market. Besides light, aquatic plants need water of appropriate pH and hardness levels, sufficient fertilizer for growth, and the absence of harmful organisms. Plants should therefore be chosen with the same care as fish.

Light Requirements

To get an idea of the lighting needs of typical aquarium plants, consider where they grow in natural bodies of water. Common sense suggests that those nearest the surface need the most light, and those capable of growing in deep water need the least amount. As is also the case in the wild, flowering plants need relatively more light than those that do not flower. Thus, aquatic ferns and mosses tolerate more shade than, say, Amazon sword plants.

Floating aquatic plants, such as water lettuce (*Pistia*), need 2,000 lux or more to thrive. Water lilies, whose photosynthetic leaves float even though the roots anchor in the mud several feet below, need about 10,000 lux to bloom. Plants that grow on the bottom, such as many cryptocorynes, need around 300 lux. Plants that grow upright though seldom reaching the surface do best with about 1,500 lux. The majority of aquarium plants will fall into this middle category. When in doubt, provide more light rather than less.

The length of the day is an important factor in regulating the growth of all plants, and aquatic species are no exception. Tropical and subtropical types, the most commonly grown aquarium plants, usually do best with 12 to 14 hours of light daily. Use a timer to control the lighting system and provide a consistent day-night cycle.

Water Chemistry

As with fish, plants have specific needs regarding water chemistry. For example, hard water has less available carbon dioxide for plant growth, because in hard water the formation of insoluble carbonates is chemically favored over the formation of carbonic acid. Plants adapted to soft, acidic water fare poorly in hard, alkaline conditions because they are starved for carbon dioxide. Plants adapted to hard, alkaline water may suffer from nutrient imbalances if placed in water that is too soft and acidic. Specific recommendations are given for each plant species mentioned in this book.

Fertilizer

Gardeners know plants need feeding from time to time. Aquatic plants also require fertilization, but should be fed sparingly. In the closed system of an aquarium too much fertilizer can be worse than none at all. Overfertilization can result in yellowing of the leaves, and may also contribute to excessive growths of algae. Fish wastes provide plenty of nutrients, so artificial fertilization may be needed only while the plants are becoming established. During the early stages of the aquarium's development, while the fish population remains low, the addition of fertilizer allows plants to overcome the stress associated with transplanting, and to develop strong roots and lush foliage. Later, when all the fish have been added, fertilization may be reduced or eliminated altogether.

Although fish wastes may provide basic nutrition, you will probably need to add an iron supplement to your planted aquarium after each water change. Iron is essential to prevent yellowing in the leaves of aquarium plants, a condition known as *chlorosis*. Yellow leaves with green veins are a sure indication that the water is deficient in iron. Iron participates in the formation of chlorophyll, without which plants cannot synthesize sufficient carbohydrates for growth. While natural waters may contain as much as one milligram per liter (1.0 mg/L) of iron, experience has shown that aquarium plants will thrive with about half this much (0.05 mg/L). Too much iron, by the way, interferes with the plant's metabolism, so it is best to monitor the level with a test kit. Replenish iron only as needed. Most shops that stock aquatic plants also stock iron test kits and iron supplements.

The chemical form of the iron makes a difference to plants. Iron can exist in either the *ferrous* or *ferric* form. Plants need ferrous iron, but in water the ferric form is chemically favored. Aquarium iron supplements get around this problem by supplying iron in "chelated" form, to help assure than the amount dosed is actually available for plant nutrition. Ethylenediaminetetraacetate, or EDTA for short (thank goodness!), will likely be listed as an ingredient on any brand of chelated iron supplement. If the tap water contains sufficient iron, it can be made available to plants by the addition of EDTA alone. An iron test kit will not distinguish between the two forms, and measures only the total amount of iron present. Therefore, before beginning a program of iron supplementation, test the water directly from the tap to establish a baseline. The baseline amount should be subtracted from the amount detected when the aquarium itself is tested. For example, if you determine that your tap water contains 1.0 mg/L of iron, you would need to add enough supplement to the tank to give a reading of 1.5 mg/L, in order to ensure that you have 0.5 mg/L of ferrous iron for the plants.

Additional elements are required in small amounts for proper plant growth. Most people know that plants need nitrogen, phosphorus, and potassium. These elements are the major components of all types of fertilizers, whether for houseplants or corn. In smaller amounts, plants also need manganese, magnesium, calcium, sulfur, and various other things. Aquatic plant fertilizers are commercially available that contain all the necessary plant nutrients. If you use these products, ignore the directions on the label, as it is impossible to predict nutrient needs. Tap water will contain varying levels of plant nutrients from one place to the next, so different aquariums will start out differently in this respect. Furthermore, any given aquarium will have a greater or lesser number of individual plants, with their needs varying by species, age, and other factors, and more or fewer fish producing varying levels of nutrient-rich wastes, than another tank sitting next to it. Because an excess of some nutrients can interfere with the uptake of others, problems can be compounded by uninformed fertilization. This can make the whole business seem too complex for most aquarists, who give up on plants altogether and resort to plastic. This need not be the case, and nearly every aquarium can successfully house a thriving garden with minimal effort. The only exceptions would be those in which plant-eating fish are exhibited, for obvious reasons.

Before adding fertilizer, make sure the plants really need it. First, the lighting should be adequate, conforming to the recommendations previously given. Without enough light, plants won't grow well no matter what other measures you take. Second, basic water conditions should be correct. Water that is too hard is often to blame for plants being reluctant to grow. Fix these kinds of problems before you try fertilization.

If you think your plants will benefit from fertilization, start with 25 percent of the dosage recommended on the label, be patient, and see if the plants look better after two weeks. Beneficial effects of fertilization on common aquarium plants would include an increase in the rate of growth. This will be noticeable after two weeks' time. Slower-growing plants may respond to fertilization by producing new leaves that are larger and more robust than was previously the case. I emphasize not to add more fertilizer on whim. If the plants don't respond on the first try, you can always slightly increase the amount of fertilizer given, but it will be difficult to undo the effects of an overdose.

Discuss with the dealer from whom you purchase plants the suitability of your local water supply. A dealer with thriving plant tanks will know which species do best in the water as it comes from the tap, and which ones will demand special care. That way, you will avoid having to do a lot of testing and experimentation to get the water chemistry right.

Another type of fertilization popular among aquatic plant enthusiasts is the addition of carbon dioxide. Carbon dioxide is arguably the most important plant nutrient, as it supplies the basic carbon skeleton for virtually all cellular activities and metabolic syntheses that the plant is capable of carrying out. Plants preferentially take up this important nutrient as the free gas. When the available supply is depleted, plants then typically turn to bicarbonate assimilation to meet their carbon needs. The harder the water, the more free carbon dioxide is needed to meet the plants' requirements. For this reason, plants accustomed to soft, acid water will benefit from carbon dioxide fertilization when grown in harder, more alkaline water, but may require no added carbon dioxide when grown in water optimized for their needs.

Aeration depletes carbon dioxide, and can reduce the level to zero in soft, acidic water. Thus, carbon dioxide fertilization may be needed for optimum plant growth even in water with low pH and hardness values if the fish population is so large, or if the ratio of surface area to volume is so low, that aeration is required for proper oxygenation. Various brands of carbon dioxide fertilization equipment are on the market. They all operate basically the same way: gas from a pressurized tank is injected into the aquarium water gradually under the control of a valve. Usually, the gas flows into a reaction chamber installed in the return pipe from the filtration system. Automated control is possible by using an electronic pH monitor. Deviations of the pH from a predetermined set point cause the CO_2 valve to open and close, in the same way a thermostat controls a heater. If you cannot afford the expense of an automated system, you must determine the valve setting by trial and error, using a device called a "bubble counter." The way it works is simple. The fewer bubbles flowing through the counter, the less CO_2 is flowing into the aquarium. You adjust the valve, wait a while and test the pH. By trial and error, you determine the proper setting to keep the aquarium at the target pH.

My friend, Sidney Arnold, was a great intuitive gardener. He seemed to know the needs of plants under his care without resorting to the library. His home was always filled with tropical foliage, and during warm weather his gardens overflowed with flowers, vegetables, and herbs. When I encouraged him to grow some aquatic plants, he gave it a try, but with disappointing results at first. Upon hearing my suggestions regarding the need for carbon dioxide in the hard, alkaline water in our city, he created his own CO_2 fertilization system. His first design consisted of a large jug in which a mixture of grape juice, sugar and cranberry juice were slowly fermented by the addition of yeast. Fermentation gives off carbon dioxide. This is what produces the bubbles in beer and champagne, for example. By running a tube from the neck of the jug to the aquarium filter box and controlling the flow of CO_2 with a valve Sidney was able to maintain a beautiful underwater garden. Early on, he fiddled with the valve until the growth and appearance of the plants were to his liking. Later, he did nothing other than replenish the fermentation jug. Of course, the contents of the jug, which were converted to wine after about two weeks, could be put to other uses.

Foods and Feeding

Aquarium shops stock dozens of kinds of fish food. Choosing the ones for your aquarium should pose little difficulty if you keep a few basic points in mind. Most common aquarium fish emphasize animal products in the diet, though they also consume small amounts of vegetable matter. Food items include protozoans, water fleas, insect larvae, adult insects, worms, snails, and other fish. The main source of vegetable matter in the aquatic diet is algae, although a few commonly kept species eat plants. Vegetarian fish include many kinds of catfish, many African cichlids, and some characins. All of these consume small amounts of animal matter incidentally while grazing on algal mats, and thus obtain a complete and balanced diet.

Commercial fish foods can consist either of a single ingredient, such as freeze-dried brine shrimp, or can be compounded of many ingredients, such as most flake foods. The trick to providing a balanced diet for your aquarium is to feed a wide variety of foods, alternating among two or three kinds during the course of a week. If your fish are primarily vegetarian, you will find products made just for them. Supplement these with small amounts of animal protein, such as frozen brine shrimp. Conversely, if your fish are primarily carnivorous, supplement their diet with small amounts of vegetable matter, such as products containing the algae *Spirulina*.

Fish food may be supplied as flakes or pellets, in freeze-dried form, or frozen. Many dealers also stock live foods, at least during part of the year.

Beginning aquarists usually give too much food. This results in an excessive load on the filtration system, since uneaten food simply decays on the bottom of the tank. The notion that fish will eat themselves to death is nonsense, but the pollution in an overfed aquarium can certainly wipe out its inhabitants.

A fish's stomach approximates the size of its eye. Obviously, it will not take a lot of food to fill it up. One rule of thumb is to feed only as much as will be consumed in ten minutes. You can determine the correct amount for your situation by trial and error. When in doubt, feed less. Fish can go for a surprisingly long time, weeks in many cases, without eating, so the likelihood of starving them is quite small in comparison to the likelihood of polluting the tank with uneaten food.

Most people find twice-daily feedings work best with their schedule. If your schedule permits, though, feed a community of smaller fish about five times daily with just a tiny pinch of food at each feeding. Feed about an hour after the lights come on in the morning, and again about an hour before darkness falls, and space out other feedings in between. You will need to modify this schedule if you have, for example, large predators like some South American cichlids. For these, the usual feeding regimen is three or four times a week. On the other hand, vegetarians feed almost continuously. These fish do best when there is plenty of algae growing in the tank to supplement the twice-daily feedings.

Be careful not to feed vegetarian fish a diet rich in animal protein, even though they may eat such food greedily. The vegetarian digestive system is not designed to cope with such a diet, and problems will develop. Similarly, fish that need plenty of animal protein will not get enough to eat if kept on a diet better suited to vegetarians.

In the natural environment, of course, fish eat mostly living foods. If you have access to live food, by all means use it, even occasionally. If there is a single secret to long-term success with a freshwater aquarium, the use of live food may be it. Some of these can be cultured at home, provided you have the time and inclination. Ideally, one would feed only live food, but this is usually impractical at home.

Live Foods from the Aquarium Store

Virtually all aquarium dealers stock "feeder goldfish." They sell by the dozen, and keep well for a week or so in a small, aerated container. Ten gallons of water will accommodate about one dozen. Instead of a glass tank, you can use a plastic trash can outfitted with an airstone. Goldfish do fine in cold water, and can be kept outside year round, as long as the water does not freeze. If you only purchase, let's say, a dozen a week, change the water between batches of goldfish. Unfortunately, only large, predatory tropical fish will consume them, so feeder goldfish are not for every aquarist.

You can also buy "feeder guppies" by the dozen at the aquarium shop. They will be eaten by any fish large enough to swallow them. Since they breed continuously, you can have many different sizes of guppies, from newborn to adult, available at all times to suit the varied sizes of fish in your aquarium. Fifty adult guppies will be fine in ten gallons of water, provided it is well aerated and the water is changed between batches of feeders. They can tolerate water temperatures down to about 50°F, and so can be kept in an unheated garage or out-building during the winter. In warm weather, they will thrive in a small outdoor pond or child's plastic wading pool located away from direct sunlight. To maintain a high population density, the aquarium or pond will require filtration or a weekly change of half the water.

Some shops stock live blackworms. These are small relatives of the earthworm that live in clean, cold water. Shops sell them in portions of a tablespoon or two. Purchase a shallow plastic food storage container at the grocery store. The ones designed to hold a sandwich are perfect. Place the blackworms in the container and cover them with no more than a quarter inch of tap water. Store in the refrigerator. Remove a few worms every day with a spoon and feed them to your fish. Rinse the worms and change their water each day. Simply pour off as much as you can and replenish with cold water straight from the tap. Repeat a couple of times until the water rinses off clear. Treated this way, the worms will keep a week or two easily. The hard part about keeping blackworms is negotiating with the other members of the household regarding the refrigerator space.

Live adult brine shrimp can be found on the menu at many good aquarium shops, particularly those that stock saltwater fish. They are usually sold in portions amounting to about two teaspoons when the shrimp are drained in a net. Because they don't keep too well without careful attention, it is best to purchase a small quantity and feed them to the tank within a couple of days. Use a net to separate the shrimp from the strong salt solution in which they grow. Rinse under the tap before adding to the aquarium. They will die within about an hour in fresh water. Therefore, make sure to feed only the amount likely to be eaten by your fish within a short time.

Earthworms not only show up in aquarium shops, but are also widely available as bait for sport fishermen. Usually sold in a container of potting soil, the worms should be cleaned before feeding them to aquarium fish. To clean them, transfer the earthworms to a container of long-fiber horticultural sphagnum moss, obtainable at garden centers. Thoroughly rinse the moss under the tap, then squeeze out most of the water so that it is barely damp. Since they cannot eat the sphagnum, after a couple of days the worms will have purged themselves of ingested soil and grit. Feed earthworms whole to large fish, or chop them into pieces for smaller ones.

Culturing Live Foods

Devoting a corner of the garage to food cultivation will pay off in healthier fish with vibrant coloration. During warm weather, you can even cultivate live foods outside, in a small "pond" set up for the purpose. Here are some suggestions for live food cultivation at home.

BRINE SHRIMP NAUPLII

Larval brine shrimp, known as *nauplii* (singular, nauplius), have been used for decades as tropical fish food. They are rich in nutrients, and can be easily hatched from the resting cysts, often incorrectly referred to as brine shrimp eggs. The ability to breed and subsequently rear many types of aquarium fish in hatcheries depends upon the use of brine shrimp nauplii. The cysts, nearly indestructible, will keep for months, even years, with proper storage. They are collected from evaporation ponds and other highly saline environments, and look like coarsely ground cinnamon. Hatching them is a cinch.

Fill an empty wide-mouth quart jar with water up to the shoulder and add two tablespoons (about an ounce, or 30 grams) of synthetic seawater mix. Seawater mix is available wherever saltwater aquariums are sold. Drop in an airstone and connect it to a pump. Aerate the water vigorously. You will want to locate your brine shrimp hatchery where the salt spray will do no harm, as it is impossible to keep it from splattering out of the container. The jar should be in a spot that remains around 75 to 80 degrees F. Bright, indirect light will improve the yield of the hatch, but keep the jar out of direct sun, or it will get too warm. As soon as the salt mix dissolves, add ¼ teaspoon of the cysts. They will hatch in 24 to 48 hours, depending upon the temperature. The warmer the water, the quicker the hatch. You can see the tiny nauplii swimming jerkily in the water. When you are ready to harvest, turn off the aeration. This will allow the empty cysts to float to the top of the container. Separating the cysts from the shrimp is the main difficulty in using brine shrimp nauplii. If the cysts are added to the aquarium, they will form an unsightly ring just above water level, and they can be harmful if fish ingest them.

The nauplii are attracted to light, and you can exploit this trait to collect them. Make a sleeve out of thin cardboard that will encircle the jar, cutting a one-inch hole just above the bottom. When you are ready to harvest shrimp, place the sleeve around the jar and shine a flashlight into the hole. The shrimp will gather at this point, from which they can be siphoned out with a length of flexible plastic tubing. Trap the nauplii with a net, and rinse under the tap before adding them to the aquarium. They will be relished by virtually all tropical fish. Like the adults, the nauplii survive only about an hour in fresh water, so feed accordingly. Try to feed your entire hatch within forty-eight hours, because the nauplii will lose much of their nutritional value during that time.

BRINE SHRIMP ADULTS

Nauplii can be grown to adulthood if you have the space. Fill a shallow container holding at least fifty gallons, such as a child's plastic wading pool, with synthetic seawater prepared at the ratio of four ounces of dry seawater mix per gallon. The container should be located in bright light but out of direct sun. Add a pinch of soluble garden fertilizer (such as Miracle-Gro) and a quart of either natural seawater collected from the ocean or water from an established saltwater aquarium. After a couple of weeks the water in the rearing container will be green with algae growth. Hatch the cysts as just described, and add the nauplii to your rearing pond. They will feed on algae and grow to adulthood in about two weeks. You can feed them to your fish at any point. About once a week, add another batch of nauplii. In this way you will be able to grow a continuous supply of adults. When harvesting the adult shrimps, use a net with relatively open mesh, so smaller individuals can escape and grow.

DAPHNIA

Culture daphnia, or water fleas, in a container holding twenty gallons or more. They feed on algae, so the rearing tank needs to be located where it will receive lots of indirect sunlight. Outdoors, locating the tank on the north side of a building or in the dappled shade of a deciduous tree works well. Fill the rearing container with tap water, and add a pinch of soluble garden fertilizer. When the water turns green, add a starter culture of daphnia. Your dealer can probably order a starter culture for you, or you can find suppliers online or in the classified section of an aquarium magazine. Wait a few weeks before harvesting the daphnia with a fine mesh net. If you try this in an area where mosquitoes are a problem, you will need to cover the daphnia tank with a screen top to prevent female mosquitoes from laying their eggs in the water. If you have a suitable spot, this is one of the easiest ways to provide your freshwater fish with a continuous supply of nutritious live food. Daphnia will survive the winter, as long as their tank does not freeze solid, but will pass the cold months as dormant cysts resting on the bottom. When the weather warms again, the tank will quickly fill with new generations of daphnia. Unlike brine shrimp, the daphnia will survive in the aquarium until eaten.

MICROWORMS

Microworms, as they are known in the aquarium world, are nematodes about a quarter of an inch in length. They can be easily cultivated at room temperature on cooked oatmeal to which a small amount of yeast has been added to cause fermentation. Shallow plastic food storage containers with covers work best for this purpose. The cover needs a couple of holes punched in it to provide air circulation. Starter cultures and recipes for culturing microworms can be ordered through aquarium magazine classifieds or online. Their main drawback is the funky smell of the fermenting culture medium. You will want to locate the microworm farm in a heated garage or basement. As they grow, the worms crawl up the sides of the container, and thus are easily harvested. Simply swab a few from the container with a cotton swab and swish them off in the aquarium. Using a small portion from an old culture to start a new one every two weeks ensures a continuous supply.

MOSQUITO LARVAE

I mentioned earlier that a water flea hatchery should be screened against the deposition of eggs by female mosquitoes. Any container of water left outdoors in warm weather will attract these little blood suckers, so they are a cinch to raise. Just leave a plastic dishpan half full of water in a sheltered spot. Check the pan daily for mosquito larvae, and feed them to the fish promptly. Your neighbors may revolt if they find you are cultivating adult mosquitoes in the back yard! Scoop the larvae from the dishpan with a fine mesh net, rinse briefly under the tap and plop them into the tank. Pour out the water in the pan and start over, lest any larvae escape. They will mature in days, producing biting adults, if left to their own devices.

Routine Maintenance

There is really only one rule for aquarium maintenance. Change water regularly. I recommend changing 10 to 15 percent per week, but you can do it biweekly or monthly, so long as roughly half the water is changed per month. This simple, low cost procedure will do more to enhance the appearance of the tank and the health of the fish and plants than anything else you do as an aquarist.

Purchase a length of plastic hose sufficient to reach from the bottom of the tank, over the top edge, and down to the floor. The inside diameter of the hose should be about three-quarters of an inch. You will also need a couple of plastic five-gallon buckets. These items will be cheaper if purchased at your DIY store instead of the aquarium shop. Just make sure you use them only for aquarium maintenance. Don't mix garden fertilizer or paint in a bucket and then later use it to carry water for your tank. You may inadvertently overfertilize your plants, or, worse, poison the fish with paint chemicals.

Before removing water from the tank, make certain to turn off all equipment, especially the heater, which should be unplugged.

To carry out a water change, place one end of the hose in the tank and suck on the other end to start siphoning water. Aquarium shops sell various types of siphons, including self-starting ones for the squeamish, if you are afraid of getting a mouth full of aquarium water. I have never heard of anyone becoming sick from aquarium water, however, so such fears are likely groundless. Fill the buckets and discard the used water until you have removed the correct amount. Refill buckets from your supply if you use distilled or softened water, or just turn on the tap. Adjust the hot and cold water faucets to approximate the temperature of the tank. Most people can judge this by feel, but use a thermometer if you are uncertain. The replacement water should be within five degrees of the tank temperature. Slightly warmer is always better than colder. A sudden chill can stress both fish and plants, and may result in an outbreak of disease. Add a dechlorinating agent if you wish. If you add anything else to the water, such as African cichlid salts or an acidifying agent, add the appropriate amount to the replacement water at this point.

> WARNING If you expose the heater to the air, it will get hot enough to blister you if it should switch on. Subsequent contact with water is likely to cause the heater to crack, which may create a dangerous electrical hazard, and will certainly ruin the heater.

Carefully pour the replacement water into the tank. I try to aim the flow toward a solid object, such as a rock or driftwood, to prevent stirring up the gravel and uprooting plants. If this maneuver is awkward, place a saucer on the gravel and pour the water on top of it. You are unlikely to do harm, but why disrupt things unnecessarily? If the tank is a large one, you may find hoisting heavy buckets to its rim too much of a chore. In this case, purchase a small submersible pump and a suitable length of hose to take care of the work. A five-gallon bucket full of water weighs over forty pounds. Please don't hurt your back trying to lift this much weight in a controlled manner, unless you are physically up to the task.

The fish, of course, will freak out over the disturbance, but it is doubtful any will suffer long-term harm. Since you have to remove the light fixture to get at the tank, the darkness will help some in this regard. Once the tank is full again, switch everything back on and check for normal operation. I suggest leaving the lights off until the next day, to allow the fish to calm down. Don't feed them, either, on water change day.

For a large built-in aquarium, the plumbing system should be designed to permit draining and filling the tank via the filter sump, as will be discussed in chapter 4.

You may want to do some housecleaning as part of your water change routine. This is a good time to clean algae from the front and sides of the tank, to prune plants or remove dead leaves, and to siphon out any noticeable accumulations of debris. It is likely that you will stir up fine debris in the course of maintenance. It will be removed once the filter is restarted. This is the ideal time to check and replace filter media, which may become clogged with particulate matter. I save the major work for once a month, but you may want to clean the inside of the glass weekly. Use a plain plastic scouring pad (such as Scotch Brite) from the supermarket for this purpose if you have a glass tank. Acrylic tanks require the use of a cleaning pad made especially for them. In either case, always be careful not to get a piece of gravel or a grain of sand between the pad and the tank wall, or you will scratch it.

Before replacing the cover, clean it thoroughly on both sides with plain water and the scouring pad you use for algae removal. Water spots, dust, and algae on the cover glass can seriously reduce light penetration, and your plants need all the light the fixture can provide. Also wipe off the fluorescent lamp itself. You will be surprised how it picks up household grime due to the electrical charge it bears when in operation. Make a note when the tank is first set up, and on the anniversary date each year replace all the lamps in your fluorescent fixture. Light output decreases as the lamps age, even though you may not notice this visually. If using metal halide lighting, follow the manufacturer's directions regarding lamp life. Most last two years before they need replacement.

Now and then you will need to replace worn parts, such as the impeller in your filter pump. Plan to do this, too, while the equipment is shut down for a water change.

Once you complete the water change and other routine maintenance, you will be amazed at how the tank sparkles. Colors will brighten on your fish, and the plants will have the lush look of a garden just after a spring rain. The benefits of a short time spent on maintenance will be clearly apparent.

Record Keeping

Get yourself a calendar, notebook, or three-ring binder and make notes regarding water changes, lamp replacement, and other routine maintenance. You can also jot down your observations about plant growth, fish spawnings, or anything that you deem important. Not only will having such a record help you remember things like when to change the filter pads, but also with time the notebook will become a history of the tank that you will enjoy looking back upon. If you find yourself wondering how old that catfish is, you can check your records and find the date you placed it in the tank. This, for me, is part of the fun, and is also a good way to spot trends.

Water Tests

I am not a huge fan of routine water testing in freshwater aquariums. In the first place, if you are keeping fish that like the conditions prevailing in your tap water, why bother? The water company will go to great lengths to make sure the water leaving the treatment plant is consistent with regard to the parameters important to aquarium fish, namely pH and hardness. If the tank has been set up properly and maintenance carried out on schedule—and if you don't overstock or fail to feed the fish with restraint—it is unlikely that ammonia or nitrite, the two major pollutants that pose a threat to fish health, will accumulate. If you do regular water changes, excess nitrate accumulation is unlikely, especially if healthy plants are growing in the tank.

With that in mind, it still pays to be prepared to take quick action in case the fish or plants show signs of distress. It is always worthwhile to have a basic water chemistry lab available for troubleshooting purposes. For that I suggest purchasing test kits for the following:

- ammonia
- nitrite

Aquarium water should never have any detectable ammonia or nitrite. The presence of either one indicates that biofiltration is not proceeding as it should. Immediate action should be taken to reduce the concentration of either of these compounds should you discover them. Change enough water to substantially reduce the level. Keep testing on a daily basis, changing water as needed, until the system returns to normal. Stop feeding during this time. The fish will not starve, and more food will only exacerbate the problem.

Nitrate is another matter. If you check nitrate just before doing a water change, you will note that it increases by about the same amount every month. Immediately after the water change, it will have been reduced in proportion to the amount changed, that is, a 50 percent water change will reduce nitrate by 50 percent. By the next water change, more nitrate will have accumulated. The difference between the nitrate level immediately after a water change and the level immediately before next month's (or next week's) change represents the normal amount of nitrate production for your particular situation. A deviation from that norm means that something has upset the equilibrium established between ammonia production, biological filtration, and absorption of nitrate by plants. Several factors can produce this deviation. Obviously, the more fish you have the more ammonia will be produced. Adding a fish produces a noticeable change, for example. Similarly, rotting food or a dead snail decomposing behind a rock adds ammonia, and this will eventually result in nitrate accumulation. Thus, it is important to keep a record of each nitrate test. Should an anomaly appear, try to identify an obvious explanation, e.g., I added new fish. Otherwise, you need to track down the culprit.

Ask yourself the following questions:

- Did I carry out the test correctly? (It is always worth doing a confirming test before looking for other explanations.)
- Have water changes been skipped?
- Have fish been added?
- Have I fed more than I normally do?
- Is everyone present and accounted for? (Snails, in particular, sometimes die unnoticed.)
- Have I added anything out of the ordinary? (Medications, especially, may disrupt bacterial activity and thus change the nitrogen equilibrium.)

Nitrate may be removed by natural processes, the most obvious being absorption by plants, but often your partial water changes constitute the main way nitrate leaves the aquarium. Remember, the amount of nitrate produced per unit of time remains constant as long as conditions do not change. Measuring nitrate accumulation allows you to spot anomalies that may be a sign of trouble.

Re-read the discussion on page 69 of the typical pattern of nitrate accumulation over time. This trend will always be upward unless 100 percent of the water is changed each month. At some point—I suggest every six months—you will need to do an extra-large water change to return the tank to a baseline position with regard to nitrate. If excessive nitrate accumulates beyond the needs of the plants, they react as if overfertilized (which is indeed the case). Leaves turn yellow and become thinner. The plant may even die. If you have ever added too much fertilizer to a houseplant, you know that it can be "burned" by the overfeeding. So, too, can aquatic plants.

Invisible nitrate, therefore, can be an indicator of the overall biological activity in your aquarium. Thus, it is worth carrying out this one test on a regular basis.

Not all nitrate tests are created equal. Some test total nitrate and some test nitrate nitrogen. Without going into the details, suffice it to say that you must always record the same parameter if your test results are to be of any value for comparison purposes. Don't switch brands of test kits, unless you are sure that the new kit is measuring the same thing your old one did. (Different brands that test the same parameter may give different results with the same water sample, but the difference will be slight.) If you simply cannot find, for example, a total nitrate test and are forced to rely on one for nitrate nitrogen, multiply the result by 4.4. Similarly, to convert total nitrate to nitrate nitrogen, divide by 4.4.

If you modify your tap water in some way, such as diluting it with softened water, or adding an acidifying agent, you will of course need test kits to make sure you are getting the results you expect. For this, you will need kits for hardness and pH. You should also, as mentioned previously, be using an iron test kit if you are adding an iron supplement for your plants.

Maintenance Service

If, after reading the foregoing, you decide that aquarium maintenance is not something you have the time or inclination to do, you can still have a beautiful aquarium by hiring a maintenance service. An aquarium maintenance service makes a lot of sense if you lack the time required to give the aquarium the weekly attention it needs. On a daily basis, checking to make sure all is well and feeding the fish are the only duties. Neither will occupy more than a few minutes, so you should be able to handle these tasks easily. On a weekly basis, however, an hour or so will be required to carry out more extensive care, and once a month some of the water should be removed and replaced with freshly drawn water. Plants require regular pruning, algae may grow in places where you don't want it, and equipment will need servicing. Depending upon the size of the tank, maintenance may thus involve more time than you can spare. Because conditions in even the best-designed system quickly tend to deteriorate without regular maintenance, if you cannot do the work yourself you will need to hire someone to carry out these chores to avoid disaster. Time may not be your only constraint. A disability, for example, might prevent you from moving heavy buckets of water.

If you decide to go this route, choose the service with care. Make sure responsibilities, yours and theirs, are clearly understood. Confirm that the price quoted covers both labor and materials, such as filter media, that will be replaced in the course of normal care. If supplies cost extra, you should have the option of shopping for them yourself, rather than purchasing only from the maintenance company. Everything should be spelled out in a written agreement. The cost for professional maintenance can be considerable, and most companies charge a monthly minimum. However, proper care is the key to long-term enjoyment from an aquarium. Failing to appreciate this fully has resulted in many a would-be aquarium owner's disappointment.

SUMMARY

You don't need a scientific background, nor a lot of experience, to have a successful freshwater aquarium with thriving fish and lush plantings. All you need to do is use common sense and stick with my basic rules. In summary, they are as follows:

- Set up the largest aquarium that your resources can accommodate.

- Know the condition of your tap water and choose fish naturally adapted to those conditions.

- Choose a lighting system adequate for the plants you intend to grow. There is no substitute for light. Otherwise, use plastic reproductions.

- Add plants first, along with an initial dose of fertilizer to get them growing. Wait until new growth appears before beginning to add fish.

- Understand the critical process of biofiltration.

- Add fish gradually. Start with no more than 10 percent of the total number you eventually will keep in the tank. This allows biofiltration to keep pace with the fish population.

- Add hardy fish first. Save delicate species for later, when the tank is more stable.

- Always choose fish and plants with care. Even if you follow a recipe from this book precisely, bringing home a sick fish will create problems. See the next chapter for suggestions.

- Understand why nitrate is an indicator of the overall condition of the aquarium.

- Feed a varied diet in small amounts.

- Carry out partial water changes on a regular schedule without fail.

- Keep a notebook of observations, such as water test results, to refer to when making changes or diagnosing a problem.

Most importantly, sit quietly near the tank for a short while each day and watch what's going on. Not only will you learn a lot about the aquatic environment, your stress level will decrease, you'll learn to relax and, hopefully, you will live longer. Not a bad trade-off, in my view.

CHAPTER 2

BRINGING OUT THE BEST IN FISH AND AQUARIUMS

Setting up a successful aquarium involves more than just placing a bunch of fish and plants in a glass box. Freshwater natural environments vary greatly in terms of water chemistry, current or lack thereof, temperature range, the nature of the substrate, the type and amount of vegetation present, and a host of other factors. Consider pH, for example. An African rainforest pond harboring killifish might have a pH around 5.0, while the cichlids of Lake Tanganyika, also in tropical Africa, swim in water with a pH up to 9.0. Like the Richter scale for earthquakes, the pH scale is logarithmic, meaning even a 1.0 difference is significant. In this example, Lake Tanganyika is 10,000 times more alkaline than the rainforest pond. Because many vital functions, such as the exchange of gases by the gills, are strongly pH dependent, such differences have profound implications. A killifish from the pond will not thrive in water from Lake Tanganyika, nor is a Tanganyikan cichlid likely to do well in the acidic water from the pond. This chapter covers how to control the important factors to optimize your aquarium for the needs of the fish you plan to keep.

Guidelines for Design

Creating an aquarium involves bringing together diverse elements, both living and non-living, and integrating them into a functioning system. An aquarium is not a true ecosystem, of course, but does tend to exhibit many of the characteristics of natural ecosystems. For example, as in a natural ecosystem, a food web forms in the aquarium. Even in the absence of added food, an aquarium will include producers, consumers, and degraders whose lives depend, at least to some extent, upon each other. Algae growing on a rock harbors small crustaceans that are eaten by a fish, which in turn excretes waste that is broken down by other organisms, ultimately producing nitrate that fertilizes another round of algae growth.

Years ago, aquarium literature often made mention of the ideal, "balanced" aquarium, in which this cycle of production, consumption, degradation, and re-uptake proceeded indefinitely in the absence of external influences such as feeding or water changes. Few, if any, aquarists achieved this ideal, not because it is impossible, but rather because it takes a huge volume of water and a great many plants to support a small population of fish. Setting up a one-hundred-gallon aquarium to house a few one-inch fish seemed like wasted effort.

Modern filtration systems are designed and deployed with one primary goal: to increase the number of fish that can be housed in a given volume of water. The aquarium remains "balanced" only so long as the filter system properly functions. The implications of this simple principle are obvious; effort must be expended on a continuing basis to keep the aquarium functioning properly. It will not "take care of itself." If we make the mistake of beginning with a collection of species having widely divergent needs, we compound the problem, because providing for one of them may simultaneously work against the interests of another. The aquarium, in effect, is constantly teetering on the brink of disaster. Eventually, a tipping point is reached, and the impending disaster becomes reality. Too often, this is the experience of the home aquarist. Therefore, the aquarium should emulate conditions that favor a natural balance, without counting on the filtration system to overcome our mistakes. This is the first priority of good aquarium design. An aquarium that is most likely to develop a natural balance has several important characteristics:

- A relatively large volume of water
- Lush and vigorous plant growth
- A relatively small number of fish

Beginners often find the huge variety of aquarium fish and plants, each with its own peculiarities and special needs, extremely daunting. The possibilities seem endless. Indeed, they almost are. If we were to try to list all possible combinations of just twenty kinds of fish and plants, for example, we would end up with more than a million billion aquarium designs. Ways exist for making sense of this overabundance, fortunately. For example, we can simply limit our choices from the outset.

By applying a simple set of guidelines, the process of designing a successful aquarium can be greatly simplified. Here are the guidelines I have developed over the years.

- Focus on a single habitat type.
- Focus on one or a few fish species.
- Focus on one to five plant species.

Habitat Types

Aquatic habitats can be characterized by a variety of factors. As mentioned earlier, freshwater habitats can vary with respect to their temperature range, water chemistry, current, and so forth. *Habitat type* refers to a particular set of these parameters. Usually, but not always, habitat type will correspond to a specific kind of geographic feature, such as a "blackwater creek" versus a "big river." Aquariums featuring fish and plants from only one habitat type are far more likely to remain free of problems than those cobbled together with species from a diversity of habitat types.

The World of Fish

Scarcely a natural body of water exists that lacks fish. From the depths of Africa's Lake Malawi to the muddy waters of the mighty Amazon, freshwater habitats support some 5,000 species of fish that can be considered suitable for aquariums. Roughly a third of these find their way into the commercial trade, though many do so only on rare occasions. No individual aquarist is likely to see them all, much less have the opportunity to keep them in a tank at home. For a given aquarium, I suggest a limit of three species for every twenty gallons of water. Thus, a twenty-gallon tank would exhibit three species only, while a two-hundred-gallon tank would house up to thiry kinds. The choice, of course, is somewhat arbitrary. Smaller tanks are likely to fare better with only one species, and a large tank devoted to only one species is truly stunning. For most aquarium displays, though, the numbers recommended will result in a design that comfortably occupies the middle ground between monotonous and chaotic.

The World of Aquatic Plants

Botanists have discovered about 4,000 kinds of aquatic and bog plants, any of which might be suited to aquarium use. Only about 250 of them are commercially available, however, and the majority of plants found in aquarium shops represent fewer than 50 species. Choosing plants, therefore, presents less of a problem than choosing fish. Plants perform numerous important functions in the aquarium ecosystem, from oxygen production to waste processing, but the primary consideration when designing a planted aquarium is aesthetics. In this regard, aquarium design mimics landscape design. The goal is to achieve a natural look, though one constrained by the special characteristics of the space it occupies. I am reminded of this principle each fall when I move my collection of tropical plants from the deck to the sunroom. My thirty-year-old Ming aralia, whose graceful proportions complement the deck's Japanese design theme so well underneath the open sky, becomes an ungainly behemoth when squeezed into a corner of the sunroom, its upper branches brushing against the ceiling. Similarly, of all the limitations placed upon the aquarium designer, the visual space within the aquarium is perhaps the most confining. Limit your design to one to three kinds of plants per twenty gallons of water. Placing many varieties of plants together in one small tank makes the aquarium look more like a collector's display case than a window into a natural habitat. However, you can have as many individuals of a given species as you wish. A twenty-gallon tank might have two dozen individual eelgrass plants, and one large Amazon sword plant as a centerpiece, for example. This will look better than five individuals each of five different plants.

Finding the Right Fit with Fish

In the old days, hale and hardy explorers sloshed through muddy equatorial streams, braving piranha and alligators, enduring mosquitoes, heat, and lousy food to bring new aquarium fish to market. Commercial harvesting operations existed throughout what we now call "the developing world" to capture a portion of the seemingly inexhaustible natural populations of colorful fish for sale to eager fanciers in colder climes.

Developing New Traits

New traits can arise in more than one way:

- **Natural mutation** can create new forms, such as a color type or tail shape. In ichthyological terms, this is a *morph*. A change in a single gene involving, say, the production of red pigment might easily create a new color morph. Mutations leading to new traits that are desirable from the breeder's point of view are rare. Indeed, most natural mutations kill the bearer, rather than resulting in flowing fins or brighter coloration. Fish are prolific, however. The availability of hundreds of offspring from a single spawning greatly increases the odds that one fish may possess something of interest. Once that rare individual appears, manipulating successive generations of its offspring to achieve further refinements of the desired new trait become the focus of the breeder. Tropical fish have relatively short generation times, with most producing several broods annually. Some may spawn almost continuously. A serious breeding operation can succeed in creating new fish varieties faster and more frequently than new plant varieties can be developed in the horticulture industry.

- **Recessive traits** in an inbred population may also generate variety in aquarium fish. Recessive traits do not appear in the offspring unless the recessive gene is inherited from each of the two parents. It should be obvious that inbreeding will increase the likelihood of this happening. Fish breeders sometimes deliberately increase inbreeding in captive fish stocks in an effort to *fix* a specific trait in the line.

- **Hybridization** offers a third avenue for development of new aquarium fish varieties. Though often difficult to achieve, hybridization of fish to produce new commercial types has been accomplished. Also, naturally occurring hybrids are sometimes discovered. Provided the hybrids are fertile and breed true to type, hatchery cultivation may follow.

Many of these wild fish adapted successfully to captivity only when a rather narrow range of optimum conditions could be discovered and duplicated in the aquarium. Indeed, the goal of many early aquarium hobbyists was to successfully maintain a species through its entire life cycle. Ideally, this would be a species that had yielded up its lifestyle secrets to no one else, and the first person to spawn and rear it successfully would enjoy the adulation of his or her peers.

These days, the challenges to the typical home aquarist are not nearly so great. While new and unusual varieties continue to be collected from the wild, the vast majority of fish offered for retail sale probably originated in a hatchery in Asia and represent strains well adapted to aquarium life. Artificial selection has been practiced on aquarium fish populations for a very long time, dating, perhaps, to ancient civilizations. Over the past fifty or so years, during which time small home aquariums have become practical and affordable, hundreds of new varieties have been developed from wild stocks.

Checking Out Varieties

Fancy goldfish provide a good example of a species with hundreds of varieties manufactured by breeders. Although the variations on the basic *Carassius auratus* species range from the gaudy to the grotesque (in some opinions) you can still tell you are looking at a "goldfish." All these varieties resulted from deliberate breeding and artificial selection for specific traits, such as the short, plump body of the "oranda" type. Traits such as fin structure, coloration, and even body shape can change without the fish's basic needs also changing. For example, the most bizarre goldfish varieties need the same temperature range and types of food as their wild counterparts.

At the level of the retail store, the end result of all the painstaking effort devoted to breeding and rearing manifests itself as dozens of kinds of colorful fish. Goldfish, plain, fancy and in-between; "black skirt" tetras; gold and opaline gouramies; dozens of different types of platies; hundreds of Siamese fighting fish color morphs. Nearly every species seems to come in an albino variety. All these and more turn up in even the smallest shops. No wonder novices are overwhelmed. Too many choices exist . . . or so it appears. In fact, all the commercial activity in tropical fish breeding over the past one hundred years has left us with comparatively few large groups into which virtually all species can be sorted. Looking at potential aquarium inhabitants in terms of which group they belong to makes more sense than trying to treat each variety as unique. Thus, we can identify five basic types of aquarium fish:

- Large, aggressive predators
- Peaceful "community" fish
- Bottom-dwelling "scavengers"
- Algae and plant eaters
- Oddballs.

> ## Fish Tips
>
> Large, aggressive predators and oddballs usually do best if provided with a tank to themselves. Peaceful fish, bottom-dwelling scavengers, and algae and plant eaters can be combined in one tank to create a community that reflects a natural biotope. A *biotope* is a small, geographically defined part of an ecosystem, containing characteristic microorganisms, plants, and animals that interact in (usually) predictable ways.

Choosing the Right Fish

Some fish are just naturally better aquarium fish than others. Keep the following in mind when choosing some for your aquarium:

- **Good aquarium fish should remain relatively small at maturity.** Space and money constraints limit aquarium size. The size of the tank defines the upper limit on fish size within it, obviously. Custom-built aquarium systems, of course, can be any size your budget permits, but most people reading this book will be considering systems holding 150 gallons or less. That translates into a six-foot-long tank, the largest most stores have in stock. Unless you intend to exhibit only one or two fish, four inches is about as large as any individual specimen should grow to be. Hundreds of possibilities exist in this size range or smaller. (That said, we won't rule out larger fish species in the model designs presented later. We'll simply use only one fish or a mated pair as the focal point.)

- **Good aquarium fish should adapt readily to captive circumstances.** This would seem obvious. Yet, plenty of fish are doomed to an early death simply because their ecological requirements are difficult or impractical to satisfy in a home aquarium. The species will only take live food, for example. Compounding the folly, such fish may be harvested from wild populations, either because the techniques for breeding them have not been discovered, or because the market for them is too small to justify an investment in a breeding operation. Arriving on the dealer's doorstep already suffering from the stresses of capture and long shipping times, wild fish need plenty of coddling before they are ready for the transition to your home. While I have not ruled out the use of wild-caught fish in the model designs presented later, I encourage you to begin with selections from the many tried and true varieties that are widely available.

Recognizing healthy fish

In many cases, a major factor in achieving success with an aquarium is the state of health of the fish at the time you buy them. Stress and starvation resulting from poor care may result in delayed mortality. That is, the fish may look okay in the store, but develop problems later, after you get them home. Beginners often fail to realize how crucial to their success is the state of health of the fish at the time they are acquired. Therefore, care in purchasing may be the most important aspect of managing your aquarium. Here are some suggestions for making wise decisions in this regard. If you want to know how to find a good dealer, check out the section "Finding a Good Dealer" on page 33.

First, become familiar with the indications of poor fish health, and be alert for them when shopping.

- **Watch out for rapid movement of the gill covers (panting or gasping).** This could indicate that the fish is infested with parasites, that the water quality is poor, or merely that the fish were being chased around the tank with a net five minutes before you walked in.

- **Beware of ragged fins, lesions, open wounds, or abnormalities.** For example, some fish become humpbacked with old age. Avoid them. Fish can, like any other creature, suffer minor injuries without serious long-term consequences. Nevertheless, any damage should appear to be healing. Without a doubt, no bloodiness or cottony growth should be apparent.

- **Look out for any fish with white stringy feces hanging from its anus.** This is a sign of poor diet, internal disease, or both. Pass 'em up.

- **Look for signs of poor nourishment.** Such symptoms as a hollow belly or a shallow indentation behind the head indicate the fish is starving. Choose another individual.

- **Steer clear from fish that hide for no obvious reason.** Unless this behavior is characteristic for that species, it indicates some kind of distress.

Above all, use common sense. Healthy fish look healthy.

- Their colors are bright.
- They search actively for food.

- Their fins are held erect.
- Fish should be convex in outline when viewed head on.
- Any fish should definitely be eating in the dealer's tank before you purchase it.

Finding a Good Dealer

Even the most adaptable species is not likely to fare well in your tank if you bring home a diseased or damaged specimen. Therefore, a fair degree of skill in selecting fish and plants from the dealer's tank will go a long way to ensuring your success with the finished aquarium. So, it is important to choose a dealer who consistently stocks good-quality fish and plants and takes proper care of them while they await your purchase.

Visit every aquarium shop in your area, ideally more than once, over a period of two or three weeks. Look for a store with a varied inventory of healthy fish living in well-maintained holding tanks. Discovering that the store is dirty, unkempt, or poorly lighted or that fish with obvious signs of disease are being offered for sale should prompt you to look elsewhere. Only a very foolish, or very careless, dealer will leave a sick fish in the display tanks. Check the dry goods section, too. Dusty inventory indicates that turnover is slow, which should tell you something about the satisfaction level of previous visitors. General untidiness signals an uncaring attitude. If the dealer cannot manage ordinary housekeeping chores, perhaps he or she is not giving the aquariums the attention they deserve, either.

Beautiful tanks filled with obviously thriving fish and plants, however, trump attentive housekeeping. I fondly remember a shop in my area that was located in the basement of the owner's house. Fish food, nets, and other paraphernalia were piled or stacked seemingly at random. The floor was wet and slippery. Cartons had been left in the one large window so long the sun had bleached them into illegibility. And the fish and plants were the finest to be found for fifty miles. Apparently, every bit of available time was devoted to the livestock, with none left over for the rest of the shop. Eventually, the dealer retired and moved to Florida. In the twenty years since, I have not found another dealer whose livestock offerings were so consistently healthy and beautiful, and that includes my own store, which was located in a busy shopping center in an upscale neighborhood. The guy must have given every single holding tank the same attention I would devote to the aquarium in my living room.

Your first visit or two to any store should be just a prospecting trip; don't plan on buying fish or plants. Become familiar with the range of offerings and the quality of the stores in your region before making any decisions, especially if there are several competitors in a relatively small area. Call ahead and ask when the store is least busy. Then you can shop when the staff is free to give you the most attention. One helpful trick in evaluating a shop is to ask a few questions for which you already know the correct answers. Of course, not everyone on the staff will be an expert, but they should all give reasonably correct answers to basic questions about water quality and the particular needs (feeding behavior, for example) of any fish in the shop. You should receive good advice regarding the prevention or cure of common problems. Furthermore, if someone is stumped by one of your questions, they should look it up in a book. Good shops always have several well-used reference books behind the counter.

Professional retailers know that the key to a thriving aquarium shop is having customers with successful aquariums. If the tanks look good and the store staff seems knowledgeable, you have probably found the right store. The next step is to look at the fish and plants with a critical eye.

In fairness to the many enthusiastic and dedicated aquarium dealers, your judgments should be tempered with reason. The shop does not have to be perfect in every respect. Don't forget that fish are commodities, not pets, to the aquarium shop. Every dealer has to make a living, and will use all the same techniques employed by other retailers to entice their customers. Sometimes, a bargain is really a bargain. At other times, the fish are marked down because the dealer wants to get rid of them before they all die.

Once you find a dealer that consistently provides good-quality fish, your best bet is to support that dealer with your business, even if a particular specimen is a few dollars less across town.

Choosing Healthy Plants

Plants present fewer problems, in terms of evaluating their condition, than fish do. Choosing aquatic plants is no different from choosing terrestrial plants: What you see is, by and large, what you get. Here are some things to look for:

- Separate tanks for plants: I prefer to shop with dealers who maintain their plant inventory in a separate set of tanks from the fish. That way, the plants remain safe from injury when the staff has to net out a fish. Some dealers keep a few fish in their plant tanks to provide natural fertilizer and to feed on potential plant pests. Usually, a sign will announce that these fish are not for sale.

- Metal halide lighting above the plant inventory: Plants that do not receive enough light will be in a weakened state, and may even respond negatively when you suddenly transfer them to your brightly illuminated aquarium at home.

- A carbon dioxide injection system: Dealers with large inventories of plants probably have a carbon dioxide injection system. This is always a good sign. It means the dealer cares sufficiently about the quality of the stock to invest in additional equipment.

Evaluating a display of plants poses few difficulties.

- Plants should be a rich green, or, in the case of those with colored foliage, of the color appropriate to the species. Yellowing is seldom normal. Avoid any plant in which the veins of the leaves are deep green but the tissue between the veins is yellowing. This is a sure sign of a nutritional deficiency.

- You should see new leaves unfurling on many of the individuals. When removed from the substrate, the roots should be healthy, firm, and pale in color, not brown or black. Avoid plants with most of the leaves broken or damaged. They may take a long time to recover, if they ever do.

- Inspect the tank closely for the presence of many small snails crawling on the plants and the glass. While some are harmless, others may munch holes in the leaves. Worse, many of them reproduce readily under aquarium conditions, leaving your tank overrun. Once they are established, eliminating them may prove exceedingly difficult. Ask the dealer how the plants are produced. Greenhouse-grown plants are less likely to be infested with snails and other pests than pond-grown plants are.

Hydroponic Plants

A major trend in recent years has been the greenhouse production of aquatic plants under continuous mist, rather than submerged in tanks. This growing method allows large-scale production of high-quality plants at low cost. As such, it is a good thing for the aquarium hobbyist. These hydroponically grown plants generally come in little plastic pots filled with rock wool. Check the pot. Healthy white roots should be growing out the bottom. The rock wool should never be black in color. When the plant is removed from the water, the pot should bear no trace of an unpleasant smell. Such a smell indicates low oxygen levels around the roots and a high likelihood of bacterial rot. The rock wool provides support for the roots while the plant is under cultivation in the greenhouse, but does not allow for good water circulation if the pot is subsequently buried in gravel or sand. Thus, an anaerobic (oxygen deprived) area develops around the roots, fostering bacterial growth. These anaerobic bacteria produce the unpleasant smell. Knowledgeable dealers place the pots on the surface of the gravel, rather than burying them. Choosing healthy plants, like choosing healthy fish, involves a little basic knowledge and a large measure of common sense.

Acclimating New Arrivals

Although plants can simply be unpacked and planted in their new habitat, new fish require a gradual process of introduction into the aquarium. Aquarists call this "acclimating" the fish to the new tank.

First, make sure your display tank is in good shape before you bring home any newcomers. Ideally, perform a water change a couple of days before you expect to bring a fish home. Placing a fish already stressed from the move into poor water conditions practically guarantees problems.

The dealer will place the fish in a plastic bag filled about halfway. Air is trapped in the space above the water to provide oxygen. Please don't make the fish store your first stop on an extended shopping excursion; head straight home with your new acquisition. Don't stop at the supermarket on the way. If you leave the bag sitting in a hot, or frigid, car, you are asking for trouble. You might even parboil the fish in the bag.

By far the best way to ensure that your beautiful aquarium display remains free of problems is to quarantine all new fish in a separate tank for a week or two after you bring them home. Any problems that develop can thus be treated without affecting the main display tank. The quarantine tank need not be an elaborate system, and needs to be only large enough for the maximum size and number of fish that you anticipate purchasing at any one time. Twenty gallons is about right for most home aquarists. Make sure to provide sufficient light if you plan to quarantine plants as well as fish. Bright, indirect sun is ideal. You can use short sections of plastic drain pipe to provide hiding places for new arrivals. Maintain conditions in the quarantine tank to match those of the main tank, to minimize stress when the fish are transferred. If you have a large display aquarium holding a valuable collection of fishes, a quarantine tank should be considered essential.

As soon as you arrive home, turn off the lights in the quarantine tank. Darkness will help to calm the new fish. Float the unopened bag in the tank for thirty minutes. Then gently open the bag and roll down the top like a sock. Next, transfer about a cup of water from the tank to the bag. Continue dipping water from tank to bag every ten minutes until the bag sinks, allowing the fish to swim out. Some aquarists do not allow the bag to sink. They scrupulously avoid introducing any of the water from the bag into their aquarium. Instead, they remove the bag and dump it through a net, straining out the fish, which is then plopped into the tank. The stress imposed on the fish by this treatment probably outweighs any benefit. You also run the risk of the fish becoming entangled in the net.

Should the fish exhibit obvious signs of distress during acclimation, go ahead and remove it from the bag and place it immediately in the tank. Leave the lights off until the next morning. By then, your new fish should be searching for food.

After a week or two in quarantine, the fish is ready for your display aquarium. When transferring a fish from quarantine, follow a modification of the acclimation procedure. Catch the fish and place it in a plastic bag or cup. Turn off the lights over the display tank, and float the container with the fish for half an hour. Assuming you have maintained water conditions in the quarantine tank to match those of the display tank, simply tip the container and allow the fish to swim out. Leave the lights off until the following day.

SUMMARY

Designing a beautiful and easily maintained aquarium poses few problems if you stick with a few simple rules. First, limit yourself to a single habitat type. Don't try to mix fish with divergent water requirements in the same aquarium. Second, stock only three species of fish per twenty gallons of water. This allows you to keep a group of several individuals of each species, without exceeding the carrying capacity of the system. Third, stock only one to three species of plants per twenty gallons of water, in order to achieve a natural look. Avoid creating a "botanical display case" in your aquarium.

Because much of your success depends upon the quality of fish and plants you purchase, spend some time investigating the dealers in your area to find the best specimens possible. Take care in transporting them home and acclimating them to your aquarium. Ideally, set up a quarantine tank and hold each new specimen for two weeks before transferring it to the display aquarium.

Part II

AQUARIUM MECHANICS

CHAPTER 3

MAKING YOUR HABITAT LOOK REAL

I endeavor to design aquariums that reflect nature. One basic approach I employ is to combine fish, plants, and other materials that come from the same geographic region. Sometimes I can create the same effect by combining elements from different areas of the world that share habitat similarities. Incorporating elements from the same geographic region or habitat type is the first step in making the artificial aquarium habitat look like a genuine stream, lake, or pond. Arranging plants and non-living elements with care completes the illusion. Natural habitats achieve a balance among the living elements. Plants, fish, and other organisms coexist in predictable ratios. Characteristic communities form because the living creatures populating them have adapted to prevailing conditions of temperature, water chemistry, and current. Controlling these factors in the aquarium, for example, regulating the temperature with a heater or pruning out plants, stabilizes the entire system in much the same way that ecosystems remain stable. Your own efforts replace natural forces, of course, but a stable balance nonetheless develops.

Taking the Tank into Consideration

The front glass of your aquarium tank is the window into the microcosm you create within. This effect is greatly enhanced with a built-in tank, which is often surrounded by molding or trim work, and gives the impression of a framed picture. If the tank is free-standing, develop your design by thinking only about the view from the front, as if it were a picture. Consider also how this picture will be framed by the support furniture. The cabinet or stand should not be a distraction. Stick with simple lines and colors that blend with the surroundings. However, while the tank captures the focus of your aquarium, it also becomes the most significant constraint on your design. In the following sections I make sure you take the space limitations and proper proportions of your tank into consideration while you create your design.

Space Limitations of Tanks

Remember that the aquarium requires a life support system. You will be forced to give up some portion of the available space to accommodate equipment. How you choose to do this will influence the overall design. For a natural look, you want the equipment to be as inconspicuous as possible. Therefore, give some thought to the arrangement of the equipment while the aquarium is in the planning stage. I suggest creating a scale drawing using graph paper, to help visualize how the tank will look with equipment in place. The photo below shows a small aquarium with the traditional arrangement of equipment.

Normally, a non-submersible heater hangs on the rear frame on one side; a power filter hangs on the other side. Aquarium equipment is usually designed to accommodate such an arrangement, but that does not mean

you are restricted only to this placement. With a little tinkering, you can use other arrangements, depending on the habitat you are trying to depict. For example, if you want to create a stream with moderate to fast current, the ideal habitat for many barbs, you can install the filter on one end of an elongated tank. The filter outflow will produce water movement parallel to the length of the tank. This simulates a stream viewed from the stream bank, with water flowing past the viewer from one end of the tank to the other.

The typical glass cover is not designed to accommodate this placement, however, so you will need either to make a custom cover (easy to do on a small scale) or dispense with the cover altogether (if the fish are types that are not inclined to jump).

Thinking about these kinds of design issues before you purchase the tank and equipment will not only help avoid headaches later, but also may save money. Always create your design on paper first, so you can identify potential problems. I have endeavored to anticipate such issues in the models discussed later, but predicting what you might encounter in a specific installation is difficult. In general, problems with a free-standing system will be far easier to correct later than is the case with built-ins.

One lesson I have gained in years of aquarium keeping is to avoid trying to do too much within a single tank. Strip down your design to its essentials. It is always surprising how an aquarium that appears quite large when empty becomes confining when you begin to add decorations. For example, a common mistake is keeping too many different kinds of fish in too small a tank. It is always better to have more individuals of a single species than one or two of many species. Similarly, plantings look more natural when individuals of one type are grouped. This principle also applies to rocks, driftwood, and other design elements. Avoid creating a "museum display case" look by exercising restraint.

Tank Proportions and Habitat Types

Unless you plan on ordering a custom-built tank, you will have to make do with one of the stock sizes. In my experience, people usually purchase the tank based on their budget. I would suggest you also consider both the size and proportions of any tank in terms of how your intended habitat will fit in. A tank that works well for a lake environment may not lend itself to a stream habitat, and vice versa. I have specified what I consider to be the optimal tank (or, in some cases, tanks) for each of the models.

Appendix B lists typical aquarium sizes from twenty to two hundred gallons. A quick inspection of this table reveals that manufacturers maintain certain proportions from one tank to the next. For example, basic smaller tanks are twelve inches deep. (In aquarium lingo, *depth* is the distance front to back, while the dimension corresponding to water depth is referred to as *height*.) Thus, a *standard* twenty-gallon tank is two feet in length, a thirty-gallon is three feet, a fifty-five-gallon, four feet. It is worth mentioning that tank capacities are nominal. The actual volume of water in the completed tank will be somewhat less.

Manufacturers also produce tanks in different proportions with the same nominal capacity. Thus, you will see a twenty-gallon *long* style (base dimension 30 x 12 in.) only twelve inches in height, and a twenty-nine-gallon *show* style with similar base dimensions but a depth of twenty inches. As a rule, long-style tanks are long and narrow and show-style tanks are exaggerated in height. The long style lends itself to river or stream habitat designs, while show tanks work well for lake habitats or for designs incorporating both aquatic and terrestrial elements. Both long-style and show-style tanks, as well as standard tanks, can of course be used any way you wish.

Lighting

Lighting plays a critical role in aquarium design, as indeed it does in many other design situations, such as home interiors. Several aspects of aquarium lighting require attention:

Aesthetic value

Plant growth

Engineering

Let us consider each of these in turn.

Aesthetic Value

Light is obviously needed to allow people to see into the aquarium. Since it is rare to be able to illuminate with natural daylight, artificial lighting will be installed above the tank. Lighting can be either fluorescent or metal halide. Manufacturers produce both types, and some also make combination units. However, fluorescent lighting predominates in most equipment packages because the initial cost of metal halide lighting is considerable.

FLUORESCENT LIGHTING

Fluorescent lamps come in many types, varying in terms of their intensity, color, and the amount of electricity they consume. The most important of these factors from a purely aesthetic point of view is the color. Each type of fluorescent lamp has its own color rendition. Ever notice how people appear unhealthy under industrial fluorescent lighting? This is because the lamps typically used in such applications are the "cool white" type. This lamp imparts a yellowish-green cast to everything, although it is supposedly the best choice for illuminating your work area. If you have ever taken a color snapshot (using film, not a digital camera) with only this type of lighting and no flash, you can see the green coloration.

Lamps sold specifically for aquarium use are the same ones sold as "plant grow" lamps at the garden center. They impart a reddish-purple color that some people say makes the colors of the fish stand out. However, better lamp choices are available. The best aquarium lamp type, in terms of color rendering, will be rated by the manufacturer in the range of 5000–5500 Kelvin degrees (°K), This lamp's color spectrum is comparable to sunlight near midday under an overcast sky. Such lighting will make the fish and plants sparkle with their natural hues. Various lighting manufacturers produce 5000–5500°K lamps under different brand names. If your aquarium shop does not stock them, check with a lighting company in your area. Be sure to purchase the correct wattage for the fixture you have.

METAL HALIDE LIGHTING

Metal halide lighting provides the very bright light needed for a larger aquarium installation. Manufacturers of metal halide equipment for aquarium use generally produce 5000–5500°K lamps. Besides providing appealing natural coloration, metal halide lighting produces "glitter lines" as it passes through the constantly moving water surface, a decidedly realistic touch. Fluorescent lighting, being diffuse rather than a point-source of light, does not produce glitter lines.

Glitter lines are basically shadows created by the constantly moving water surface. As water moves up and down in surface ripples, light is reflected to a greater or lesser degree. This causes a pattern of bright patches and dark, squiggly lines on the sand and rocks below.

Plant Growth

Lighting must be sufficiently intense for the needs of plants living in the aquarium. I generally suggest plastic plants for smaller tanks, and live plants for larger ones, because larger tanks simply allow for more lighting equipment. I recommend against the "plant grow" type of fluorescent aquarium lamp because they are low output compared to other types. Despite their undeniable aesthetic appeal, plant grow lamps are a poor choice for intensity.

For larger aquariums, metal halide lighting will be absolutely required to provide enough light for proper plant growth. A single lamp provides enough light to illuminate four square feet of water down to a depth of eighteen inches.

One reason larger aquariums need more light is the *Inverse Square Law*. Simply stated, light becomes less intense the farther you are from the source. This is common sense, of course, but the Inverse Square Law tells us how much the intensity decreases. Double the distance and intensity drops to a quarter of its previous level. Most light fixtures use a reflector to direct as much of the lamp output as possible into the tank. This only partially overcomes the Inverse Square Law effect, however, and can be seen from the table below. The following table demonstrates how light intensity diminishes in relation to various distances from a light source with a reflector. The researchers took measurements with a light meter underneath a "shoplight" fluorescent fixture with two forty-watt cool white lamps. Note that the brightest light is at the top center of the tank, with intensity decreasing toward the bottom and ends.

Lighting Table

Height	Lumens				
6 in	100	320	520	320	100
12 in	140	250	300	250	140
18 in	130	180	200	180	130
24 in	110	140	150	140	110
	12 in	6 in	Center	6 in	12 in

Horizontal Distance from Center

Data from Hosizaki, Barbara Joe and Robbin C. Moran. (2001) The Fern Grower's Manual. Portland, OR: Timber Press. p. 31

Engineering

Not only must aquarium lighting provide sufficient intensity and good color rendition, it has to physically fit the tank. Lighting equipment generates heat, and this must be dealt with to avoid overheating. The lighting equipment must also be protected from water, both to avoid electrical hazards and to prevent damage from corrosion and water spots. All of this, not to mention cost, must be taken into account when engineering an aquarium lighting system.

FLUORESCENT LIGHTING SYSTEMS

Fluorescent lamps come in stock sizes. The longer the lamp, the greater the light output and the amount of electricity consumed. Thus, forty-watt lamps are four feet long, twenty-watt lamps are two feet, and so forth. If you are going to use a fixture that sets on top of the tank (the most common design), you will be limited to the lumen output of a certain lamp size, for example, two feet for a twenty-gallon tank. You can always purchase an additional fixture, or one that accommodates two lamps. For small tanks, however, it may be hard to justify the additional expense. That is the main reason I suggest live plants for larger tanks only. Once the tank reaches four feet in length, the lighting options are greater. For example, you can purchase an inexpensive fluorescent fixture, or shoplight, at a DIY store and hang it above the tank. Two of them will fit nicely side by side, giving you a total of 160 watts of lighting, enough for most submerged plants. You will need to allow for some headroom when working on the aquarium, as well as protect the units from water damage. Hanging them with a pulley system that allows the height to be adjusted works well.

Hanging lights over the tank may not appeal to you, and the finished look is certainly industrial. If the tank is built-in, of course, you can hide the lighting on the other side of the wall. For most of us, neither of these will be an option, and we will use an enclosed hood or canopy that provides both a top for the tank and a housing for lighting equipment. Wood or laminate canopies that match the aquarium cabinet create a finished look to free-standing tanks that is hard to beat. You can purchase a canopy with up to four fluorescent lamps.

The heat-producing transformer, or ballast, needed for fluorescent lighting may be dealt with in one of two ways. In the most common design, the ballast is located in the power cord and sits underneath the aquarium or on the floor, out of the way. Protect the floor finish with a cork pad if you place it there, as the ballast may get too hot to touch. For multiple lamps, the ballast is often located within the lighting hood itself. This is because the needed wiring gets complicated, and you would have a fat bundle of cable running from the ballast up to the lamps. To prevent overheating, the manufacturer may install a small fan, such as the one in your computer, to ventilate the hood. A multi-lamp fluorescent hood may offer you the best balance between cost and lighting efficiency for tanks up to four feet long.

METAL HALIDE LIGHTING SYSTEMS

My personal preference for aquarium lighting is metal halide. As mentioned previously, these lamps are hard to beat for light output, color rendering, and durability. The lamps usually last about three times as long as comparable fluorescent lamps, which lose intensity with age. On the downside, metal halide costs considerably more, both for the initial installation and for replacement lamps. Further, the lamps get hot in operation and can be extremely dangerous if broken. Proper design, though, deals with these issues adequately. There are two options: Hang fixtures at intervals above the aquarium (sort of like the lighting above the bar in many restaurants), or use an enclosed hood similar to that described for fluorescent lighting. Hoods containing metal halide lamps absolutely require ventilation via one or multiple fans, and the lamps must be shielded from any contact with water by a clear, heat-resistant plastic panel or tempered glass. All these features contribute to the greater cost. If you are planning a tank much larger than a fifty-five-gallon, however, metal halide will give the most satisfactory results. A four-foot tank will need two lamps (about 150 watts each) and a six footer will require three.

SAFETY AND MAINTENANCE

Every precaution must be taken to avoid an electrical hazard. We all know water and electricity don't mix! I'll have more to say in general about electrical safety and aquariums in the next chapter. For lighting equipment, specifically, look for units that are made of water-repellent materials, that is, plastic, laminates, or properly finished wood. If the design incorporates a protective panel between the water and the lamps, as metal halide systems always should, check to see how easy it will be to remove this panel for cleaning. Water spots can significantly reduce the amount of light reaching the plants. No electrical connections should be exposed. When no protective panel is used, the end caps for mounting fluorescent lamps should be waterproof. The best advice regarding safety is to choose equipment made specifically for aquarium use.

Other than keeping dirt and water spots from blocking the light, maintenance for lighting equipment will be minimal. Replace fluorescent lamps annually. Follow the manufacturer's recommendations on metal halide lamp replacement. Periodically inspect for damage that might admit water, and take any necessary corrective action.

Backgrounds

I confess an aversion to see-through aquariums. Looking past the fish and plants to view the room or persons on the other side just destroys the whole illusion of a natural scene. Nevertheless, I have included a couple of see-through model designs in the book. Most tanks will need a background of some kind, both to block the view of the room or wall on the other side, and to hide wires and hoses running up from the cabinet. Numerous options exist for backgrounds.

Solid Colors

My first preference for an aquarium background is paint. Simply use masking tape to protect the areas you don't want painted, and cover the back outside glass with an exterior-type paint. It will scratch easily, but since it is in the back, it should not receive too much contact. If the tank is built-in paint the ends also. The outside of the glass will not be seen, and paint will prevent a viewer from looking into the equipment space behind the tank.

I like paint for several reasons. First, it comes in any color you want and can be mixed to match anything you like. Second, it is cheap. Any leftovers can be saved to touch up or to do another aquarium. Exterior paint will stand up to the inevitable water spills. It can also be easily removed with a razor blade if you want to change it. Just remember not to try painting a tank unless it is empty. Paint solvents can be fatal to fish if they find their way into the water.

Aquarium shops sell solid color background materials that come in rolls like wallpaper. Any of them can be taped to the back of the aquarium on the outside. Use freezer tape or package sealing tape for this, as other kinds will eventually come loose in the humid environment around an aquarium. Make sure to use a continuous strip of tape along the entire length of the tank at top and bottom and along both sides. If not, foreign matter, dust, and even insects and cobwebs will get lodged between the glass and the background. Nothing detracts more from the appearance of the tank.

The color choice for a solid background is, of course, up to you. I strongly recommend restraint here. Flat black is my favorite choice, because it creates an air of mystery. Something lies beyond the aquarium scene that cannot be seen in the murky water. Black also works with any color of fish, plant, or decorative object. Shades of blue would be my second choice. Light blue for an open water scene, navy for a more shadowed look close to shore. Green and brown tones can also be used, for example, to suggest a distant wall of rocks. Stay away from white, or the aquarium will look like a box of water, which is precisely the opposite of the effect you are seeking. Please do not use bright foil or patterned materials. You don't want the background to be a distraction from what's going on in the aquarium.

Photography

Aquarium dealers also sell backgrounds that are photographs of underwater scenes. These can be effective and attractive backgrounds, provided that the objects in the photo are their normal size and are appropriate to the rest of the aquarium. For example, you do not want a photo of a submarine in the background. This just

Using Your Computer to Make a Tank Background

For smaller tanks, you can make a realistic-looking background with a digital camera and your PC. The cave habitat in Model Design 66 (see page 176) could be enhanced without the time and effort expended to paint a background on the tank. Find a natural rock formation or stone wall that you think will serve the purpose. Take several shots with a digital camera. Use your computer and photo manipulation software to change the color to match the natural rocks you have available. Also crop or stretch the photo to correspond to the proportions of the tank. When you are satisfied with the result, print out a copy using the highest quality your printer will produce. Take this to your nearest copy shop and enlarge it to the correct size. Attach the enlargement to the outside back of the tank, using bits of transparent tape. To protect it, tape a piece of black plastic film, such as a heavy-duty garbage bag, on top of the photo. Then seal all around the edges, using a water-resistant tape or duct tape. This prevents dust or moisture from reaching the color ink on the background.

There is nothing new about this idea, by the way. Shops have sold photo backgrounds for eons. What *is* new is the availability of technology to the average aquarist that enables shooting a customized background and enlarging it to the appropriate size cost effectively.

You can use this basic technique to create a background scene of any size. Remember, however, that a high-resolution image, meaning lots of megapixels, enlarges best. The larger you go the more likely the image will become grainy. This may not matter, however, for an amorphous background such as rock strata.

Think about the many possibilities for using this technique for other designs described in this book. You could, for example, shoot a planted tank and enlarge the image to place behind your tank, containing similar plants. Obviously, you will need some degree of expertise with the camera and software. If you lack these skills, perhaps you know a friend who can teach you.

If you have a generous budget for the aquarium project, you can produce a much higher quality background image by enlarging the photo directly from the digital file. Doing so may require the services of a professional print shop, however, depending on how large a sheet your printer can handle. Don't forget that a large color image will drain those costly ink cartridges, too. Professional inks and paper should also help to increase the longevity of the print, especially if you are careful to protect it from moisture as much as possible.

How about planting your tank, allowing it to grow in, shooting a photo of it and enlarging that photo for the background? Depending upon the tank location, this might be a challenge to install correctly after the tank is in place, but the effect might actually be worth the trouble. Someone once said about Gertrude Jekyll, a famous garden designer, "no amount of trouble is too much for her, to achieve some desired effect." Aquarists can be equally dedicated to their tank designs.

looks silly. On the other hand, if the photo contains elements that can be repeated in the tank, such as plants or driftwood, you can create the impression of a scene stretching infinitely away from the viewer. Some large custom installations feature a photo background shot from nature and then duplicated with real objects in the aquarium. These are sometimes illuminated from behind the tank, creating a striking effect. Such museum-quality designs are, of course, expensive.

Dry Installations

One of the most effective backgrounds is the diorama. Basically, this is a shallow wooden box placed behind the tank, visible through the back glass. It is illuminated, and contains an appropriate scene, recreated without water. Using this technique permits the use of materials, such as tree roots, that might decompose if submerged, or large, heavy rocks that might damage the aquarium tank if used within it. On the downside, the display requires considerable time and expense to create and must remain dust-free, or the illusion is destroyed, and so requires regular cleaning.

Including Terrestrial Components

Aquariums that incorporate some aspect of the shore appeal to those of us interested in tropical plants as well as tropical fish. Many of the aquatic plants described in this book live at least part of their lives out of water. Some plants sold as *aquatic* are, in fact, bog dwellers, or fully terrestrial species that survive only a short time if grown underwater. Fish often seek shelter in the shade of plants overhanging the stream bank. Terrestrial and bog plants can become part of your aquarium display in two ways, either by actually being planted above the water line, or by means of mere suggestion. The latter approach is easier.

Bamboo, for example, is often found in wet locations. It also tends to be associated with the tropics when used as a decorative or construction material. Its widespread use in traditional Chinese, Japanese, and other Asian landscape designs may immediately suggest "Asia" when it appears in the aquarium. Extremely durable, bamboo canes can be had for a few dollars at garden centers. Using a saw with a fine-toothed blade, lengths can be cut and placed vertically at the rear of the aquarium tank. Spacing them randomly gives the illusion that the canes are growing up and out of the water, suggesting the shallow water at the edge of the stream bank. A dark, mud-colored paint background enhances the effect, making the pale bamboo canes stand out. True aquatic plants positioned in front of the bamboo mimic lush vegetation in the shallows.

Cheap enough to replace when you need to, bamboo will last a year or more in the aquarium. If the canes float, use a piece of slate to anchor them. Most aquarium shops sell slate. Using a masonry bit in an electric drill, make a hole in a slab. Cut a bamboo cane at a point just below a segment. Insert a stainless steel screw through the hole in the slate and into the bottom of the cane. Drive the screw through the natural plate that separates two segments of bamboo. Repeat with additional holes, screws, and canes to create a "stand" of bamboo. Cutting one or two pieces of the bamboo at a slight angle will permit attaching the canes to the slate at a tilt. Randomly space these barely tilted canes among the others, to avoid the appearance of telephone poles in perfect alignment and plumb. Natural bamboo canes do not grow that way. Bamboo canes projecting toward and beyond the surface fool the eye into believing that something more lies above the water level of the aquarium.

Terrestrial plants in pots can also be grown above the aquarium and their leaves allowed to droop over the edge. A long, narrow planter situated on wall brackets behind the tank works well in such a design. Make sure the plants will receive enough light, and do not use plants treated with pesticide of any kind, which can find its way into the water and poison all your fish. Also take care when fertilizing. Drips of plant fertilizer reaching your aquarium will result in excessive algae growth. A larger amount of fertilizer will also harm your fish.

Creating a terrestrial zone, that is, actually having part of the scene above the water level, results in an even more realistic look. Such displays sometimes go by the name *vivarium* or *paludarium*. Though more complex to design and build than an aquarium, a paludarium in a suitably large tank is the ultimate recreation of a tropical paradise in the confines of your living space.

In the simplest type of paludarium, the tank is filled only about halfway, and bog plants rooted in the substrate are allowed to grow above the water line. A bolder design would have plants rooted in a growing medium that does not remain saturated. This means the terrestrial area must be separated from the aquatic area by a substantial barrier. Again, the tank is only partially filled, so the growing area remains, literally, high and dry. One solution is to build a platform, supported by rocks or driftwood, above the water line. This platform supports a plastic container of growing mix. Drainage is supplied by a layer of coarse material below the growing medium. Ferns and other houseplants will thrive in this arrangement, benefiting greatly from the high humidity. Additional rocks and driftwood are strategically placed to mask the edges of the container, maintaining the illusion of a natural landscape. Extra-high aquarium tanks lend themselves best to this type of design. Periodically, the plants must be removed, divided, and replanted in fresh medium to keep them in bounds. Vivariums require more maintenance than traditional aquariums, but reward good care with a strikingly beautiful display.

In several designs I suggest including tropical terrestrial plants to create a paludarium. As a rule, in the limited space you will be working with, plants with finely divided foliage and relatively small leaves will look best. Many plants are miniatures that remain under about six inches in height. These may be ideal for the design you have in mind.

Mosses look right at home in the paludarium. You can count on them to have tiny leaves, and their habit of covering everything creates a green carpet. Mosses also appreciate the high humidity in an enclosed growing space. Ferns constitute another group that contains many great choices for a humid, tropical environment. Spike mosses are fern relatives with tiny leaves on creeping stems.

Among the flowering plants, orchids and bromeliads present obvious choices, although they must be chosen carefully. Often these plants have specific cultural needs. Good choices among bromeliads might include small *Tsillandsia* varieties. For possible orchid selections, look for jewel orchids (*Anoectochilus*, *Goodyera*, *Ludisia*, *Macodes*) whose colorfully patterned foliage looks exotic and beautiful even when the plant is not in bloom. Other good orchids include *Paphiopedalum*, *Phalaenopsis*, and a host of lesser-known genera.

Common houseplants, such as philodendrons, creeping fig (*Ficus pumila*), miniature African violets, and *Streptocarpus* should also do well.

Aquascaping

The art of underwater interior design has been dubbed *aquascaping*. Just as naturalistic landscaping involves combining the living and non-living elements of a garden in ways that reflect natural relationships, naturalistic aquascaping seeks the same goal underwater. Although aquariums are built on a much smaller scale than most gardens, you will discover that similar design principles apply to both.

Materials

SUBSTRATES

Substrate refers to the material covering the bottom of the aquarium. It may be purely decorative, may anchor the roots of plants, or may serve as part of the filtration system. Natural gravel, sand, or a combination serves these needs best:

- **Gravel** with grains averaging about ⅛ up to about ¼ inch in diameter is the most commonly used substrate. Many colors, ranging from charcoal to eggshell, are available. Gravel dredged from a river will have rounded edges, while gravel produced by crushing quarry rock is rough and angular. Natural gravel tends to be less uniform in color and grain size. You can mimic the visual effect of the natural material by mixing different types of crushed gravel in varying proportions. Aquarium gravel comes bagged, and is priced by weight. As a rough guide, twenty pounds will cover a square foot of aquarium bottom to a depth of about two inches. Thus, a one- by two-foot tank will require forty pounds of gravel.

- **Sand,** with grains generally smaller than ⅛ inch, can be used instead of, or in addition to, gravel. I find that most aquatic plants grow better if rooted in pure sand or a mixture. Natural river sand or sand made by crushing sandstone is the best choice. Beach sand should be avoided, as should any similarly fine-grained material. You will need a little more sand than gravel to cover the same surface to the same depth, about twenty-five pounds per square foot. The one- by two-foot tank in the previous example will thus require 50 pounds of sand.

A combination of gravel and sand works best for most plants. Use one part sand to three parts gravel.

For installations calling for large amounts of sand or gravel, you can save a lot of money by purchasing from a DIY store, garden center, or even directly from the quarry. Sand sold for sand blasting works great, and is usually sold in fifty- to one-hundred-pound bags. For still larger quantities, these materials can be as cheap as five dollars a ton, even if you purchase only a couple of hundred pounds. Industrial materials need a thorough washing before being used for the aquarium. That chore is up to you, of course.

Please do me a favor and avoid that brightly colored dyed gravel. Some dyes can leach out and harm your fish. They all tend to detract from the natural look of the aquarium and to compete with the bright colors of the tank's inhabitants. Colored glass, while completely inert, creates the same jarring detraction from the aquarium's natural beauty.

DRIFTWOOD

Many aquarium shops sell driftwood. As a decorative material for a variety of habitats, it is indispensable. Natural driftwood is collected and then "cured" for a period of time, usually by soaking it in water with some added bleach. After bleaching, which kills any organisms tagging along, the wood is treated to remove the chlorine and allowed to dry out before being sold. Often, pieces are mounted on a slate base (as previously described for mounting bamboo).

If you collect your own driftwood, you will need to cure it yourself.

1. Use one cup of liquid bleach per five gallons of water and soak the wood for a week. You may need to weight it down until it becomes waterlogged. Invert an old dinner plate over the wood and use a rock to hold it down in the bucket, or simply tie the wood to a large rock to keep it under water.

2. After soaking, use a stiff brush and a garden hose to remove any loose material, and then return the wood to a bucket of fresh water.

3. Add tap water and a tablespoon of sodium thiosulfate. You can also use commercial aquarium dechlorinator at four times the dose recommended on the label.

4. Soak the wood overnight.

5. Allow it to dry in the sun before mounting it on a slate base.

If cured as for driftwood, dead tree roots can also be used. They are particularly effective suspended as a backdrop to suggest the water's edge. The piece should be placed at the top of the tank, with smaller roots hanging down into the water in a natural position. Trimming may be required to achieve just the fit and effect you are seeking. Clamp the piece to a work surface and use an electric saber saw or a small hand saw to shape a flat surface where it will meet the glass near the top edge of the tank. Use heavy scissors or a pair of garden pruners to trim smaller roots so they will dangle to your satisfaction. Once trimmed to fit the tank, the piece can be anchored to the back glass with a blob of silicone sealant.

Rocks

Smooth, water-worn rocks look best in most aquarium designs, for obvious reasons. Some specialized setups call for other types of rock. When layers simulating rock strata are desired, slate looks appropriate and can be stacked without fear of its tumbling down unexpectedly. For tanks featuring African cichlids, limestone of various kinds can be used. Other types of tropical fish would find the water rendered too hard by leaching of carbonates from the limestone, but cichlids from the African rift lakes thrive in hard, alkaline water. Some types of limestone are sufficiently soft to be shaped with relative ease.

If you collect your own rock, make certain you know its geology well enough to avoid introducing harmful substances to the aquarium. Natural deposits may contain metal ores, for example, that can poison the water. If in doubt, only purchase rocks from an aquarium shop.

When selecting rocks, choose several pieces of one specific type or color, rather than one each of several colors. Sticking with one type of rock looks more natural and less distracting.

Besides larger pieces of rock choose a few pebbles of various sizes. Scatter these over the gravel to reduce the monotony of a uniformly colored substrate material. The visual connection between the pebbles and larger rocks somehow makes the scene look more enclosed. Omit the pebbles for a more "open," expansive look. Pebbles can range from the size of a marble to the size of an egg. Smooth, rounded rocks and pebbles suggest flowing water, while flat, angular pieces give the impression of a lake habitat.

Faking It

Aquarium manufacturers have succeeded in creating plastic rocks, driftwood, and plants that look remarkably like the real thing. By all means use them if you wish, alone or in combination with natural materials. Plastic plant reproductions, in particular, may be the best choice if you do not want to invest in the additional lighting and care that living plants require.

Placement

In all cases, when arranging driftwood, rocks, pebbles, gravel, and sand in any combination, bear in mind how these materials sort themselves out in flowing streams and rivers. Here are some helpful guidelines:

- The largest pieces will dominate everything else when confined to an aquarium tank, so exercise the greatest care in choosing them, and the greatest amount of restraint in their number.

- For smaller tanks, limit yourself to three to five larger pieces of rock or only one to three pieces of driftwood. One large piece of driftwood usually looks better than several smaller ones.

- Large objects should be placed firmly on the tank bottom to avoid the possibility of them toppling. Secure them in place with dabs of silicone aquarium sealant, if necessary. (Silicone must be allowed to dry and cure for several days before continuing with design.)

- It is often convenient, though certainly not necessary, to place the larger items near the rear of the tank, where they do double duty by hiding an unsightly hose or heater.

By doing all the following first, before you add fish, you avoid stressing them needlessly. So, try following this order when putting your materials together in your aquarium:

1. Move the tank into its permanent position, then place larger rocks first, followed by smaller pieces.

2. Add most of the washed substrate, making sure it fills the crevices between the rocks.

3. Plants come next, whether living or plastic. Partially filling the tank with water facilitates planting because the leaves will float above the substrate, out of the way. Plants often grow in between rocks or other objects. You may want to mimic this arrangement. Locate a plant near one of the larger rocks, then carefully place one or two smaller rocks on the substrate around the base of the plant. The plant thus appears to have grown from a crevice among this group of rocks.

4. Place pebbles last. Bear in mind that water tends to sort materials by size. Smaller pebbles perched on top of larger ones, for example, contradicts the natural look we are seeking. Keep rearranging until you are satisfied.

5. Sand, when used as a component of the substrate rather than as the sole substrate, should be added last, allowing it to sift naturally into crevices and holes.

6. All this activity will probably leave you with cloudy water. You can start running the filter system at this point. The tank should clear up after a few days, and you can make adjustments to your design. If fine debris settles on plant leaves or in crevices, use a turkey baster to direct a jet of water at the debris,

re-suspending it to be picked up by the filter. You may need to do this several times to remove all the debris.

7. Keep a close check on the filter, and replace or clean the medium when it becomes dirty.

Borrowing from Japanese Gardeners

People seldom fail to notice the similarities between aquarium design and garden design. Good gardeners often make good aquarists, and vice versa. The primary difference lies with scale. Gardeners generally have more than four square feet to work with, whereas a fifty-five-gallon aquarium provides only this much space. Among gardeners, the Japanese have mastered the art of making an impressive garden in a minimum of space. Whether it be the *tsuboniwa*, or courtyard garden, the *bonseki*, or dish garden, or *bonsai*, pruned dwarfed trees, the design draws upon basic principles to create the illusion of spaciousness. Four basic principles, developed over hundreds of years, exemplify this technique. Aquarists can apply the same rules. They are:

- Inspiration from nature
- Wildness versus control
- Personal expression
- Idealization

Let's consider how each of these works in designing an aquarium.

Inspiration from Nature

Throughout this book I emphasize the value of taking inspiration from natural habitats to create aquarium habitats. This, however, should not limit us *solely* to combinations of fish and plants from the same geographic region. Creating a harmonious aquarium community lies in selecting fish and plants for the ecological roles they play. For example, Asian rasboras will do just as well when paired with South American *Corydoras* catfishes as will South American tetras. Rasboras and tetras inhabit similar environments and fulfill similar ecological roles. Importantly, their roles do not overlap with those of the catfish. Catfish are bottom feeders, the others feed at midwater level. In the model designs presented later, I combine species with compatible ecological roles.

Wildness versus Control

A simplistic example of this principle is the separation of predators and prey. Although the angelfish may feed on neon tetras in the wild, we avoid combining them in the aquarium. Similarly, live aquatic plants need regular pruning and thinning. We don't usually allow them to grow rampantly. Another, more subtle kind of control has to do with manipulating the viewer's perception of space. By the controlled placement of natural objects it becomes possible to fool the eye into thinking a space is larger or smaller than it is in reality. This technique is known as *forced perspective,* and proves invaluable time and again.

For example, to make the aquarium look deeper, place an especially interesting, tall plant with bold, colored foliage near the front glass, positioned slightly to one side of center. A good choice might be *Hygrophila corymbosa* var. *gracilis*, giant red hygrophila. (This plant may be identified in older literature as *Nomaphila stricta*.) Use a pale green, wispy plant, such as *Echinodorus tenellus*, to create a monotonous lawn along the rear wall of the tank. In between, place a piece of driftwood to obscure the "middle ground." This arrangement distorts perspective, and fools the eye into thinking that the space is larger than it is. The trick is to keep the view toward the back less well defined than the one in front. The eye will be drawn first to the more interesting object. When the forward object is taller than those in the rear, we tend to perceive the distance between them as greater than it actually is. This arrangement reverses the usual aquascaping advice to keep tall things toward the back.

Conversely, if your intention is to allow the viewer an imagined glimpse into an enclosed space, place the larger, more boldly colored *Hygrophila* toward the back of the tank. Plant the *Echinodorus tenellus* near the front, creating a uniform, medium-textured lawn. Frame this view with curving pieces of driftwood or tall, bushy plants such as *Limnophila aquatica* placed in each corner. The eye will again be drawn to the bright colors, which are now at the back, and in effect bring them forward. This effect, when combined with the "frame" at the front, gives the impression of a window into a secluded corner.

Personal Expression

Allow yourself to experiment with aquascaping until you achieve the look you want. An artistic design maximizes the stress-reducing value of the aquarium. You may evoke calmness or excitement with your choices. For example, fish that constantly dart around, such as zebra danios, and a strongly directional current create an upbeat mood. Enhance the effect by using bright lighting, a pale-colored substrate, and skinny plants that will accentuate the water movement as they bend with the flow.

On the other hand, you may find this look too busy. You can aquascape for a calming effect. Use a dark substrate, a plain black background, minimal current, and dense plantings. Choose fish more laid back in their behavior, a school of timid pencilfish, perhaps. Filter the light with floating plants. This design will appear more relaxed.

Idealization

One of the many pleasures of aquarium keeping is the feeling of accomplishment when the design comes together just right. As with the Japanese gardener, the aquarist strives not to imitate nature precisely, but actually to enhance it. We achieve this by incorporating pleasing elements (calmness, brightness) and avoiding unpleasant ones (predation, decay). Aquarists often admit to me the value they place on feeling a sense of control over the microcosm they have built. Like calm, a sense of control is highly to be desired amid the stress and hurry of our daily lives.

SUMMARY

For an aquarium to appear most like a natural underwater scene, its design must include elements that would naturally occur together. For example, if you create a display of fish from a flooded Amazon forest, the tank should have plenty of driftwood to simulate submerged roots or stumps and lots of vegetation. Fish from a swift Asian stream will encounter smooth rocks and pebbles, but few plants can take root in a strong current, so you need not include a lot of greenery in a stream tank. Regardless of the habitat you select for the basis of your design, such seemingly inconsequential factors can make all the difference between a natural look and a contrived one. Keep this in mind as you execute the model designs I suggest, and when developing new designs of your own.

CHAPTER 4

NUTS AND BOLTS

To retain the aquarium's decorative value over the long term requires planning. Unlike non-living art, the aquarium is dynamic, always changing due to the growth, maturation, and yes, death of its inhabitants. Anticipating these changes and making allowances for them from the beginning will maximize your enjoyment long into the future. For example, as fish grow they place bigger demands on the filtration system. You need a filtration system adequate to the task of caring for mature specimens, despite the fact that what you bring home from the shop may be diminutive juveniles. Make sure you are aware of the mature size of any fish you are considering. Your choice of equipment packages will depend upon the needs of the fish, as well as upon practical considerations, such as how to hide the filtration equipment so it does not distract observers of the tank. In this regard, different design considerations apply to built-in aquariums as opposed to free-standing ones. Both types are discussed below.

Built-in Installations

A built-in aquarium offers many advantages over a free-standing design. Unattractive equipment hides behind the wall. Spills and splatters mostly occur behind the scene, also. The aquarium can have its own plumbing. Equipment, such as the lighting system, can be of an industrial type; no need for an expensive, finished housing. On the downside, of course, installation is a major project and the cost can be much greater than a more traditional, free-standing system. Only you can judge if the added expense is worth it.

A built-in aquarium should be at least one hundred gallons in capacity. Anything smaller is hardly worth it, considering the cost of building a new interior wall or cutting through an existing one. You will need at least four by eight feet of floor space. The aquarium is essentially enclosed in a closet. The tank itself will be up to two by six feet, assuming you use the largest available stock size, holding about two hundred gallons. Of course, custom tanks can be any size, but I will discuss what might be possible as a do-it-yourself (DIY) project on a relatively limited budget.

Electricity and Water Supplies

Let's say you happen to have a closet of appropriate size that you can spare. What else must be taken into account before you begin installing the aquarium? Before cutting a window into the wall you must first determine if this is a load-bearing wall. If any doubt exists, consult a licensed contractor. Otherwise, you could seriously weaken the structure of your house! Next determine if electrical service is located within the wall section to be removed. If so, you will need to re-route the wiring. This may gain you the electrical circuit you need inside the closet to supply the aquarium. On the other hand, this circuit may already be carrying all the load it can handle, and you will require new service for the aquarium equipment. In either case, I strongly recommend obtaining the services of an electrician, unless you thoroughly understand basic home wiring skills. Wiring in the vicinity of the aquarium should be enclosed in waterproof conduit connecting waterproof junction boxes. Proper installation requires practice, but still lies within the DIY realm if you are the handy type. All circuits must be protected by ground-fault circuit interrupters (GFCI). This is an extremely important safety precaution. The device monitors the circuit, comparing the current in each of the two conductors, which should be equal unless there is a "fault" or break in the insulation protecting the conductors. A ground fault means electricity is no longer confined to its intended path, and instead is taking an alternate route through the aquarium water to reach ground. When a heater element, for example, contacts water because the protective glass tube around it has broken, you have a ground fault. The current in each conductor will cease to be equal when this happens. The GFCI detects the inequality and instantly shuts off power, protecting you against a shock. This is why codes often require GFCI protection for wet locations such as in a bathroom or near a spa. Again, consult a professional unless you thoroughly understand the nature of the work involved. Some municipalities may require that all wiring be done by a licensed electrician. Always check local codes before attempting a do-it-yourself project.

You may also need a plumber if you intend to have a laundry sink near the aquarium. Plumbing only the filtration system you can probably handle yourself, with the help of the instructions that come with the equipment. You may want to provide a drain valve as part of the filtration system. Ideally, a large tank should drain directly to the sink. If this is impossible, you can install a drain valve that can be connected to a garden hose to direct water to the nearest drain.

Floor Load

You must also make certain the floor can carry the weight. Water itself weighs eight pounds per gallon. Water to fill the 210-gallon tank in our example will, therefore, weigh almost 1,700 pounds. Substrate will add more weight, not to mention the tank itself, especially if it is made of glass. You should assume the completed aquarium weighs a ton. Dividing by the tank's footprint of twelve square feet yields a load on the floor of 167 pounds per square foot. Typical building code requirements for a load-bearing residential floor call for it to support one hundred pounds per square foot when the flooring is supported by wooden joists. Your floor may need shoring up to support the weight of a large tank. Fortunately, this is relatively easy to do using steel posts, cinder block columns, or similar means. Here again, you will need a contractor unless you fully comprehend the nature of the work involved.

The tank itself will need to be supported at a convenient viewing height. Space should be provided beneath the tank for installing the filter equipment. Sturdy construction using framing lumber works best. The wood can be given several coats of an exterior-grade paint to prevent water absorption.

The opening in the wall should be approximately ¼ to ½ inch larger than the outside dimensions of the tank. This ensures no undue stress will be placed on the glass as a result of too tight a fit. Molding will frame the tank on the viewing side of the wall, hiding the gap. The aquarium should fit snugly against the molding all the way around. Any gaps should be filled with painter's caulk or silicone before applying finish to the molding. This step prevents dirt from accumulating between the glass and the molding. Generally, the trim on the room side of the aquarium should match the other woodwork in the room.

Apartment dwellers should limit themselves to smaller aquariums, or have the entire project overseen by a professional. Improper installation could result in great risk of damage to the floors below the apartment.

Lighting

The least expensive lighting system for a built-in consists of multiple fluorescent fixtures suspended on chains about a foot above the water surface. For the six-foot tank in our example, I suggest a bank of six four-foot fixtures, each holding two forty-watt lamps. This provides three rows of two fixtures each placed end to end. Each pair stretches along the length of the tank. They will extend about a foot beyond each end if the aquarium is centered under them, but this should create no problems and will merely provide additional light for the work area.

Ideally, electrical service for the lighting will be located on or near the ceiling, thus affording maximum protection from splashing water. Alternatively, suspended metal halide fixtures of the industrial variety can be used. You will need three of them, spaced equally along the length of the tank. Control individual metal halide fixtures, or each of the three pairs of fluorescent units, with separate timers. This enables you to vary the lighting to simulate the changing patterns that occur over the course of a day, or to temporarily create special effects for dining or entertaining. Ballasts for all of this lighting equipment, whether metal halide or fluorescent, will create heat.

The enclosure should be vented, ideally to the outside, or at least into adjacent rooms. Passive vents through the wall, both above the aquarium and near floor level below it, can be installed during construction. Warm air from the aquarium enclosure flows out the upper vents and is replaced by cooler air from the floor. This is a simple approach that consumes no additional energy. Fan-driven vents, such as a bathroom ceiling fan, can be installed to move air from the enclosure to the outside via duct work. For this, once again, you may need to consult a pro.

Filtration

Although many different types of aquarium filters exist, none is more satisfactory for the installation we are considering than the so-called *wet-dry* system popular with saltwater aquarists. I value this type of filter more for the basic plumbing scheme than for its superiority as a biological filter. In its simplest form, a second aquarium tank, known as a *sump*, sits underneath the main display tank. The display tank has a drain hole in the bottom, with a standpipe projecting above this drain. The height of the standpipe determines the water level within the tank. The standpipe is connected to the sump by pipes or hoses. An electric pump moves water from the sump via a pipe that reaches the top of the aquarium, where it discharges into the tank. When the pump is turned on, water from the sump causes the display tank to overflow the standpipe, which then drains water back to the sump, completing the circuit. The total capacity of the system equals the tank capacity plus the capacity of the sump.

The standpipe inside the main tank is usually surrounded by an opaque plastic box with notches at the top, over which water flows. The idea behind this design is to trap floating debris and surface film while also protecting surface-dwelling fish. Some species of fish, however, may be so inclined to dive over this waterfall that in order to exclude them you need a fine plastic mesh instead of narrow notches. Maintenance will be required to keep the mesh free of obstructions, such as dead leaves.

Efficient biological filtration occurs when a filter medium is placed in a box or on a tray between the tank drain and the sump, where it is showered constantly with water. Beneficial bacteria colonize this material and detoxify pollutants produced by the metabolism of the fish and plants in the display tank. When live plants grow in abundance as part of the display, much of this filtration capacity is redundant, and the filter medium can be dispensed with, although it does perform the valuable function of trapping particles of sediment.

The sump also provides a convenient location for the heater. Not only is it out of sight, it is protected from accidental damage during tank maintenance.

Accumulating biologically active debris is a further benefit of the sump. Fine particulate matter will accumulate on the bottom. Thus, it can easily be siphoned out. Placing one or more baffles between the inlet side and the outlet side of the sump enhances debris collection. While the debris would be unsightly if left in the display aquarium, it is teeming with beneficial microorganisms that break down and recycle wastes, resulting in improved water quality. Saltwater enthusiasts sometimes refer to this material as *magic mud* in recognition of its benefits to the aquarium's ecology.

The sump can facilitate changing water, as well. By installing valves in the return line from the pump to the display tank, water can be directed either into the tank or to an external drain line. To operate this system:

1. Shut down the pump.
2. Close the valve leading to the aquarium and open the drain valve.
3. Turn the pump back on.
4. When the sump is nearly empty, shut off the pump and switch the valves back to their operating positions.
5. Refill the sump with replacement water.
6. Restart the pump to complete the process.

The capacity of the sump must be such that all the water in the plumbing system can drain into it without overflowing in the event of a power outage or pump failure. I suggest a sump of half the capacity of the main tank, although a much smaller sump may be enough to contain the water. Having a bigger sump makes working in it easier, increases the total water volume in the system, and minimizes any risk of overflow.

Some aquarists worry about designs that require drilling a hole in the bottom of the tank. Although a catastrophic leak is unlikely with proper workmanship, leaks do occasionally happen. You can have a truly fail-safe system by locating the sump above the display tank. In this case, the sump is called a *header tank*. A submersible pump located inside the display tank transfers water to the header tank. Near the top of the header tank, a drain hole allows water to escape, falling into the main tank through a connecting pipe. If the pump fails, a small amount of water drains into the display tank, and that's that. This arrangement presents additional engineering challenges, such as supporting the weight of the elevated header tank and making allowances for the lighting equipment, which must be located below the header tank and above the display tank.

Another way to eliminate the drain hole in the bottom of the display tank is to install a siphon to drain water to the sump. Unfortunately, this arrangement may also be vulnerable to problems. If the pump stops operating, water will continue to siphon into the sump until the main tank is drained below the intake point. You can easily avoid such a disaster by drilling a small hole in the siphon just below the desired water level in the display aquarium. When water drains to a point below this siphon-break, air rushes into the pipe and the siphoning stops.

> WARNING   Be extremely cautious about making major modifications to your house without first checking code requirements and making sure you have the right skills for the job. A licensed professional will likely be needed to modify wiring and plumbing, in particular. In some jurisdictions, even renovations that do not involve wiring and plumbing require building permits if they exceed a certain cost. Aside from concerns about regulations, improperly installed wiring can create a fire hazard, and improperly done plumbing may result in leaks that will lead to water damage. Hiring a contractor, whose job it is to navigate the labyrinth of building regulations, may be your best bet.

Maintenance

Built-in aquariums are frequently simpler to maintain than their free-standing counterparts. Factors contributing to ease of maintenance include having a sink adjacent to the aquarium, valves for drain and refill, and easier access to equipment. If maintenance is easy to carry out, chances are you will stick to a regular schedule. This is crucial to the long-term success of your aquarium, regardless of its size. Just make sure your nets and the all-important algae removal tool have sufficiently long handles for the height of the tank.

Finishes

All surfaces that might be exposed to water should be protected with an exterior-grade paint or varnish. If the drywall through which the tank projects is made of sheet rock, be certain that any exposed edges are covered. I recommend finishing the opening as if it were a pass-through or doorway prior to installing the tank itself. For the tank support structure, treated lumber can be used for an extra measure of protection against water damage.

The floor beneath the aquarium is likely to take the most abuse from spilled water. Choose from the array of flooring materials one might use in a bathroom. Sheet vinyl, vinyl tile, or ceramic tile are all good options.

Cost Estimating

The cost of a built-in aquarium will approximate that of a bathroom addition. This can be $15,000 or more, depending upon construction costs in your area. You can save by doing most of the work yourself, but you should attempt this only if you are qualified. Not only can shoddy construction hamper your future enjoyment of the aquarium, it can pose danger to you and your family, and even reduce the value of your home. You may also need a building permit for an aquarium installation, if certain modifications to existing wiring or plumbing are required. Check with your local code enforcement authority.

Free-Standing Installations

If you cannot afford a built-in aquarium, you can have plenty of fun—not to mention impress your guests—with a skillfully done free-standing system. When making the recommendations that follow, I am assuming that one of the aquarium's main purposes is to be an artistic focal point for your living space. Some of my suggestions, therefore, merely enhance the look of the finished tank without affecting its functionality. You can cut corners on these purely decorative options to save money. Do not scrimp, however, on the recommended filtration or lighting, as doing so will make a big difference in the health and longevity of your fish. Building a successful aquarium with off-the-shelf equipment poses few problems if you know what to look for.

Electricity and Water Supplies

I agree with the commonly given advice to choose a location for your aquarium that is away from windows and exterior doors, free from drafts, relatively stable with respect to temperature, and lacking in excessive noise or vibration. I have yet to find the perfect spot anywhere in my house, so you will probably have to compromise a bit on one or more of these criteria. Temperature stability should be the main goal. Above all, though, choose a spot with adequate electrical outlets and a sink within a reasonable distance. You are going to need electricity to operate the filter pump, lighting, and probably a heater. If not enough outlets are handy, you can always use one of those power strips that nearly everyone has under their computer desks. Do not just leave it lying on the floor. Mount the outlet strip on the wall next to the outlet or vertically inside the aquarium cabinet so the receptacles are not pointing upward, just waiting for water to spill into them. For safety's sake, purchase a power strip with a GFCI device (see page 58) to protect against shocks. Alternatively, replace the existing wall outlet with a GFCI receptacle (if you know what you're doing) or hire an electrician to do so.

Having a sink near the aquarium makes doing water changes much easier. The farther you have to lug heavy buckets the less likely you are to do this important chore on a regular basis. One way to avoid buckets altogether is to use a drain/fill device with a garden hose. Aquarium dealers sell these gadgets. The cost is minor in comparison to the amount of labor they save. The device attaches to a faucet, and a hose connects to a side arm. Basically, you connect up everything and turn on the water full blast. As tap water flows rapidly through the device suction is produced in the side arm by the Venturi effect. A valve on the unit is first set to suction water through the hose to drain the tank. Tank water mixes with the flow from the tap, and drains into the sink. Then, when you are finished draining, you switch the valve's position, and tap water now flows through the side arm to the hose, refilling the tank. About halfway through the refill, you can dose the tank with a dechlorinator, if you use one.

Floor Load

Floor load, as mentioned earlier, is the weight of the aquarium per square foot of footprint. In a typical frame house, floors support 100 pounds per square foot. If the tank you choose exceeds this limit, you must install additional support below to avoid an accident. A 60-gallon hexagonal tank, for example, weighs about 600 pounds when full. Dividing by its 4.5 square foot base gives 134 pounds per square foot. This tank would require additional support. How you position the tank relative to the floor's construction also matters. If the floor joists run parallel to the wall against which the tank sits, all the weight will be supported only by the single joist nearest the wall. On the other hand, if the joists run perpendicular to the wall, the tank will be supported by more than one joist, a sturdier arrangement.

Lighting

For free-standing tanks, the most decorative approach to lighting is an enclosed hood that matches the cabinet. For growing plants, up to four fluorescent lamps can be hidden inside in the hood. Metal halide lighting can also be used, but this is overkill on anything under about seventy-five gallons, unless the tank is quite deep and you want to grow plants that demand high light levels. One drawback to any type of enclosed lighting hood is its bulkiness. The thing needs to be moved out of the way in order for any work to be done in the tank. Another issue is heat. While not a problem with fluorescent lighting on a small tank, metal halide lamps or multiple fluorescent ballasts may require forced air ventilation of the hood to avoid overheating. This is accomplished with one or more small computer fans installed in the hood, adding to both cost and weight. Some people may find the audible whirr of the fan annoying. If you are using plastic plants, lighting can be selected for viewing only, and you need nothing more complicated than the traditional single lamp fixture. You may want to review the discussion of lighting in Chapter 2 before shopping for equipment.

Filtration

Filtration systems that incorporate a sump offer as many advantages to a free-standing tank as they do to built-ins. The only real difference will be in the size of the sump, which must fit beneath the aquarium, hidden by the support cabinet.

If you don't want to bear the extra expense of a drilled tank and sump filter system, plenty of other options exist.

CANISTER FILTERS

In this design, the filter media are contained within a sealed canister through which water is pumped. The inlet and outlet pipes are connected to the canister by hoses. Since the only equipment in the tank are the two pipes, they can easily be hidden with plants or decorations. The canister sits underneath the cabinet.

HANG-ON FILTERS

The hang-on design is an old and reliable one, especially for smaller tanks. Water siphons out of the tank into a box that hangs from the top rim. After passing through filter media, it is pumped back into the tank over a spillway. Various brands add other features to this basic design.

FILTER MEDIA

Either type of external filter can contain two basic types of media: particle and chemical. The most commonly used chemical medium is activated carbon. It excels at removing compounds that tint the water yellow, and even traps some large molecules, too. Carbon has a short lifespan, however, and needs regular replacement. The pores in the carbon pieces become saturated with the substances extracted from the water. Despite this, the carbon does continue to function as a biological filter, because each piece becomes colonized with beneficial bacteria. Though not absolutely necessary, carbon filtration benefits almost any tank.

All sorts of plastic and fiber products are sold as particle filter media in aquarium shops. Their function is to trap suspended debris, giving the aquarium a tidier appearance. Like carbon, a particle media will become colonized by beneficial bacteria, and thus does double duty. In fact, this may be the main value, especially in an aquarium that lacks living plants to help with fish waste removal.

I have found that external filter media supplied as a cartridge ready to slip neatly into the canister or hang-on box are the least trouble to work with. Periodically, any filter medium will require flushing out and/or replenishment. Many aquarists find it most convenient to do this when performing a partial water change. If you are merely rinsing the particle medium, do so in the bucket of old aquarium water. That will help to maintain bacterial activity. Because changing the carbon or rinsing particle media with tap water drastically reduces the population of beneficial bacteria, I recommend only replacing a portion with new medium at each maintenance time. If you are using cartridges, you can leave the old cartridge sitting in the filter box for a week or so after you install a new cartridge, in order to keep those bacteria on the job. If the box is not large enough for both cartridges, you can place the old one in a mesh bag (available from aquarium dealers) and suspend it temporarily in the tank.

UNDERGRAVEL FILTERS

In this type, the gravel on the bottom of the tank is the filter. A perforated plastic plate sits on the bottom of the tank, with standpipes that reach the surface. Water is pumped up through the standpipes by small electric pumps called *powerheads*. This causes more water to flow downward through the gravel bed. Each piece of gravel becomes coated with beneficial bacteria.

The undergravel filter offers the least expensive option for efficient biological filtration, but has some drawbacks. First, some plants do not like water movement around their roots, which occurs if they are growing above the filter plate. This won't matter, of course, if you are using plastic plants. Second, the gravel bed also acts as a particle filter, and will become hopelessly clogged with debris if it is not periodically "vacuumed" with a specially designed aquarium siphon. Despite these negatives, I have enjoyed many a tank outfitted with only an undergravel filter. Combining an undergravel filter with an external filter also works well, giving you an extra measure of pollution control.

Maintenance

Maintenance for any freshwater aquarium involves the same procedures regardless of size. In this regard, the only difference between a free-standing setup and a built-in one is convenience. Carrying out weekly partial water changes is the most essential chore. You will also need to remove algae from the glass. A monthly cleaning or partial replacement of filter media will also be necessary. It is more convenient, as mentioned above, to do all of this when the tank is located in its own enclosure with plumbing and a sink. Even so, with a free-standing tank, weekly maintenance will take only around an hour, even for tanks as large as one hundred gallons. If you cannot spare an hour a week for aquarium care, you should either hire a maintenance service, or look for another way to add interest to the den.

The inside of the cabinet will be cramped, hindering access to the filter system. I suggest storing food, nets, and other supplies elsewhere, to leave more room to get at the equipment. It will also be dark under there unless you install a work light. Battery-powered closet lights work just fine. You can find one at any department or DIY store.

Finishes

Aquarium furniture manufacturers offer an impressive range of cabinets, stands, and hoods in wood, laminate, even stainless steel finishes. Choose whatever looks best with the décor of the room. You can browse the available options at manufacturer's Web sites, and even order online if your local dealer does not carry what you want.

A cheaper alternative, though with drawbacks, is a wrought-iron aquarium stand. In the right setting, painted wrought iron can be quite attractive. Choose a stand with scrollwork for a Victorian conservatory look, or a simple rectilinear design for more modern surroundings. The major drawback is the open space underneath, revealing all the equipment and marring the overall look of the aquarium. Many people use plants, either live houseplants or silk ones, to disguise a canister filter sitting under the tank. Rust can also be a problem. If you buy a wrought-iron stand, take the time to give it several coats of exterior paint, which will last far longer than the cursory paint job applied at the factory.

Wood stands are widely available, and have the same advantages and disadvantages as wrought iron. You can paint the wood as you prefer, using exterior paint for water resistance.

Cost Estimating

A free-standing tank will cost a lot less than a custom built-in one, of course, but be prepared to spend around $500 and up for a complete system with a nice cabinet, proper lighting, live plants, and the fish.

SUMMARY

Whether free-standing or built-in, your aquarium must meet certain specifications if it is to provide you with long-term satisfaction and enjoyment. Foremost is the requirement that every aspect of the installation be completed without creating a hazard for your household. Modifications to the water or electrical supply, to the ability of the floor to support the weight of the tank, or to structural components of the house are best carried out under the supervision of a licensed contractor. Do-it-yourselfers should content themselves with a free-standing installation. Although the fish will not know the difference, a safe, sturdy, and durable aquarium will be the most pleasing one for its human audience.

CHAPTER 5

TROUBLESHOOTING

E ven though you may follow my instructions to the letter, your aquarium may develop problems. This may occur through no fault of yours. A power outage, for example, may cause a chill (heater cannot operate) or a rise in ammonia (filtration is interrupted), or both (double whammy). Fish, and to a lesser degree, plants, are stressed by these disturbances of their environment. A disease outbreak may be the ultimate result of any form of stress.

Stress underlies most aquarium problems, and can usually be traced to environmental conditions outside the optimum range. The cause of the stress may be invisible. Ammonia in the water can only be detected by testing, for example. But this chapter can give you an idea of what to be looking for and what to test for so you can discover and correct the problem. Knowing how to cope will save *you* from becoming stressed.

Disease Prevention

Ich

By far the most common disease resulting from environmental stress is *ich*. The causative agent is a single-celled parasite that alternates between a free-swimming infective stage, and a reproductive phase that remains attached to the fish, feeding off its body fluids. At the proper time in its life cycle, the parasite falls off the fish, sinks to the bottom, and produces more free-swimming parasites that spread the infestation. Ich is usually discovered during its attached phase. Look for:

- Individual lesions that look like tiny white dots, making the fish appear as though it has been sprinkled with salt

- Fish scratching themselves in an effort to dislodge the parasite

- Fish hanging near the surface or in the current from the filter return because their gills have been affected and they are seeking oxygen.

In the confines of an aquarium, the problem will quickly claim every occupant. Fortunately, various commercial remedies are available. Make sure you select one that will not harm live plants. Also, be wary of medications containing methylene blue, which is toxic to beneficial bacteria. If you wipe out the biological filter, you will increase stress as ammonia begins to accumulate. Used according to manufacturer's instructions, medication can halt the progress of the parasite, and the fish will recover.

That said, you must also take action to correct whatever was inducing stress in the first place. The following sections describe some common reasons and their solutions.

Temperature Fluctuations

If the tank is getting too cool, you may need a larger heater or you may have to move the tank to a location with a more stable temperature. Choose a heater that provides five watts or more per gallon of water. Keep the tank away from floor registers and outside doors.

If the aquarium is too warm, the most likely culprit is sunlight from a nearby window. You can fix this with shades or draperies, or by relocating the tank.

Overcrowding

Stick to the stocking recommendations made in this book, and you should have no problems with overcrowding. Too many fish in too small a tank will lead to water pollution because the filtration system is overtaxed. Pollution rapidly leads to stress. Crowding also increases the likelihood of aggression among the fish. Many species need sufficient space, or they may not remain peaceable toward their tank mates. Fighting is also stressful, and may leave the weaker fish injured, inviting disease.

Overfeeding

Review the feeding recommendations I offer in chapter 1, and in the discussions of some individual fish species in the model designs to follow. Exceeding the amount the fish need not only wastes food but also leads to the accumulation of uneaten food in the tank. This material decays, adding to the load on the biological filter. In effect, overfeeding creates the same undesirable condition as overcrowding: not enough capacity to meet the demand placed on the filter. Pollutants therefore accumulate to the detriment of the fish.

Medicating Unnecessarily

Beginners often make two kinds of mistakes with medications. The first is thinking that exceeding the dosage recommended on the label will lead to a quicker cure. The second is regularly adding medication as a preventive measure. The best preventive measure is following the rules laid down here (and in every other book on the subject) for proper care and feeding.

Adding Antibiotics

Never add antibiotics to a display tank. Apart from the fact that choosing an appropriate antibiotic treatment may require the diagnostic skills of a veterinarian, many will kill beneficial filter bacteria along with the disease-causing ones. If you knock out the filter, your problems will multiply rapidly. If you conclude that only an antibiotic will save a valuable specimen, carry out the treatment in a separate hospital tank.

OSMOTIC PRESSURE

Aquarists seldom give thought to this stressor. To understand it, a little background explanation is needed. Freshwater fish are "saltier" than the water in which they swim. Their body fluids contain more dissolved substances than the surrounding stream or pond. Because water tends to move, by the process known as osmosis, from an area of low concentration of solutes to an area of higher concentration, freshwater fish tend to take on water. They have consequently evolved physiological mechanisms to cope with whatever level of dissolved minerals is present in their natural habitat, to maintain the correct balance inside their bodies. Only a few kinds of fish are able to inhabit both dilute environments and more concentrated ones.

In the aquarium, dissolved substances accumulate that would not do so in a natural setting. Nitrate, the end product of biological filtration, is one such substance. Some nitrate removal by plants does occur, but the tank will usually produce an excess beyond their needs. If the tap water is hard, it will also contribute to the load. Tap water may also contain phosphate. Phosphate does not contribute to hardness, but nevertheless increases the osmotic pressure of the water. Similarly, dissolved organic compounds, including those responsible for yellowing of the water, add to the load. If these multiple accumulations of dissolved substances are not somehow dealt with, they will eventually reach a concentration beyond which the fish cannot cope, and stress results.

Despite numerous attempts over the years to devise a filtration strategy to eliminate the need for water changes, this simple procedure remains the surest way to cope with the buildup of dissolved compounds. Every author stresses the importance of carrying out regular partial water changes. Now and then, a major overhaul of the aquarium will be necessary to restore the appropriate balance.

The baseline of water quality is the initial water conditions when the tank is set up. With time, the level of dissolved substances increases, until a partial water change results in an abrupt reduction. Because only part of the water is changed, however, the overall trend will always be upward. This is because the fish continue to excrete wastes at a steady rate. Doing a partial water change will return the tank only part way to the baseline, and by the time the next water change is due, additional accumulation of dissolved compounds will have occurred. For example, assume zero waste is present at setup and that twenty milligrams of waste per liter are generated by the fish each month. A fifty percent water change will reduce the first month's accumulation to ten milligrams, but during the second month another twenty will be added by the fish, a total of thirty milligrams by the end of the month. Another fifty percent change now leaves behind fifteen milligrams, and so forth each month.

Now and then, therefore, it is necessary to do a water change of 100 percent, or nearly so, to return to baseline conditions. How often should this occur? I suggest about every six months. You may need to catch all of the fish and hold them in a separate container as you drain the aquarium. To do this, you may need to remove all the plants, although avoid this if you can. Take precautions, to prevent plants from drying out if you are forced to remove them. You can hold them in a separate container of water, or pile them on newspapers and use a spray bottle to mist them every few minutes while you are working. When I do a major change, I have replacement water standing by, so that as soon as I drain the tank I can begin filling it again. Prior to draining, it is a good idea to do a really thorough job with the algae scraper, thus allowing you to siphon out a lot of algae along with the old water. As you remove water, you can also use a gravel vacuum to eliminate accumulated debris from the substrate, taking care not to damage the roots of any plants remaining in the tank. A major upheaval like this need not be unnecessarily stressful to the tank's inhabitants. Just make sure the replacement water is the same temperature as the tank, and that any treatment, such as the addition of African cichlid salts, has been carried out. If you act with care, you will be amazed how much better the aquarium looks the next day.

Velvet

This condition is similar to ich symptomatically, but may be harder to detect. The parasite causes a brownish or golden film to appear on the fish's skin. There may not be any obvious lesions or dots, and the fish may simply look dull rather than shiny. Sometimes the only obvious symptoms are scratching, hiding, or hanging out where oxygen is most abundant, as described earlier for ich cases. Treatment for velvet is the same as for ich, using a commercial remedy.

Fungal Disease

Any white, yellowish, or gray cottony growth on the body or fins is usually referred to as a *fungus*. In reality, many cases are due to bacterial growth. This condition commonly results from an injury. Perhaps two fish have been fighting and one has suffered a wound. The problem can also result from severely degraded water conditions. Excess food may be providing a rich breeding ground for bacteria. Coupled with the inevitable stress resulting when water quality deteriorates, the presence of abundant bacteria leads to an infection.

Euthanasia

Often the best course of action is to euthanize a debilitated fish. A simple, painless way to do this is available. Place the fish in a plastic cup of aquarium water and set the cup in the freezer. Discard cup and all the next day. Do not flush a sick fish down the toilet. This condemns the fish to slow suffocation.

If the cottony growth is localized, the best treatment is simply to remove the fish and dab the infected area with ordinary mercurochrome, diluted by half with tap water, using a cotton swab. Hold the fish gently in the net, and return it as quickly as possible to the aquarium. Anything more than a small, localized area of fungus requires transferring the fish to a hospital tank and treatment with either an antifungal agent or an antibiotic. If the fish has a large area of cottony growth, chances are treatments will not be effective. It may be best to consider euthanasia in such circumstances.

Dropsy and Popeye

The condition known as *dropsy* is characterized by swelling of the body. Often the body becomes so distended that the scales turn outward. This problem results from internal organ failure. Affected fish should be euthanized. Dropsy seldom affects fish that receive proper care.

A similar condition, known as *popeye*, occurs when fluids accumulate behind the eyeball, which protrudes grotesquely. Probably resulting from injury or seriously degraded water conditions, popeye is seldom treated effectively, and the fish should be euthanized.

Diet-Related Problems

Improper diet leads to several debilitating conditions. Certain African cichlids may succumb to *Malawi bloat*, thought to result from a diet too rich in animal protein. Treatment is rarely effective, because once symptoms are apparent, too much damage has already occurred.

The majority of tropical fish feed mostly on small invertebrates, and will eventually starve if fed too much plant matter. Similarly, the several popular vegetarian species fare poorly on an animal diet. Make certain your fish are receiving the proper type of food. White, stringy feces that remain attached to the vent provide a sure sign of the need for changes in the diet. Switching to a live food for a while will frequently reverse this condition.

Fish that are not getting enough to eat lose weight, but the process takes weeks. A hollow belly or a concave appearance behind the eyes indicates weight loss due to starvation. Fish that lose weight even though they are eating an appropriate diet may be suffering from internal parasites or other troubles that you cannot treat successfully without a veterinarian's help.

Parasites

All sorts of flukes, worms, and crustaceans parasitize fish in the wild. These problems are not as likely to occur in hatchery-raised specimens, but the possibility remains, since the fry are reared in outdoor ponds. Frequently, the parasite requires an intermediary host, such as a snail, in order to complete its life cycle. If the snail has not been imported along with the fish, then the parasite dies out in one generation.

If you purchase a fish and discover a parasite attached, the best approach is to remove it with a pair of tweezers and swab the wound with 50 percent mercurochrome. Most parasites, however, will be internal, or located on the gills, inaccessible to your intervention. To treat an internal infestation, you will need a veterinarian.

Plant Problems

Several plant problems mentioned in chapter 2 deserve review. Chlorosis develops in response to iron deficiency. Leaves become yellow while retaining bright green veins. Overfertilization and under-illumination can also result in yellowing, though usually without the green veins.

Too low a level of carbon dioxide may cause some plants, especially those that normally grow under acidic conditions, to accumulate tiny nodules of calcium carbonate, lime, on the surfaces of the leaves. These hard, white encrustations indicate that all the free carbon dioxide has been exhausted, and the plants are now getting their carbon from dissolved bicarbonate ions. Besides the chemical stress this creates for the plant, the lime deposits reduce the amount of light reaching the leaf. Carbon dioxide fertilization offers the only solution.

In addition to their adaptations to specific water chemistry, plants have specific temperature requirements. At temperatures lower than optimal, growth becomes stunted or ceases altogether. At too high a temperature, abnormal growth manifests itself as smaller-than-normal leaves and elongation of the stem between leaf nodes. The plants look stretched. One should remember that both temperature and light intensity affect plant growth. As the temperature increases, the amount of light must also increase. For these reasons, growing plants with different temperature requirements in the same aquarium is a bad idea.

As a rule of thumb, brown spots appearing on the leaves should be taken as a sign of water quality problems. Usually, the spots enlarge, leaf tissue dies, and the spot becomes a hole. The whole leaf may eventually die. Medications or other chemical added to the water may be at fault, a good argument for carrying out such treatments in a separate tank. More commonly, the problem may be traced to an overdue water change. The obvious correction: Make a large water change immediately and return to a regular routine thereafter.

Aquatic plants will do poorly if regularly nibbled on, as you might guess. Herbivorous fish eat leaves from the edges inward; snails perforate the leaves with a random pattern of holes. In either case, removal of the offender(s) provides the only remedy. New plants should always be carefully inspected for the presence of snails. Make sure you know the eating habits of the fish you purchase if you keep live plants in your tank.

Algae Problems

When conditions deteriorate for aquatic plants, a *bloom* of excessive algae growth may develop. Similarly, in a tank with plastic plants only, algae may grow because it has no competition. In either case, maintaining a regular routine of partial water changes, thus providing stable, appropriate conditions, deters most algae growth. Various fish can be added to control algae, but their efforts will not amount to much under poor water conditions; algae will grow faster than the fish can feed.

In a planted tank, algae may appear under conditions of insufficient lighting despite proper water chemistry. Usually, the problem can be traced to aging fluorescent tubes or metal halide lamps. Changing them solves the problem, although established algae may require physical removal or cautious treatment with an algicide before it abates.

As with many aquarium situations, preventing undesirable algae from gaining a foothold proves easier than eliminating a bloom. The keys are regular water changes to maintain appropriate chemistry, carbon dioxide fertilization, and abundant light.

SUMMARY

Being dynamic, living systems, aquariums sometimes unexpectedly develop problems despite our best efforts. Knowing the signs of disease in fish or plants and having knowledge of appropriate remedies allows you to take action before problems become too severe to correct. You will note, however, that the best insurance against trouble comes from maintaining the aquarium properly on a regular basis. Partial water changes, regular vacuuming of the substrate to eliminate debris, cleaning algae from the glass, changing filter media appropriately, and keeping the lighting at the proper intensity all contribute to a healthy, trouble-free aquarium.

Part III

FRESHWATER AQUARIUM MODEL DESIGNS

The world's tropical freshwater habitats teem with colorful, interesting fish and an astonishing variety of plants. I have chosen approximately one hundred fish and some sixty plant varieties with which to create aquariums. Most of them can be found in any well-stocked aquarium shop. A few will require you to search them out, but are well worth the effort. In addition to recommendations for designs that reflect specific regions of the world, I have provided some purely artistic designs. The former seek to replicate the natural conditions to the greatest extent possible, while the latter include compatible, easy-care choices that will look great in any room.

An infinite number of aquariums can be created with the materials and live creatures available to enthusiasts. I hope you will look upon my suggestions as guidelines, rather than rigid dictums. You can dream up new designs with ease if you keep a few simple rules in mind.

- All species in the tank must live within the same range of temperature.
- All species in the tank must share optimal water conditions (pH, hardness).
- The tank must not be overcrowded.
- The needs of live plants must be met in addition to those of the fish.
- All fish in the tank must thrive on a diet that you can readily supply.

Your design should also reflect a specific biotope, such as a stream, pond, or vegetated river margin. Fish and plants from a particular biotope will thrive together even though they may come from different parts of the world. One sure-fire method of designing a successful aquarium is to limit yourself to a single species. Every aspect of the design can be tailored to suit the featured fish. Yet most people want a community aquarium. Accordingly, the majority of my suggestions here include several species.

Some enthusiasts find aquatic plants just as fascinating as the fish. Several designs that feature plants form part of the purely artistic group. Some reference books refer to plant tanks as *Dutch* aquariums, a nod to those who pioneered and perfected this approach.

I have previously mentioned that plastic plants can substitute for their living counterparts. Doing so reduces the lighting requirement for the aquarium, and eliminates certain chores, such as pruning. Several designs specify plastic. Nevertheless, growing aquatic plants adds another dimension to enjoyment of the aquarium, bringing welcome green into the house all year long. In winter, especially, you will appreciate the charms of your underwater garden. I urge you, therefore, to give plants a try.

Still another variation is the bog or swamp aquarium, containing both aquatic and terrestrial elements. This can be the most difficult type to design, but the finished product is striking when well done. The chief limitation is the size of the tank, which must be big enough to accommodate several inches of water as well as the terrestrial area above. These designs go by a variety of names; *aquaterrarium*, *vivarium*, *paludarium* and even *orchid spa* can be found in the literature and on the Internet. For a serious enthusiast, this type of design can be his or her masterpiece.

In a large city you are likely to find many kinds of fish not mentioned in this book. Take the time to research the needs of any that strike your fancy. Doing so will enable you to design an appropriate habitat, or perhaps to assess the fish's suitability for an aquarium you already own. Base your design on one given here, then tweak it to suit your particular situation.

As you read through this section, you will note that some localities are particularly favored in the aquarium trade. This results not only from the diversity of species found in a particular locale, but also from changing collecting patterns in the past fifty years. Early in the history of aquarium keeping, most species were collected from their native habitats. Today, considerably more than half of tropical fish sales comes from captive rearing. The adaptability of a particular species to hatchery culture, coupled with its popularity with aquarists, has imposed artificial selection for hardy, easily bred fish. I have given preference to these species as good choices for a non-expert aquarist.

Other factors also influence which species show up in the retailer's shop. For example, few fish surpass killifish for sheer beauty in a compact package. Killies are found in South America, North America, Africa, and Asia. Most remain small enough to be accommodated in a modest home aquarium. Yet, they are seldom seen in shops. One explanation is the difficulty of maintaining the huge variety of species. Another is the ease with which many killies can be mailed long distances as resting eggs. You can locate sources of killies and their eggs online.

CHAPTER 6

SOUTHEAST ASIA

The vast region stretching from India to Indonesia offers numerous biotopes, and a huge array of both fish and aquatic plant species. The region also provides many of the captive-bred aquarium fish. Typically, spawning and rearing are carried out in Asia, where labor and land costs are comparatively cheap. The fry are shipped in bulk to grow-out ponds in Florida, from which they are sent to retail markets all over North America. It is here that we encounter some of the most popular aquarium species, along with several oddballs with much to offer. Here we begin our ichthyological journey around the world, and here we meet our first killifish.

Ponds, Ditches, and Rice Paddies

From brackish coastal creeks to seasonally flooded river margins, to man-made canals and reservoirs, the freshwater biotopes of Southeast Asia teem with fish. Only South America has more species that adapt well to life in an aquarium. Slow-moving streams or still-water biotopes often harbor insects that attract surface-feeding fish in variety and abundance. Many of them are among the most durable species available.

The region has an abundant and varied aquatic flora. The numerous species of *Cryptocoryne* that occur here usually adapt so well to the aquarium that some enthusiasts specialize in only this genus. Water lilies and other types of floating plants often grow in shallow, still waters, their leaves shading the depths and providing cover for the fish lurking below. Add to these two of the hardiest and most useful species, Java moss (*Vesicularia dubyana*) and Java fern (*Microsorium pteropus*).

To represent the still-water biotopes of Southeast Asia, I have created ten model designs that draw upon a full range of the region's abundant aquatic resources.

MODEL DESIGN 1 Shallow Pool in Southern India

In southern India, tidal creeks connect the mangrove-lined shore to freshwater streams descending the country's mountainous interior. Here, and in similar habitats in Sri Lanka, we encounter our first members of the killifish clan, known as *panchax*. These colorful species, seldom more than three or four inches long, are peaceful surface dwellers with elongated bodies. Coloration tends toward blue and brown with bright, contrasting speckles on the flanks and touches of orange and red on the fins. Feeding on insects and tiny crustaceans that multiply by the billions in and around mangroves, in canals, and stagnant, brackish pools, panchax benefit from the addition of small amounts of seawater to their aquarium.

This tank should be perfect for one to three pairs of the peaceful and wide-ranging *Aplocheilus blockii,* the green panchax. Other panchax, such as the aptly named sparkling panchax, *A. lineatus*, display serious aggression. If you want to display *A. lineatus*, keep only one pair in the tank.

Panchax will take flake foods, but if you can arrange to feed them mosquito larvae they will reward you with eggs, spawning almost every day. Eggs will be attached to the strands of Java moss. Peaceful toward tank mates as well as their own kind, they will nevertheless devour their own offspring. If you want to raise them, transfer the moss containing the eggs to a separate aquarium, where they will hatch in about two weeks. The fry must be fed extremely tiny foods.

Aquarium Capacity . . . . 20 gallons

Water Conditions .neutral, moderately hard

Optimal Temperature . . . . .75°F

Plants

    Java fern (*Microsorium pteropus*) . . . . 1, mounted on a piece of driftwood

    Java moss (*Vesicularia dubyana*) . . . . several clumps

    red mangrove (*Rhizophora mangle*) . . . . . 2 (optional, see text)

Other Décor . . . . .driftwood, mangrove roots, water-worn rocks

Background . . . . .dark brown or black

Substrate . . . . .dark gravel

Filtration . . . . .hang-on external filter

Lighting . . . . .1 20-watt fluorescent lamp

Special Requirements . . . . .live foods, 0.5 percent seawater (about 12 ounces in 20 gallons)

Fish . . . .*Aplocheilus blockii*, 2–3 pairs

Install the background and place a two-inch-deep layer of gravel on the floor of the tank. Position the mounted Java fern right of center and toward the back. On either side of the fern, place additional small pieces of driftwood or dead mangrove roots. The mangrove roots should be placed with the curved portion toward the left. This establishes the right side of the tank as the shore of the creek. Attach Java moss to the roots, where it might be found growing in the wild. Install the filter on the left rear side. The current it produces simulates deeper water away from the shore. Other possibilities exist for including mangroves in this display. You can sometimes find mangrove seeds, already sprouting their thick, oval leaves, in shops that stock brackish and marine fish. They will eventually grow up and out of the water, becoming too large for the tank, but they add a nice touch of green in the meantime. Plant them with just the tip of the elongated seed buried in the substrate. Place them behind the dead roots for the most natural look. Add water-worn stones randomly to relieve the monotony of the substrate. Choose stones in colors that echo those of the substrate, but a slightly lighter or darker hue.

MODEL DESIGN 2 Large Pond in Thailand

Thailand, home of fabulous food and splendid architecture, also harbors one of the most popular of all aquarium fish, *Betta splendens*, the Siamese fighting fish. It is often identified simply as *betta* in aquarium shops, although the genus contains several other good aquarium species that are also correctly called betta. For this reason, I prefer Siamese fighting fish, although I deplore the practice of fighting them for sport. Admittedly, though, part of the allure is their aggressive nature.

Bettas have been maintained in captivity for a very long time. Wild bettas have rather drab coloration, but perhaps a rare colorful fish turned up in the nets of local fishermen from time to time. Possibly thought to be a token of good luck, the fish was cared for in a pond or container. Eventually, Thais got the notion to practice artificial selection, creating the beginnings of the vast array of captive modern breeds. Selected for vivid colors and long, elegant fins for more than a century, brilliant new breeds no longer resemble the wild type. Thai people call the Betta *pla kat,* meaning *tearing fish* or *biting fish*. Males defend their territories against all comers, and particularly against other male bettas seeking territories of their own. Wild betta fights, limited to threat displays such as flared gills and spread fins, occur mostly for show; confrontations rarely end in death. In the aquarium, aggression intensifies because of confinement and the lack of escape routes. Keep only one male betta per tank. Tank mates can include rasboras, danios, and other popular aquarium fish originating in similar biotopes. This model design exploits the barrel-like shape of a hexagonal tank.

Aquarium Capacity . . . . 30 gallons, hexagonal

Water Conditions .neutral, moderately hard

Optimal Temperature . . . . .75°F

Plants

     common crypt (*Cryptocoryne willisi*) 7

     red tiger lotus (*Nymphaea lotus*). 1

     eelgrass (*Vallisneria americana*) . . . . 12 (optional)

Other Décor .a few water-worn rocks

Background . . . . .dark brown or black

Substrate .dark gravel with a small amount of sand added

Filtration . . . . .canister filter

Lighting . . . . .metal halide, 100 watts, suspended

Special Requirements . . . . .custom tank construction (optional)

Fish

   Betta splendens 1

   Rasbora heteromorpha 9

Hexagonal tanks offer dramatic design possibilities, but they can be devilish to aquascape. The model design presented here permits a full 360-degree view, but will only work if you have a floor outlet. Otherwise, the power cord will not only need to be disguised from view, but also must be secured against creating a hazard that could trip someone. Suspending the light fixture above the tank will provide the strong illumination required for the tiger lotus to produce its floating lily pads and fragrant, four-inch flowers. Installing a canister filter underneath minimizes the amount of equipment in the tank, since only a pair of hoses is needed. These can be tidily routed along two corners on the side of the tank least visible from the main portion of the room.

The overall effect of this model design can be greatly enhanced by customizing the tank. By drilling drain and fill holes in the bottom center and installing a dark covered overflow around them, all equipment can be completely hidden. The overflow can itself be hidden among the stems of the *Nymphaea*. You could also add a dozen *Vallisneria americana* around the overflow in addition to the tiger lotus. Underneath the cabinet, the sump can hold a 150- to 200-watt heater, maintaining the warm temperature preferred by the betta. With these modifications, the design becomes an exhibit worthy of a public aquarium.

Regardless of whether you use the optional filtration system, plant the tiger lotus approximately in the center of the tank. If you are using the *Vallisneria* plants, locate them where they will hide equipment. Randomly place the *C. willisi* plants. They will eventually carpet the bottom. After planting, arrange three water-worn stones around the base of the lotus, visually anchoring it in the substrate.

MODEL DESIGN 3 Community Featuring Gouramis

Here is a highly adaptable design. You can use any size tank from thirty gallons up, varying the plant and fish population appropriately. Long tanks lend themselves to fluorescent lighting. Choose multiple tubes if you go with live plants. With plastic plants, of course, only a single tube is needed. The viewer should feel as if he or she is seeing beneath the surface of a flooded depression near the edge of a river. In the rainy season, the river escapes its banks, refreshing the pond formed by the depression. As the river recedes, clouds of insects lay their eggs in the warm, stagnant water. They will hatch to provide food for the fish. Low oxygen levels in hot, stagnant pools such as this undoubtedly led to the evolution in gouramis of the ability to breathe atmospheric air. Freed from reliance upon their gills, gouramis can exploit the rich food sources to be found in the swamps.

Aquarium Capacity . . . . 30–75 gallons

Water Conditions .soft, acidic

Optimal Temperature . . . . .80°F

Plants

    hygrophila (*Hygrophila corymbosa*) 3–15

    Indian hygrophila (*Hygrophila difformis*). . . 3–15

    orchid lily (*Barclaya longifolia*) 1–3

    round-leaf rotala (*Rotala rotundifolia*) 3–15

    floating fern (*Salvinia auriculata*) . . . . 1 clump

Other Décor . . . . .driftwood and/or roots

Background . . . . .dark brown or black

Substrate . . . . .dark gravel with a small amount of sand added

Filtration . . . . .canister filter

Lighting . . . . .fluorescent or metal halide, for plants

Special Requirements . . . . .none

Fish

    Colisa laelia . . . . 1 male, up to 4 females

    Trichogaster leeri . . . . 1 male, up to 4 females

        Or *Trichogaster trichopterus*. . . . . 1 male, up to 4 females

        Or *Trichopsis pumila*. . . . . 1 male, up to 4 females

    Rasbora borapetensis . . . . 7–21 individuals

    Rasbora heteromorpha . . . . 7–21 individuals

    Botia morleti . . . . 1–5 individuals

Select an appropriate number of fish for the tank size. In the case of *C. laelia* and *T. leeri*, you can place more than one male in the same tank, provided there is plenty of room. A male *T. trichopterus* may not get along with another male gourami of any species, however, regardless of the available space. Other small fish that prefer soft, acid water, such as *Barbus titteya*, can also be included, again paying attention to the tank capacity.

Arrange the roots and driftwood on opposite ends of the tank, leaving an open area in the center. With suitably bright lighting, the plants will tend to grow toward the center, creating an arch effect. The *Barclaya* takes center stage in this model design. You could also use an *Aponegeton* species if *Barclaya* is unavailable. Plant the *Hygrophila difformis* along the back of the tank between the two arrangements of driftwood, then place the *Barclaya* slightly left or right of center. The placement as well as the reddish coloration of the *Barclaya* will tend to draw the viewer's eye. *Hygrophila corymbosa* var. *gracilis*, which is red under bright lighting, will balance the *Barclaya*. Plant it on the opposite side of the tank. Fill in with *Rotala*, planting the individual stems in groups of three to five. The *Salvinia* merely floats on the surface, and should be periodically thinned as it begins to shade the tank too much.

Streams and Rivers

The waters draining the Asian continent supply many of our most desirable aquarium fish, especially the cyprinids, or carp-like fishes. Asian carp were most likely the earliest aquarium fish. Fancy carp, or *koi*, remain popular with pond keepers after centuries of cultivation. Although koi grow much too large for an indoor tank, their relatives among the barbs and loaches are among the hardiest choices for aquariums.

MODEL DESIGN 4 Sri Lankan Stream

Sri Lanka supplies a nearly perfect example of a mountaintop island. More than 90 percent of Sri Lanka's surface consists of rocks dating back two billion years. The central highlands were created by the transformation of ancient sediments under intense heat and pressure. Sri Lanka experiences few earthquakes or volcanic events because it is located near the center of an ancient landmass it shares with India, much of which is now submerged. Streams flow down the sides of the central highlands toward the Indian Ocean, radiating in all directions like the spokes of a wheel. In addition to a rich fish fauna, Sri Lanka's streams harbor a wide diversity of aquatic plants, including many species of *Cryptocoryne*. This model design takes advantage of that biological diversity.

Aquarium Capacity . . . . 30 gallons

Water Conditions .moderately hard, neutral to slightly acidic

Optimal Temperature . . . . .75°F

Plants

    Beckett's crypt (*Cryptocoryne beckettii*) . . . 3

    Wendt's crypt (*Cryptocoryne wendtii*) 7

    common crypt (*Cryptocoryne willisii*) 7

    ambulia (*Limnophila aquatica*) 3

Other Décor	driftwood, water-worn rocks
Background	gray or light blue on back, dark brown or black on right end
Substrate	dark gravel with a small amount of sand added
Filtration	hang-on filter
Lighting	fluorescent or metal halide, for plants
Special Requirements	laeterite substrate additive, iron supplementation, bottom heater, CO_2 fertilization (optional)

Fish

Barbus nigrofasciatus 5

Or *Barbus titteya* 7

Or *Danio aequipinnatus* 5

Lending itself to a long tank style, the arrangement of the filter in this model design may require you to customize the tank cover. The giant danios, especially, are prone to jumping. Using a relatively light background helps to convey the notion of a sunny stream, and the fish will welcome dense plantings to make them feel more secure. I suggest you also place a dark background on the end where the filter is located, to help hide it. Install the filter on the right-hand end of the tank, and build up a "riffle" of rocks beneath it. As the water from the filter return cascades over the rocks, it simulates the turbulence of a stream. You will need to choose rocks carefully, since water-worn pieces tend to be rounded and difficult to stack. It may be necessary to arrange the rocks in a dry tank, trying various positions until you have a stable one. If in doubt, use silicone adhesive to secure them. For the most natural appearance, the rocks should be in place before you add the gravel. Also spread the laeterite on the bottom prior to adding the gravel. Locate the driftwood a bit downstream (toward the left side) and toward the back, with the *Limnophila* grouped between it and the riffle. The larger *Cryptocoryne beckettii* should be placed toward the left side, with the other plants arrayed toward the front. All *Cryptocoryne* plants do best when planted in groups, and the arrangement looks good, too. Think through the arrangement before you plant; *Cryptocoryne* hates to be transplanted. For the same reason, you can expect them to sulk for a few weeks after being moved from the dealer's tank.

If you find *Cryptocoryne* too much trouble to grow, you could substitute three to five plants of *Aponegeton crispus* and increase the number of *Limnophila* clumps. Being taller, the *Aponegeton* will look better in a larger tank, such as a fifty-five gallon. If you have the floor space, another alternative arrangement would be to omit the pale background and allow the tank to project into the room, with the end holding the filter nearest the wall. This creates a room divider, and permits viewing from either side. Locate the plantings more or less down the middle, with taller specimens toward the center.

For a low-maintenance system, set up a large tank, furnish it with plastic plants, and keep a school of tinfoil barbs, which like to eat live plants. Bear in mind that the barbs will grow quickly to about a foot in length. The clown loach provides an extra touch of color.

Aquarium Capacity . . . . 125 gallons

Water Conditions .neutral, moderately hard

Optimal Temperature . . . . .78°F

Plants

    hygrophila (*Hygrophila* sp.) . . . . plastic, 7–13

    rotala (*Rotala* sp.) . . . . plastic, 7–13

    aponegeton (*Aponegeton* sp.) . . . . plastic, 3–5

    crypt (*Cryptocoryne* sp.) . . . . plastic, 7

Other Décor . . . . .driftwood, water-worn rocks

Background . . . . .gray or pale blue

Substrate . . . . .natural gravel

Filtration . . . . .large canister filter or sump filter

Lighting . . . . .fluorescent, 1 or 2 tubes

Special Requirements . . . . .none

Fish

    Barbus schwanfeldi 5

    Chromobotia macracanthus. 1

Leave plenty of swimming room for the active barbs. Arrange the plants toward the back of the tank, and place the driftwood underneath the filter return to create turbulence. Strew medium to small water-worn stones on the substrate to relieve the monotony of the gravel. The fish in this model design are quite hardy and robust, so they should offer few challenges in husbandry. Make certain, however, to perform regular partial water changes, ideally once a week, to compensate for the lack of plants and the hearty appetite of the fish.

If you haven't the room or cannot afford the six-foot tank suggested, scale down to a forty- or fifty-five-gallon size, and keep either a red-tailed or red-finned shark, *Epalzeorhynchus bicolor* and *E. erythrurus*, respectively. Because these largely vegetarian species are aggressive and territorial, either does best in a single-species tank. They are quite hardy, and should pose few problems for a beginner.

China remains a lifetime vacation destination for many of us in the Western Hemisphere. This aquarium evokes a uniquely Chinese ambience for a fraction of the cost of a trip. Featuring not only the endemic White Cloud Mountain minnow, but also delicate hornwort, this biotope would be perfect for a child's room. Any aquarium shop will stock all of the affordable ingredients.

The minnow showcased here boasts an interesting history. It was discovered by a boy in a stream flowing down White Cloud Mountain in southern China near Canton. The scientific name, *Tanichthys albonubes*, means "white cloud boy fish." A great choice for boys or girls, this hardy little minnow thrives in cool, clean water. Think mountain stream. Paired with equally hardy plants, the bright coloration really stands out. Usually under an inch and a half in length, the body of the White Cloud minnow is dark olive. A shiny gold stripe runs from the snout to the tail, terminated by a jet-black dot. Thirteen fish are recommended for this display, because they prefer to travel in schools.

If you prefer larger fish, a single pair of paradise fish will do nicely in this small aquarium, and you need not alter any other aspect of the design.

Aquarium Capacity . . . . 20 gallons

Water Conditions . . . . .neutral, moderately hard to hard

Optimal Temperature . . . . .70°F

Plants

    hornwort (*Ceratophyllum demersum*). . . . . 1 clump

    spiral eelgrass (*Vallisneria spiralis*) 10–12

    Java moss (*Vesicularia dubyana*) . . . . 1 clump

Other Décor . . . . .smooth, water-worn rocks

Background . . . . .light blue or pale gray

Substrate . . . . .dark gravel in a range of sizes, natural colors

Filtration . . . . .hang-on filter

Lighting . . . . .dual lamp fluorescent system for plants

Special Requirements . . . . .possibly a few small snails for algae control

Fish

    Tanichthys albonubes 13

        Or *Macropodus opercularis* . . . . 1 pair

Choose a filter that provides about one hundred gallons per hour of water flow, since this is a stream habitat. Place it at the back, on either side, depending upon what looks best to you. Select three to five smooth rocks in colors similar to the substrate material. Each should be about the size of your fist or larger. You will also need a handful of pebbles in assorted sizes. Anchor the Java moss to the largest rock, using a length of monofilament fishing line. After a few months, the moss should have attached itself, and the monofilament can be removed. Use the larger rocks to hide the filter intake. You could also use a piece of driftwood, and attach the moss to it. If you go that route, anchor the driftwood with an arrangement of smooth rocks at its base. Also scatter pebbles elsewhere on the gravel. On the end of the tank opposite the filter, create a stand of the *Vallisneria*. The hornwort simply floats on the surface. If your lighting is good, it will need regular pruning. The minnows will move around the tank in a school. One nice feature of this aquarium is the temperature. All the inhabitants will do fine at normal room temperature, since they come from a more temperate climate than most other aquarium fish.

Model Design 7   Community Tank Featuring Barbs

Southeast Asia and the Indian Subcontinent provide us with numerous hardy aquarium barbs. The term, *barb*, refers to the barbels, often tiny, which project from the fish's lip. These sensory appendages are common among the cyprinids. Although sometimes inclined to be aggressive toward tank mates, most barbs make splendid community fish.

Aquarium Capacity . . . . 30–55 gallons

Water Conditions .neutral, moderately hard

Optimal Temperature . . . . .72–76°F, depending upon species chosen

Plants

    hygrophila (*Hygrophila corymbosa*) 3–5

    common hygrophila
       (*Hygrophila polysperma*) 3–15

    ambulia (*Limnophila sessiliflora*) 3–15

    round-leaved rotala
       (*Rotala rotundifolia*) 3–15

Other Décor . . . . .driftwood and/or roots

Background . . . . .black or dark gray

Substrate . . . . .natural gravel with a small amount of sand added

Filtration . . . . .canister filter

Lighting . . . . .fluorescent or metal halide, for plants

Special Requirements . . . . .none

Fish

Barbus conchonius

Barbus everettii

Barbus oligolepus

Barbus tetrazona

Brachydanio albolineatus

Brachydanio nigrofasciatus

Brachydanio rerio

Pangio kuhlii

No numbers are given above for fish, because the final mix is up to you. Choose from among the species listed in varying combinations, depending upon temperature preferences and tank size. *Barbus conchonius*, *B. oligolepus*, and *B. tetrazona* all prefer the cooler temperature setting, while *B. everettii* needs warmer conditions. The *Brachydanio* species all prefer cool conditions, too, with the exception of *B. rerio*, which is equally at home in cool or warm water.

Tiger barbs, *Barbus tetrazona*, should be maintained in a school of seven or more, depending upon the size tank you choose. Expect some chasing and fin nipping as *B. tetrazona* establishes a pecking order in the school. It is worth noting that these fish can be disruptive because of their high activity level. You may want to consider devoting this tank only to a school of tiger barbs.

Choose a piece of driftwood sufficiently large and interesting to be used as a centerpiece, although, as always, place it slightly off center to avoid a too-formal look. Arrange the plants in clumps to the rear and sides of the tank, leaving the center space open for the actively swimming barbs and danios.

These highly active fish need plenty of top-quality food to supply their energy requirements. Accordingly, you should choose a filter somewhat larger than normally recommended for the tank capacity. The extra flow will also provide the current that all these fish appreciate. Although it is secretive, one to three coolie loaches, *Pangio kuhlii,* will perform the valuable service of cleaning up bits of food missed by the others. All the species suggested may jump; make sure the tank is covered.

If I were choosing only one Asian-themed model design, it would be this one. Incorporating all of the elements of a biotope tank, the aquarium can offer maximum interest even on a small scale.

Aquarium Capacity . . . . 30 gallons

Water Conditions . . . . .neutral to slightly acidic, soft to moderately hard

Optimal Temperature . . . . .75°F

Plants

    ruffled aponegeton
        (*Aponegeton crispus*) 1

    crypt (*Cryptocoryne affinis*) 5

    thread-leaved crypt (*Cryptocoryne*). 5

    corkscrew eelgrass
        (*Vallisneria americana v. biwaensis*) . . . 15

    red floating fern (*Azolla filiculoides*) . . . . . (optional)

Other Décor . . . . .driftwood and/or roots, bamboo stakes

Background . . . . .dark brown or black

Substrate . . . . .dark gravel with a small amount of sand added

Filtration . . . . .canister filter

Lighting . . . . .fluorescent, 2 lamps, for plants

Special Requirements . . . . .regular additions of live food to staple diet

Fish

    Kryptopterus minor 7

    Rasbora kalchroma 5–7

I suggest a canister filter because you can control the direction of the output. The glass catfish will orient themselves facing into the current. You therefore want to arrange it so they will be front and center most of the time. Keep the driftwood and the large *Aponegeton* to one side, and arrange the *Vallisneria* along the back to form a curtain. Bamboo is obtainable from garden centers, and it is inexpensive. Choose untreated canes about the diameter of a pencil or slightly larger. Cut lengths of the bamboo, using garden pruners, heavy scissors, or a fine-toothed saw, that will extend from the bottom of the tank to the rim. After planting is completed, insert the stakes into the gravel at random, to give the impression that the bamboo is growing up out of the water at the river's edge. In all, use about seven to eleven pieces of bamboo. The natural oils in the bamboo will preserve the stakes for about a year, after which time they should be replaced.

Cryptocoryne affinis is one of the best choices for aquarium use. Plant it in front of the *Vallisneria*, opposite the *Aponegeton*. *Cryptocoryne ciliata* is a tall, pale green, slow-growing species that should be positioned as a focal point. It can be located near the *Aponegeton* or balancing it on the opposite side of the tank or used as a substitute for the *Aponegeton*.

The clown rasboras provide a colorful contrast to the glass catfish. Both species will remain in schools, and both appreciate the security afforded by the plantings. Add the optional *Azolla* to provide additional cover to help keep the catfish out of hiding, but do so only if you are prepared to thin this tiny floating fern ruthlessly. Without thinning, it will cover the surface quickly and block most of the light from the other plants.

Other plants that would work in this aquarium include any of the other *Cryptocoryne* species, such as *C. balansae v. crispatula* or *C. cordata*, and either *Rotala macrandra* or *R. rotundifolia*. The latter two will create additional interest with their colored foliage.

The two fish featured in this aquarium require more care than most, and will benefit from weekly partial water changes and regular feedings with live food.

Estuarine Habitats

An estuary forms where a river meets the ocean, with concomitant mixing of fresh and salt water. Add about 10 percent synthetic seawater to your tap water to create the brackish water preferred by estuarine fish. Some aquarists cause the salinity to fluctuate by alternately doing water changes with fresh and salt water. If you go this route, keep tabs on the specific gravity (an indirect measure of the salt content of the water) with a hydrometer. This inexpensive instrument, along with synthetic seawater mix, is certain to be found on the shelves of a dealer who stocks saltwater fish.

MODEL DESIGN 9 Estuary I

Plant choices for brackish water are limited to those species that can tolerate salt. In this simple model design, plastic plants eliminate the worry about making correct choices.

Aquarium Capacity . . . . 30 gallons

Water Conditions . . . . .brackish

Optimal Temperature . . . . .80°F

Plants

    plastic, your choice . . . . 3–5 (optional)

Other Décor . . . . .mangrove roots, driftwood, limestone rocks

Background . . . . .dark brown or black

Substrate . . . . .dark gravel, black, if available

Filtration . . . . .hang-on filter

Lighting . . . . .fluorescent

Special Requirements . . . . .synthetic seawater mix

Fish

Chanda ranga. 7

Since greenery is not going to be the focus for this model design, fill the tank more or less evenly with mangrove roots. If these are unavailable, try to find driftwood that came from tree roots. Locate some chunks of limestone near the back of the tank to suggest the eroded shore; the roots should project forward from this, as if one were looking at the mangroves from the middle of the river. If you use the optional plastic plants, select only one kind and place them among the roots, where they would be found in the natural habitat.

The glass fish will spend time in the open area toward the front of the tank. If you want to observe the spawning behavior in this fish, it can be done rather easily, although the fry are extremely tiny and difficult to raise. Spawning is stimulated by an influx of fresh water (the rainy season), a rise in temperature, and an increase in the amount of light reaching the tank during the morning hours. Increase the temperature slightly and set the lighting timer earlier over a period of a week. Then do a water change with fresh water. The glass fish will do the rest, placing their eggs on the plants or roots.

Glass fish do best when their diet includes live foods. If live food is not available, be sure to use a good-quality frozen food to supplement flakes.

MODEL DESIGN 10 Estuary II

The archer fish surely ranks among the most interesting freshwater/brackish water fish available to the hobbyist. This remarkable species, placed in its own family by biologists, is able to shoot insects from the leaves of plants located as much as five feet away. Its mouth is specially designed for this function, and the accuracy is absolutely mind boggling. They can be trained to shoot at dead insects, or even a piece of freeze-dried shrimp, by dangling the food enticingly above the water surface. Archers will also forgo the target practice and take food from the surface, like other fish. To provide them with overhanging plants and shallow water, we will create a paludarium using a tall, narrow tank kept only half full, with a terrestrial area at one end.

Aquarium Capacity . . . . .77 gallons

Water Conditions . . . . .brackish

Optimal Temperature . . . . .80–83°F

Plants

    water sprite (*Ceratopteris thalictroides*) . . . 5–7

    Java fern (*Microsorium pteropus*) 3–5

    Terrestrial houseplants. . . . . see following text

Other Décor . . . . .driftwood, mangrove roots, limestone, bark slabs (optional)

Background . . . . .dark brown or black

Substrate . . . . .coarse sand, with a little finer sand mixed in

Filtration . . . . .undergravel filter with powerhead

Lighting . . . . .fluorescent (four lamps) or metal halide, for plants

Special Requirements . . . . .plastic planter for terrestrial plants

Fish

    Toxotes jaculatrix . . . . 1–3 individuals

The most readily available stone for this design is coral rock, fossilized coral that is quarried in Florida and sold by the ton for aquarium decoration. It is soft enough to be shaped with a masonry chisel and hammer. Be sure to wear eye protection!

The seventy-seven-gallon tank is two feet deep, allowing you a foot of water for the fish, and ample space above for terrestrial plants. Imagine a tropical forest extending right down to the edge of the estuary. Start constructing this biotope by installing a narrow plastic planter near the back of the tank on one end. Elevate the planter so its rim is just above the water line. You can do this by choosing a length of PVC drain pipe with a diameter slightly less than the width of the planter. Using a fine-toothed saw, cut sections of the drain pipe the correct length to raise the planter to the desired position. If you can find a PVC planter, so much the better. Plug any holes in the planter with a blob of silicone sealant, and attach the pipe sections to the bottom with PVC cement. (Try one piece of pipe first. If it fails to bond, choose a more general-purpose plastic cement.) Allow the assembly to dry for several days before placing it in the tank.

Apply the background to the end nearest the planter, as well as on the back glass. Install the undergravel filter, adjusting the length of the uplift pipe to position the powerhead in one rear corner with the outlet a little below the rim of the planter. Next, install the planter, locating one end within an inch or so of the powerhead. Using the rocks, build up a shoreline in front of the planter, leaving room for the powerhead to direct water between two pieces. Several pieces of rock should extend above the water line, completely hiding the powerhead and the planter. You may need to glue some of the rocks in place with silicone to make a stable structure. If so, leave the whole thing to cure for a week before you continue.

When the preceding steps are complete, test the system by filling the tank half full with tap water. (You may need to weight down the plastic planter with a couple of chunks of rock, to keep it from floating.) Plug in the powerhead. Water should flow vigorously from between the rocks. Imagine a tiny rivulet carrying water from the forest into the estuary. When everything is working to your satisfaction, remove most of the water and continue with the installation.

Arrange roots or driftwood so they extend from the planter end toward the opposite end. A shorter piece or two can point forward, toward the viewer. If you like, portions can project above the water line. To the submerged portions of a few roots, you will attach the *Microsorium* plants using monofilament fishing line. (Once the Java ferns attach themselves, the line can be clipped off.) Be sure to allow room for the Java ferns when placing the wood.

Next, add the substrate, sloping it away from the shore end of the tank, but maintaining a depth of about two inches on the opposite end. Near the opposite end, plant the *Ceratopteris* after the tank is filled.

Depending upon the size of the planter you have chosen, a number of Asian houseplants can complete the biotope. For an upright specimen, you might select a *Croton* variety for its colorful foliage. It will need pruning to keep it in proportion to the aquarium. Smaller *Ficus* species can also be used. *Ficus benjamina*, the weeping fig, grows into an enormous tree, but can easily be pruned to size like *Croton*. Creeping fig, *Ficus pumila*, is a ground-covering vine that will climb a rough surface. The optional bark slabs can be obtained from orchid suppliers. You can cut them with a fine-toothed saw and glue them to the back glass above the planter, suggesting a large tree near the edge of the estuary. The creeping fig will quickly climb up the heavily textured bark. Another vine you could use is the very slow-growing *Hoya*. Check the Internet or visit the houseplant department of your local garden center for additional ideas. Regardless of your plant choices, place a layer of coarse pebbles in the bottom of the planter to provide drainage. Most terrestrial plants will grow poorly without this. Use a sterilized commercial potting soil or other growing medium recommended for the plants you select. I suggest limiting yourself to only three kinds of plants. Not only is the growing room limited, but fewer varieties in one place looks more natural. At least one plant should have branches or stems that overhang the water, to provide a spot toward which the archer fish can aim. Very few plants can tolerate salt, even in the low concentrations needed for the archer fish. Make sure water from the tank cannot leak into the planter.

Once the aquarium is completed, leave it in place for a month or more to condition the filter system and allow the plants to begin growing. During this time, keep the water slightly salty by adding up to 10 percent synthetic seawater. Finally, add the archer fish. Try to select specimens of equal size, as larger ones may harass smaller ones. When the fish have settled in, you can try training them to shoot as described above.

This model design takes a lot of work to establish, but maintenance is relatively simple, since you have only a few fish. Properly done, an archer fish paludarium ranks among the most arresting and beautiful designs in this book.

CHAPTER 7

AUSTRALASIA

The island nations of Australasia were at one time all connected to the larger Asian landmass. As a result, many Asian fish genera, and some species, are found throughout this region. A good example is the pearl gourami, *Trichogaster leeri*, which occurs in Malaysia, Sumatra, and Borneo. Barbs, danios, killifish, and others also live here. The region is perhaps best known, however, for a unique fish family known as *rainbowfishes*.

Oceanic Islands

Borneo, Irian Jaya, Java, Sulawesi, Sumatra—the names alone conjure images of exotic lands cloaked in tropical forest. Each island has a backbone of highlands, from which freshwater rivers flow to join with the sea. These rivers are home to an astonishing variety of fishes, many of which lend themselves to single-species aquariums.

MODEL DESIGN 11 Borneo, Sumatra

The large islands of Borneo and Sumatra are represented by several popular aquarium fish. A small species tank for any of them makes a beautiful display. I have chosen two different fish with somewhat different water needs. For this twenty-gallon setup, select one or the other, not both.

Aquarium Capacity . . . . 20 gallons

Water Conditions . . . . .soft, acidic, or neutral and moderately hard

Optimal Temperature . . . . .72–80°F, depending upon species chosen

Plants

    Indian hygrophila (*Hygrophila difformis*). . . 15

        Or corkscrew eelgrass (*Vallisneria americana v. biwaensis*) 15

        And floating fern (*Salvinia auriculata*) . . . . 1 clump

        Or ambulia (*Limnophila sessiliflora*) . . 7

        Or crypt (*Cryptocoryne affinis*) 7

Other Décor . . . . .driftwood and/or roots, water-worn rocks

Background . . . . .dark brown or black

Substrate . . . . .dark gravel with a small amount of sand added

Filtration . . . . .hang-on filter

Lighting . . . . .2 fluorescent tubes, for plants

Special Requirements . . . . .none

Fish

    Trichogaster leeri . . . . 1 male, 1 female

        Or *Barbus tetrazona* . . . . 7 individuals

Combine the *Hygrophila* or *Vallisneria*, and the *Salvinia* with the gouramis, using soft, acidic water and a warm temperature, around 80°F. Use one of the other plants with the tiger barbs, and keep the tank water at neutral pH, moderately hard, and cool, around 70°F. Since the tank is small, limit yourself to a single rooted plant selection. (The *Salvinia* is included because gouramis like floating plants.) Regardless of which combination of plants and fish you use, the aquarium will be easy to maintain, and would look good in a cozy room where the tank would be relatively close to the viewer. Use driftwood to hide equipment, and anchor the plantings with carefully placed smooth rocks. Above all, keep the design simple for this small tank. To a great extent, the finished look will depend upon the shape of the piece of driftwood you choose. Find one you think looks interesting, and arrange the rooted plants attractively around it.

MODEL DESIGN 12   Irian Jaya, Ajamaru Lakes

This western portion of the island of New Guinea contains some of the most remote tropical forest in the world. Fortunately, the Ajamaru Lakes has been visited by fish collectors. They brought back the spectacular Boseman's rainbowfish featured in this model design.

Aquarium Capacity . . . . 40 gallons, breeder type

Water Conditions . . . . neutral to alkaline, hard

Optimal Temperature . . . . 82–85°F

Plants

    Java fern (*Microsorium pteropus*) 9

    hornwort (*Ceratophyllum demersum*). . . . . 1 clump

Other Décor . . . . driftwood and/or roots, water-worn rocks

Background . . . . dark brown or black

Substrate . . . . gravel similar in color to rocks

Filtration . . . . canister filter

Lighting . . . . 4 fluorescent tubes, for plants

Special Requirements . . . . none

Fish

    Melanotaenia bosemani 5–7

Leave plenty of swimming room for the active rainbowfishes when decorating this tank. I have suggested a forty-gallon breeder tank, with a thirty-six- by eighteen-inch footprint, so you can confine the decorations to the rear third, leaving the front area open. Place the driftwood near the left end, at a slight angle so it points toward the right front corner. Anchor it with a large stone at the far left. Place small stones around the base of the driftwood, as if it were lodged among them on the bottom of the stream. Arrange some larger rocks along the back glass. Choose dark colors for the rocks, pebbles, and gravel. This will show off the metallic blue and bright orange coloration of *M. bosemani* to best advantage. Keep the tank covered, as this and other rainbowfishes can jump.

MODEL DESIGN 13   Irian Jaya, Fly River

The southern part of Irian Jaya is drained by the Fly River, which is home to the unmistakable and relatively rare threadfin rainbowfish. Although the females are rather plain, the gorgeous males sport a sail-like first dorsal fin tinted in yellow-green. The second dorsal fin as well as the anal and caudal fins possess elongated, threadlike extensions that can be confused with no other fish, except perhaps the Celebes rainbowfish mentioned next. These dorsal and anal fin extensions are emphasized with black pigmentation. The narrow, elongate pectoral fins are also black. The base of the second dorsal fin and the outer edges of the caudal fin are tinted orange.

Aquarium Capacity . . . . 40 gallons, breeder type

Water Conditions . . . . .neutral, moderately hard

Optimal Temperature . . . . .78–80°F

Plants

  water sprite (*Ceratopteris thalictroides*) . . . 1 clump

  crypts (*Cryptocoryne*, various species) . . . 10–15

  round-leaved rotala (*Rotala rotundifolia*). . . 2

Other Décor . . . . .driftwood and/or roots

Background . . . . .medium gray or blue

Substrate . . . . .natural, medium- to light-colored gravel with sand added

Filtration . . . . .canister filter

Lighting . . . . .2–4 fluorescent tubes, for plants

Special Requirements . . . . .none

Fish

  Iriatherina werneri 7

As with the previous model design, keep the front of the tank open to provide swimming room for these active swimmers. Since these fish do not require hard, alkaline water, the variety of plants that can be used in this model design is not limited to tolerant Java ferns. Use the driftwood to hide the filter hoses, and locate stands of plants toward the rear and outer edges of the tank. The relatively pale background, foliage, and gravel will set off the pretty black fins for which this fish is rightly famous.

MODEL DESIGN 14 Sulawesi (Celebes Islands)

The main island in this archipelago is the E-shaped one (if you have a good imagination). Formerly Sulawesi was known as the Celebes Islands, and an interesting fish found there retains this older name. This species is *Telmatherina ladigesi*, commonly known as the Celebes rainbowfish, though it is not in the same family as the other rainbowfishes we will discuss, being more closely related to the silversides (Family Atherinidae). Most members of this family are found in the ocean, so *Telmatherina* probably evolved from silversides that ventured up the increasingly freshwater rivers from the sea. It does best with some added seawater.

Aquarium Capacity . . . . 30 gallons

Water Conditions . . . . .hard, neutral to slightly alkaline, with added seawater

Optimal Temperature . . . . .78°F

Plants

    Java fern (*Microsorium pteropus*) 3–5

    dwarf arrowhead (*Sagittaria graminea*) . . . 3–15

Other Décor . . . . .water-worn rocks, small driftwood pieces

Background . . . . .deep blue

Substrate . . . . .fine mixed gravel with a few pebbles on top

Filtration . . . . .canister filter

Lighting . . . . .2 fluorescent tubes, for plants

Special Requirements . . . . .none

Fish

    Telmatherina ladigesi 5

This beautiful fish needs swimming room and fairly constant water conditions. If you wish, substitute one tablespoon of non-iodized aquarium salt per two gallons of water, instead of using the added seawater. Keep the pH near neutral with regular weekly water changes of about 10 percent. Drastic changes in water conditions are to be scrupulously avoided.

Attach the Java ferns to small pieces of driftwood by tying it in place with monofilament fishing line, and locate them near one end of the tank. (You can clip off the monofilament later with scissors, after the Java fern has attached itself to the wood.) Plant the *Sagittaria* toward the middle, where it will receive plenty of light. Arrange the water-worn rocks to create a focal point off center and opposite the driftwood. Leave plenty of swimming room for the school of *Telmatherina*. The males can be recognized by the extended, dark-colored rays of the dorsal and anal fins. Both males and females sport electric blue and yellow-orange markings on the transparent body. A school of these fish makes a stunning display.

MODEL DESIGN 15 Sumatra

I developed this model design specifically to showcase one of the most popular fish species commonly maintained alone in a single-species tank.

Aquarium Capacity . . . . .55 to 75 gallons

Water Conditions . . . . .neutral, moderately hard

Optimal Temperature . . . . .78–80°F

Plants

    none, or plastic

    perhaps a floating plant, such as *Azolla*

Other Décor . . . . .driftwood and/or roots, water-worn rocks

Background . . . . .dark brown or black

Substrate . . . . .soft sand

Filtration . . . . .large canister filter or sump filter

Lighting . . . . .1 fluorescent tube

Special Requirements . . . . .live foods, especially at first

Fish

    Mastacembelus erythrotaenia 1

For aquarists who want a tank with a single large and stunning specimen, the fire eel is hard to beat. The only difficulty you are likely to encounter is its preference for live foods and a penchant for escape. Keeping the tank well-covered solves the second problem. Feed live and frozen foods until the eel becomes accustomed to captivity. Although it is a nocturnal predator, with proper care and feeding it learns to come out during the daylight hours. Arrange the tank decorations to provide ample hiding places, and use a floating plant, if you wish, to reduce light penetration.

Other species of Southeast Asian spiny eels, Family Mastacembelidae, can also be maintained in this setup. Do not try to combine them, however, or you may have a fight on your hands.

Australia

Isolated from the rest of the world during much of its long geological history, Australia is home to many unique kinds of plants, animals, and fish. Popular Australian aquarium fish include several varieties of rainbowfishes. Combining these with the interesting water clovers results in a display sure to call forth images of the land down under.

MODEL DESIGN 16 Australian Rainbowfish Community Tank

Because the various species of *Melanotaenia* are peaceful schoolers, they can be combined to good effect in a large tank. If you do not want to care for a large tank of live plants, simply substitute plastic for the species recommended in this model design.

Aquarium Capacity . . . . 75 gallons

Water Conditions . . . . .neutral, moderately hard

Optimal Temperature . . . . .75–78°F

Plants

    hygrophila (*Hygrophila corymbosa*) 3–15

    Indian hygrophila (*Hygrophila difformis*). . . 3–15

    ambalia (*Limnophila sessiliflora*) 1–3

    water clover (*Marsilea drummondi*) 3–5

        Or *Marsilea exarata* 3–5

    red tiger lotus (*Nymphaea lotus*) 1

    round-leaf rotala (*Rotala rotundifolia*). 3–15

Other Décor . . . . .driftwood and/or roots, water-worn rocks, and pebbles

Background . . . . .dark brown or black

Substrate . . . . .dark gravel with a small amount of sand added

Filtration . . . . .large canister filter or sump filter

Lighting . . . . .4 fluorescent tubes, or 2 150-watt metal halide lamps,
for plants

Special Requirements . . . . .none

Fish

    Melanotaenia exquisita. 3–5

    Melanotaenia nigrans. 3–5

    Melanotaenia splendida australis 3–5

    Melanotaenia trifasciata 3–5

You may have to do some searching to find the rainbowfishes. If you cannot find a particular species, simply substitute more individuals of an available one. If using either or both species of *Marsilea*, plant them toward the front of the aquarium, where they will form a lush carpet on the bottom. Use the bunched plants along the back and edges, leaving the center open for the rainbowfishes. The driftwood or roots can be used to hide equipment. Rocks and pebbles placed here and there in groups will help convey the impression of a river habitat.

Rainbowfishes are of great interest to biologists because they demonstrate how isolated populations of related species can evolve into different types. Multiple color forms of the same species occupy different tributaries. Since fish spawn with the others in the neighborhood and little mixing between tributaries occurs, the color forms can become fixed in a given population. You could devote an entire tank to the varied forms of *M. trifasciata*, for example. On the other hand, you could modify this model design to fit into a thirty- or forty-gallon tank: Keep only one of the color forms, and designate the biotope as that of the appropriate river. *Melanotaenia trifasciata* from the Giddy River, for example, has more blue on the body and red in the fins, whereas this species from the Goyder River has yellowish body coloration and orange in the fins.

CHAPTER 8

AFRICA

The central portion of the African continent teems with fish. So many similarities between Africa's fish fauna and that of South America exist that the ichthyological data are taken as strong evidence the two continents were once joined. Three families with many representatives in the aquarium trade are shared: the characins, or tetras; the cyprinodontids, or killifish, and the vast cichlid family.

Once the source of numerous aquarium species, Africa no longer supplies large numbers of wild-caught fish. Collectors no longer work in many areas, largely due to political turmoil. Fortunately, some of the most popular Africans present few impediments to successful hatchery culture. Virtually all rift lake cichlids are raised in captivity these days, for example. Every now and then, some highly interesting African species do appear on wholesalers' lists. Any of them is worth seeking out for a unique single-species tank.

Hard-to-Find Africans

When I owned an aquarium store, in the 1980s and 1990s, the fish in this section could be obtained about once a year. Alert your favorite dealer of your interest in non-cichlid African fish (most shops routinely stock African cichlids). Dealers are usually willing to order specific oddballs when they have a guaranteed sale.

MODEL DESIGN 17 | All-Purpose African Barb Tank

Only a few African barbs are available. The clipper barb, *Barbus callipterus*, comes from rivers and streams in west Africa. *Barbus holotaenia* can be found in running waters from tributaries of the Sanaga and Dja Rivers of Cameroon south through the Congo region to Angola. Overlapping the southern part of this range, from the lower reaches of the mighty Zaire River to Angola, *Barbus hulstaerti* occurs. Arguably the most beautiful of the three, *B. hulstaerti* is also, unfortunately, the least commonly available. The clipper barb sports an orange and black dorsal fin on an otherwise silvery body. *B. holotaenia* is handsomer, silvery white with a narrow black stripe from the snout to the base of the tail; the stripe bisects bright red eyes. *B. hulstaerti* has iridescent, pale blue scales. The dorsal fin is orange and black, and the orange is repeated on the anal and pectoral fins. The eye and gill cover are black, and there is a large black blotch on the side and another at the base of the tail. Probably the black spots serve to camouflage the eye, often a predator's preferred target.

The clipper barb adapts to most reasonable water conditions, but the others are more demanding. This aquarium model design will accommodate *B. hulstaerti*, the most finicky. The other two would be equally at home, too. You could also include rasboras or small South American tetras in this tank, as the preferred conditions are closely similar.

Aquarium Capacity . . . . 30 gallons

Water Conditions . . . . .soft, acidic

Optimal Temperature . . . . .74°F

Plants

    dwarf anubias (*Anubias barteri v. nana*) . . 1 (optional)

    red cabomba (*Cabomba furcata*) . . . . . . 3 (optional)

    floating water sprite
       (*Ceratopteris cornuta*) 5

    water sprite (*Ceratopteris thalictroides*) . . . 3

    African water pest (*Lagarosiphon major*). . . 3

Other Décor . . . . .driftwood and/or roots

Background . . . . .dark brown or black

Substrate . . . . .dark gravel with a small amount of sand added

Filtration . . . . .canister filter

Lighting . . . . .2 fluorescent tubes, for plants

Special Requirements . . . . .peat filtration (optional)

Fish

    Barbus callipterus. 5–7

       Or *Barbus holotaenia* 5–7

       Or *Barbus hulstaerti* 5–7

Ideally, add sterilized peat to the canister filter to acidify the water and tint it brown. This will be absolutely necessary only if you are lucky enough to find a school of *B. hulstaerti*; the other two can get along fine without it. Select a large piece of driftwood nearly as long as the tank. Place the larger end of the driftwood near the left rear corner of the aquarium, angling it slightly away from the back glass and toward the right front corner. Locate the intake for the canister filter at the left rear, and its return hose at the right rear. This creates a moderate current parallel to the length of the tank.

Plant either or both *Ceratopteris* species at the left rear to disguise the filter intake. Take care not to bury the crown, the point at which the roots and stalks join. Burying them too deep will cause them to rot off. These ferns are viviparous, meaning small plantlets are produced in the notches of the leaves. These will detach themselves and float, providing surface cover much appreciated by all the barbs, and that seems to be required for *B. hulstaerti* to thrive. Eventually, the floating plantlets will grow large enough to be planted in the substrate. When you run out of room, give them away to your hobbyist friends.

The clump of *Lagarosiphon* should be placed in the right rear of the tank and along the right side. Together with the *Ceratopteris*, it forms a frame for the piece of driftwood. The other plants are optional. If you want to add a touch of color, go with *Cabomba furcata*, which has finely textured, reddish foliage. You can place a small clump near the *Ceratopteris*, where it will contrast beautifully with the coarser, light-green leaves of the fern. It needs a lot of light, however, and is not native to Africa. Enough light for the *Cabomba* will probably rule out *B. hulstaerti*, but won't bother the other barbs. *Anubias barteri v. nana* has a much greater tolerance for shade, but is a bit harder to grow than *Cabomba*. Use *Anubias* as a centerpiece, attached to the driftwood with nylon monofilament. It will grow toward the light.

Leave the central area of the tank open, the better to display your school of African barbs. If you decide to make this a community tank, some good fish choices would be neon or cardinal tetras, *Paracheirodon innesi* and *P. axelrodi*, or any of the rasboras.

MODEL DESIGN 18 Congo Tetra

Certainly the most readily available non-cichlid African fish is the Congo tetra, *Phenacogrammus interruptus*. Either as a member of a large community tank or as the focus of a species tank, this active swimmer stands out. Easily frightened, the fish is not a good choice for a child's tank. Since it sometimes supplements its diet by nibbling at plants, they are omitted entirely from this model design.

Aquarium Capacity . . . . 30–75 gallons

Water Conditions .soft, acidic

Optimal Temperature . . . . .78–80°F

Plants

    none, or use a few plastic ones

    any floating plant, such as *Azolla* or *Salvinia* is OK

Other Décor . . . . .driftwood and/or roots, several pieces

Background . . . . .dark brown or black

Substrate . . . . .dark gravel

Filtration . . . . .hang-on or canister filter, depending on tank size

Lighting . . . . .1 fluorescent tube

Special Requirements . . . . .none

Fish

Phenacogrammus interruptus 5–15

The concept here is to suggest a tangle of driftwood caught in tree roots at the shaded edge of a sluggish stream. Details of the decoration will depend upon what you find in the way of wood. If possible, select several pieces of root. These should be suspended from the rear glass, so they hang down in the water. If they are large enough, place the root tips on the bottom, allowing the larger portion to reach the top of the tank. To provide support, cut a length of gray (known as schedule 80) PVC pipe that will just fit across the tank along the back. Using a hacksaw, notch out the ends so they rest on the tank frame. Driftwood can be suspended from this "curtain rod" using black plastic cable ties. Floating plants will hide your work from the viewer. If you cannot find roots, pick up some bamboo canes, ranging in diameter from one half to one inch. Using a hacksaw, cut lengths of bamboo that can be inserted into the gravel to form a "fence" along the back of the tank. This simulates a clump of bamboo growing close to the shoreline. Decorate the rest of the tank with driftwood, arranging it to create a maze through which the fish will swim. If you want greenery, place one to three plastic plants in whatever arrangement pleases you. Let the tank age for a week or so, then add the tetras over a period of weeks, placing only two at a time until you have reached the number you desire. The fish will feed on a variety of readily available foods. Make sure their diet includes small amounts of plant matter. This aquarium should receive a 20 to 50 percent weekly water change because the Congo tetra dislikes nitrate build-up.

If you have the room and want a community tank, any of the species mentioned in the previous model design will also work in this one.

MODEL DESIGN 19 African Lungfish

Three species of lungfish are known, only one of which occurs in Africa. The African lungfish, *Protopterus dolloi*, so differs from the others that it is placed in its own family by ichthyologists. It lives in streams in the lower portion of the Zaire River, where the alternating rainy and dry seasons have greatly influenced the fish's lifestyle. During the rainy season, it hunts among the submerged roots and thick vegetation for insects, worms, crustaceans, and other fish. The smooth, elongated body looks much like a submerged branch, and the two sets of paired fins are worm-like feelers. The dorsal, caudal, and anal fins are fused, forming a continuous band around the posterior two thirds of the body. It reaches about three feet in length, and is a fascinating subject for a large paludarium. This model design is recommended only for an experienced aquarist who can provide a suitably large tank.

Aquarium Capacity . . . . 210 gallons

Water Conditions . . . . .not critical

Optimal Temperature . . . . .80°F

Plants

    leopard orchid (*Ansellia africana*) . . . . . . 1 (terrestrial, see following text)

    smooth anubias (*Anubias barteri
      v. glabra*) 5

    dwarf anubias (*Anubias barteri v. nana*). . . 15

    African water fern (*Bolbitis heudelotii*). . . . 30

Other Décor . . . . .driftwood and/or roots

Background . . . . .dark brown or black

Substrate . . . . .sandy mud

Filtration . . . . .see text

Lighting . . . . .metal halide, 600 watts, for plants

Special Requirements . . . . .see text

Fish

    Protopterus dolloi 1

Lungfish are one to a customer, since the species is intolerant of its own kind, and will eat anything it can catch. They will also bite, so beware. Make sure you can provide plenty of live food. Fish, such as guppies or goldfish, will no doubt constitute the staple diet, supplemented with crayfish, shrimp, snails, tadpoles, earthworms, or insect larvae. Make sure you can meet the lungfish's dietary requirements before you attempt this model design.

Another peculiarity of this aquarium is its muddy bottom. Not only will it support the growth of terrestrial and aquatic plants, the mud serves an important function in the life of the lungfish. During the rainy season, river banks flood, and the fish can venture into the swamped lowlands to hunt. Because numerous other species take advantage of the rainy season to breed, food is abundant and the lungfish stores fat for the coming dry season. With the dry season, the waters recede, leaving nothing more of some streams than damp mud. To survive, the lungfish buries itself in the soft mud. Secreting a slime which causes the mud to harden like concrete, the fish provides itself with a breathing hole extending to the outside. Using its lungs to obtain oxygen

Live shrimp and crayfish can often be obtained from seafood vendors. Crayfish are in season only in the spring months. Tadpoles can be found, during spring and early summer, in shops catering to pond enthusiasts. You may also be able to collect live tadpoles. The tadpoles sold for ponds are likely to be bullfrogs, by the way, and should not be released into the wild unless you live in the frog's natural range. They have become a pest in some parts of the country.

and feeding off its stored fat, the lungfish remains curled in this cocoon to wait out the dry season. Collectors intrepid enough to locate the lungfish by the presence of the breathing hole on the surface of the mud can actually dig out the mud ball containing the fish. The fish can remain like this for the entire six-month duration of the rainy season. When water returns, the emaciated fish escapes the mud to hunt again among the roots and reeds of the flooded stream bank.

It is probably not necessary to repeat the annual cycle of flood and drought for the benefit of the lungfish. Specimens may do well in a strictly aquatic environment for years. Nevertheless, I have designed this aquarium so you can allow the mud to dry out if you wish. First, determine where the water level will be. Install a standpipe to this height, directly in the center at the rear of the tank. From the sump beneath the tank, pump water to a point along one end, say the right, almost to the front glass. Imagine viewers standing in the river, looking into a small cove just downstream from the point at which a small creek runs into the main channel. Along the right end, build up a ledge using slabs of rock. Water from the return hose will cascade down the rocks and into the river below. Set this up and test the arrangement before proceeding. See the description of plumbing, including a tank drain valve, on page 60 for more details on how to arrange the system. Once the waterfall is performing to your satisfaction, drain the tank. Let everything dry out thoroughly, and set the rocks in place permanently, using silicone adhesive. For a more professional look, quick-drying concrete with added fiberglass works better. Allow the concrete to cure at least a week, then paint with swimming-pool paint, tinted to match the rocks. You can also tint or stain the concrete, although achieving professional results takes practice.

Give some careful thought to the background you want for this paludarium. The viewer should receive the impression of endless rain forest in the distance. You could use a painted background and arrange bamboo canes in front of it, as I described on page 86. Bamboo canes can be attached to a piece of slate to keep them in place. Choose a leafy green paint color for the area above the water line, and black for the area below. A trailing vine trained upon the emergent part of the bamboo will complete the illusion.

Search out a piece of driftwood that is a relatively uniform log three or four inches in diameter and about three feet long. You will need to cut this piece to fit diagonally across the left side of the tank, beginning at a point about six inches back from the front glass and ending at the back glass about two feet to the right of the left rear corner.

Once you determine the exact position in which the driftwood log looks best, hold it in place and trace its path along the tank bottom using a wax pencil or a black marking pen. Using this line as the center, lay one or more rows of slab rocks, using the same material as for the waterfall. Place them on a bed of concrete about an inch thick. You will build up this foundation to a point at which the log, when cemented in place on top, is just above the predetermined water level. Treat this dam as you did the waterfall, and allow it to cure for at least a week. You should have a triangular shore area on the rear side of the dam, with the riverbank, upon which a fallen log has landed, toward the front. If you want the shore area to be fully terrestrial, caulk any cracks that would allow water through the dam, using silicone sealant. Otherwise, you can fill it about halfway full of cypress chips and place a thick layer of horticultural sphagnum moss on top. Cypress chips are sold in bags for garden mulch, and will not decay in water. They provide a cheap filler for your planting area.

To create the layer of mud on the bottom of the river, use bagged mud sold for growing water lilies, mixed with one part coarse river sand to two parts mud. You will want a layer that is six inches thick somewhere, to allow the lungfish room to bury himself. The mud will make the water extremely cloudy when the aquarium is first filled. Deal with this by running a canister filter with a fine particle cartridge on the sump for a week or so until the water clears up and all the mud settles out.

Disguise the standpipe with driftwood and roots. You can scatter a few smooth stones on the mud to complete the effect of the river's edge.

The featured terrestrial plant is the native African leopard orchid, *Ansellia africana*. It produces bright yellow flowers with brown spots and a haunting fragrance. The flowers are borne on arching spikes, many per plant, and they last a long time, perhaps a month. This is an easy orchid to grow, and it will thrive in the warm, humid environment of the paludarium. Plant it in the center of the terrestrial area, using a mixture of orchid potting bark and long-fiber sphagnum moss (both available at garden centers). Position the plant so the bases of the upright, jointed stalks, properly known as *pseudobulbs,* are just at ground level. Leaving a few roots exposed does no harm. It is important that the growing mix remain moist but never waterlogged. If necessary, build up a mound of mix above the water level. If you have done everything correctly, the cypress bark filler will remain waterlogged, allowing moisture to wick up through the growing mix. If you are not up to the challenge of an orchid (although this one is among the easiest to grow) you could substitute almost any tropical plant. Philodendrons and ferns would thrive in these conditions. You could also place small tropical plants around the base of the orchid or another tall, centerpiece plant. Another approach, particularly if you would like the option of changing the plants now and then, is to set the plants in flowerpots elevated on bricks to the proper height. The spaces between the pots should be filled with cypress chips or coarse aquarium gravel, and the rims hidden by a layer of long-fiber sphagnum placed on top.

I should mention my purpose in specifically including the *Ansellia* orchid in this model design. Its long flower spikes will grow in the direction of the light, arching gracefully over the water and providing a seasonally breathtaking display. The overall effect is likely to be so sensational you will want to invite friends over during the flowering time.

As for the aquatic plants, all those listed are bog varieties that do not spend all their time underwater in their natural habitats. Further, they all grow best if the roots are only partly covered by substrate. *Bolbitis* can even be attached to a piece of driftwood. All three are also rather slow growing, so little pruning will be needed and the plants can remain in the paludarium undisturbed for a long period of time. Plant them in groups near the edges of the aquatic portion of the display, leaving the center relatively open. You can arrange some additional driftwood in these areas, also, if you wish. Placing the coarse-textured *Anubias* closer to the viewer and

Saving Money When You Want a Really Big Tank

I enjoy home construction projects, and have always been inclined to do it myself in order to save money. If you are equally handy and have the tools, you can save a small fortune on a really big tank by building it yourself out of plywood. The front of the tank, of course, is glass to permit viewing. You will need thick plate glass for the purpose, half an inch for a water depth up to 2 feet. For a large paludarium, you can purchase an entire 4 x 8-foot sheet of half-inch plate glass, and keep the water level at 2 feet or less. Even so, an 8 x 4 x 2-foot volume of water is 480 gallons, weighing over 3,800 pounds.

Don't try constructing your own tank unless you are sure you know what you are doing. I've only included basic instructions—enough to allow a person with some experience to design and build a workable system. Some of you reading this will get it immediately. If you are not one of them, go with a custom-built glass or acrylic tank instead.

Of course, you can scale the tank down as much as you like. Our current example will assume you are using both glass and plywood in four-by-eight-foot sheets. It should go without saying that you should make careful drawings and measurements prior to launching a project of these dimensions.

The bottom and three sides of the tank are constructed from three sheets of 3/4-inch marine-grade plywood. Two of the sheets form the back and bottom; the third sheet is cut in half to make the ends. All cuts must be as perfectly square and uniform as humanly possible. The front of the tank is framed with two-by-fours, planed down so the edges are square and smooth. The top, back, and sides are braced with more two-by-fours, and the top corners are held in place by plywood gussets. The plywood pieces are held together at their edges with three-inch exterior-type wood screws set in pre-drilled holes every six inches. Waterproof wood glue is spread on the edges before installing the screws, as an extra measure of protection against the tank's separating at the seams.

Once the tank is assembled, its interior receives three coats of swimming-pool paint. The glass is mounted inside the front frame with a wide bead of silicone sealant. Water pressure from the inside helps to hold it in place securely when the tank is filled, but install it with the tank supported on planks, front side down. The weight of the glass helps to create a uniform seal. Make sure the lower edge of the glass is in contact with the tank bottom, where it will rest securely when the tank is filled. When the glass is in place and the sealant has cured, caulk all edges and seams with more silicone. After curing, neatly trim away any excess.

The plywood can easily be drilled to accommodate plumbing. To avoid having to install a standpipe, you can simply cut drain holes in the rear of the tank at the desired water level. Remember not to exceed 24 inches of water if you are using ½-inch plate glass. Two drains, each 1¼ inches in diameter, should handle a system flow rate of 120 gallons per hour. For a more robust waterfall, increase the number of drains or the water will rise above your predetermined level. I strongly recommend thoroughly testing the completed tank and plumbing system prior to installing any other components.

the dark, more finely textured *Bolbitis* toward the back will promote the illusion that the paludarium is much deeper than it actually is.

When everything is in place and the equipment is running properly, allow the tank to age for a month before introducing the lungfish. This will give the plants time to become established both above and below the water line.

When I had my aquarium store, our first African lungfish prompted much discussion about the best aquarium for it. When I described essentially the design just presented, my partners scoffed at spending so much money and effort on a single lungfish. You could, however, use the same design and fill the watery portion with more traditional fish, as suggested in the next model design.

MODEL DESIGN 20 *Distichodus*

The lower reaches of the Zaire have yielded up an amazing number of aquarium fish species, some of which are rare in the trade. Among these are some unusual, vegetarian characins, the genus *Distichodus*. If you can find one, they make a valuable addition to either a community aquarium lacking live plants or a single-species tank. Make certain of your identification. In my experience, when these are offered at all it is one of the barbed species (*D. lusosso* or *D. sexfasciatus*) that is available. Neither of these is suitable for any but the most specialized aquarium. The former grows much too large, while the latter matures from an attractive juvenile to a drab, gray adult. Bottom line, only buy the one described here.

Aquarium Capacity . . . . 30 gallons, long style

Water Conditions . . . . neutral and moderately hard

Optimal Temperature . . . . .75–78°F

Plants

    plastic only, or none

Other Décor . . . . .driftwood and/or roots, water-worn rocks

Background . . . . .pale blue or green

Substrate . . . . .natural gravel

Filtration . . . . .large hang-on filter or canister filter

Lighting . . . . .1 fluorescent tube

Special Requirements . . . . .vegetable diet

Fish

    Distichodus affinis 3

Think of a big river when you think of this fish. You will need extra filtration for this or any other vegetarian species, as they run through a lot of food. Set up the tank with the filter on one end, to create a brisk, length-wise current. Place a few interesting pieces of driftwood with their tips pointing in the direction of the current. Position water-worn rocks in groups here and there. Add the substrate. Done! You can stop at this point or add some well-chosen plastic plants, if you prefer greenery. *Distichodus* will munch live plants down to their stems. Reaching only about four inches long, *D. affinis* has a silvery body and striking orange-red fins.

The dorsal fin bears the added decoration of a black stripe. Feed them a variety of vegetable foods, from specially formulated flakes to fresh greens from the grocery store.

You could add some other kinds of peaceful community fish to this tank. Good choices would be the zebra danio, *Brachydanio rerio*, or the cherry barb, *Barbus titteya*.

MODEL DESIGN 21 Elephantnose

It is a shame aquarium fish are not exported more regularly from Africa. If properly managed, the industry could be a source of income and an incentive to preserve natural aquatic habitats. With research into their breeding habits, some species can be brought into hatchery production. Seldom is there a better place to do this than near the fish's native biotope, from which breeding stock can be collected. The subject of this model design probably appeals only to serious aquarists, but it represents one of the most remarkable groups of freshwater fish on the planet.

Aquarium Capacity . . . . 40 gallons, long style

Water Conditions .neutral and moderately hard

Optimal Temperature . . . . .75–78°F

Plants

    dwarf anubias (*Anubias barteri v. nana*). . . 1 to 3

    Wendt's crypt (*Cryptocoryne wendtii*) . . . . 3 to 5

    crypt (*Cryptocoryne willisii*) . . . . 3 to 5

    Java fern (*Microsorium pteropus*) . . . . 1 to 3

    Java moss (*Vesicularia dubyana*) . . . . 1 to 3 clumps

Other Décor . . . . .driftwood and/or roots, water-worn rocks

Background . . . . .dark brown or black

Substrate . . . . .a mixture of coarse and fine, soft sand

Filtration . . . . .canister filter

Lighting . . . . .2 fluorescent tubes, for plants

Special Requirements . . . . .rocks to build a cave, blue night light

Fish

    Gnathonemus petersii 1

Gnathonemus petersii is known in the aquarium trade as elephantnose. I chose this representative of the mormyrid family because it is the only one with which I have had experience. It is a nocturnal predator that searches bottom sediments for small invertebrates, which it locates with the aid of a fleshy extension of its lower lip. It is also amazingly adept at jumping. The one I owned had a habit of leaping into the hang-on filter on its aquarium. Make sure yours is securely covered.

Install the filter return on one end of the tank, directing its outflow toward the opposite end. Underneath it, position a long piece of driftwood with the narrow portion pointed in the direction of the current. On the end opposite the filter outflow, create an arrangement of stones that simulates a cave. With any luck at all, the elephantnose will spends its days in here.

The elephantnose and others of its kind are the ecological equivalent of catfishes. Sensory structures around the mouth enable them to find food in bottom sediments. The nose of this fish is soft and smooth, however, while the whiskers of most catfish are more durable. The elephantnose needs a soft substrate in which to search, or damage can occur. For this reason, I suggest a particular arrangement of the substrate. Start by building an oval island of coarse sand near the center of the tank. The long axis of the oval should be shifted to the left or right of center to avoid a formal look. Use one to three smooth rocks on the downstream side of the oval to help hold this bed of sand in place. (Downstream is the direction opposite the filter outlflow.) Into this bed you will place the plants, as if debris collected behind those large rocks provided fertilizer. This, in fact, is the arrangement one sees in natural sandy-bottom streams. Seeds are also trapped in such pockets; that, of course, is where the plants come from!

Before you plant, cover the remainder of the tank bottom with the fine sand, building it up to the same depth as the central area. The soft, sandy area encircling the plants will make it possible to observe the fish on its feeding forays. To accomplish this, I suggest installing a blue night light of the type often sold for saltwater reef aquariums. You can find them advertised in magazines and online. Sold primarily to simulate the light of a full moon, they are perfect for observing any nocturnal behavior in the aquarium.

The elephantnose is not a particularly pretty fish, unless you have a fondness for the unusual. The smooth skin is uniformly dark brown or black, relieved only by lighter areas near the base of the tail. The tail itself is elongated, roughly a third of the total length of the body, somewhat stiffened, and deeply forked at its outer end. The dorsal and anal fins set far back toward the base of the tail. The portion of the body anterior to this unusual fin arrangement is elongated. The pectoral fins emerge just behind the gill covers. The most noticeable aspect of the head region is the lip extension; the small eyes disappear into the dark background of the head.

By now you must be wondering why this fish holds any interest at all. For me, the fascination comes from the knowledge that the fish bears an electric organ. Speculation as to the function of this structure has fueled a debate that can only be answered by careful study. Possible functions include self-defense, prey location, and, most interestingly, mate location. Perhaps its electrical capabilities serve the fish in all these capacities. It emits electricity in bursts of rapid pulses. Like radar, the pulsations could help to identify telltale shapes, either a morsel in the muddy bottom, or danger lurking among the reeds. It could also be a signaling method analogous to the calls of birds or frogs seeking mates, albeit a silent one. According to one reference, the fish has been used to monitor water quality. Its pulsing pattern changes in response to changes in water quality. Perhaps females swim toward the electrical song of a male, basing her choice on his virtuosity. Perhaps different species of mormyrids produce different songs.

Mormyrids accept a wide selection of living and prepared aquarium foods. Feed, of course, at night. Perform regular partial water changes to keep water quality good. Harmless to other fish, the elephantnose can share the tank with smaller, peaceful species preferring similar conditions, such as colorful livebearers, rasboras, or danios. A community tank provides interest during the day, when the elephantnose will rest in its cave.

The Zaire and Other West African Rivers

West Africa has supplied virtually all the aquarium fish exported from the continent, with the exception of the rift lake cichlids to be discussed later. The Zaire River and its tributaries might be called the African Amazon, alluding to the variety of interesting species to be found there.

MODEL DESIGN 22 Jewel Cichlid Paludarium

Surely one of the most beautiful freshwater fish available is the jewel cichlid, *Hemichromis bimaculatus*. Its red-orange body is overlain with iridescent, baby-blue dots. The species name *bimaculatus* refers to the two black spots, edged in yellow, on the fish's side, one on the gill cover and one about the middle of the body. There is a smaller dark spot at the base of the tail. The colors of the male become brighter than those of the female at spawning time, but the two are otherwise difficult to distinguish. If you can obtain an already mated pair, so much the better.

A pair of jewel cichlids would be spectacularly at home in the previously described paludarium, if the African lungfish is not to your liking.

Aquarium Capacity . . . . 210 gallons

Water Conditions . . . . .not critical

Optimal Temperature . . . . .72°F

Plants

    leopard orchid (*Ansellia africana*) 1

    smooth anubias (*Anubias barteri*
      v. glabra) . . . . 7 to 15

    dwarf anubias (*Anubias barteri v. nana*). . . 7 to 15

    African water fern (*Bolbitis heudelotii*). . . . 5 to 7

    red tiger lotus (*Nymphaea lotus*). 3

Other Décor	. . . . .driftwood and/or roots, water-worn rocks
Background	. . . . .dark brown or black
Substrate	. . . . .natural gravel with added sand
Filtration	. . . . .see text
Lighting	. . . . .metal halide, 600 watts, for plants
Special Requirements	. . . . .see text

Fish

> *Hemichromis bimaculatus* . . . . 1 mated pair

Jewel cichlids are territorial, but generally remain peaceful toward their tank mates, except when spawning. Using a huge, well-planted tank minimizes these problems. Optional tank mates could include a school of Congo tetras, *Phenacogrammus interruptus*, and any of the Zaire River catfishes, such as *Synodontis angelicus*, *S. decorus*, or *S. notatus*, to name but three possibilities. Lay out the tank as described in the lungfish tank model design, substituting gravel for the mud. Group the tiger lily plants to create a centerpiece, though, as always, you should actually place them off center to achieve a more natural look. They should be placed in the rear half of the tank, with the other plants nearer the edges as in the lungfish tank.

Toward the front, place some water-worn rocks. Arrange them in three groups, separated as far as possible from each other. Individual groups should consist of three to five rocks, in a color that complements that of the gravel. At least one rock in each group should be flattish and quite smooth. On one of these, the pair of cichlids will lay their eggs. It is difficult to keep a healthy pair of cichlids from raising a family in the aquarium. You will not be able to keep many of the offspring, however, so be prepared to remove the eggs before they hatch. If the pair is permitted to raise its brood, expect about 300 fry. The parents are scrupulous in caring for their babies. They will dig shallow depressions near the rock groupings and move the fry to these "spawning pits" once they are free-swimming. The adults usually dig more than one pit, and move the kids around, probably in an effort to foil predators.

MODEL DESIGN 23 | Soft Water African Tank

This aquarium is for the rest of us who cannot afford and/or lack the space for the giant tank used in model designs 19 and 22. You could keep a pair of jewel cichlids in this one, but they may become too aggressive for the smaller fish.

Aquarium Capacity	. . . . 65 gallons
Water Conditions	. . . . .soft, acidic
Optimal Temperature	. . . . .75–78°F

Plants

    smooth anubias (*Anubias barteri v. glabra*) 3

    dwarf anubias (*Anubias barteri v. nana*) . . 5

    red floating fern (*Azolla filiculoides*) . . . . . floating

    dwarf bacopa (*Bacopa monnieri*) . . . . 3 clumps

    African water fern (*Bolbitis* heudeloti) 3

    floating water sprite (*Ceratopteris cornuta*) 3–5

    Wendt's crypt (*Cryptocoryne wendtii*) 3–5

    crypt (*Cryptocoryne willisii*) 3–5

    spiral eelgrass (*Vallisneria spiralis v. spiralis*) 12–15

    red tiger lotus (*Nymphaea lotus*) . . . . 1 (optional)

Other Décor . . . . .driftwood and/or roots, flat rocks, coconut shell

Background . . . . .dark brown or black

Substrate . . . . .natural gravel with added sand

Filtration . . . . .canister filter

Lighting . . . . .4 fluorescent tubes, for plants

Special Requirements . . . . .none

Fish

    Hemichromis bimaculatus . . . . 1 mated pair

       Or *annochromis parilus* . . . . 1 mated pair

    Synodontis nigriventris 3–5

    Phenacogrammus interruptus 3–5

The first time I saw *Nannochromis parilus*, it was known as *N. nudiceps*. You may find it still given that name in the aquarium trade. It is a beautiful, peaceful cichlid that seldom exceeds three inches in length. This species is a cave spawner, meaning the parents shelter the eggs in a rocky enclosure. You can provide them with an arrangement of flat rocks, but they will readily accept an empty coconut shell with the eye drilled out to make a sort of tropical igloo. Because they remain on the bottom, encounters with the somewhat nervous Congo tetras are unlikely.

Synodontis nigriventris is known as the upside-down catfish, for its habit of swimming inverted. Every aquarist should keep them at some point, because they are so amusing to watch. Many species of synodontid catfishes can be found in the rivers and streams of central Africa, and the competition has no doubt been intense. *S. nigriventris* has solved the problem of securing enough food by abandoning its cousins who, like most other catfishes, grub for food in the bottom sediments. Instead, it seeks mosquito larvae and other surface dwellers. Because its mouth points downward (when the fish is viewed in the normal position), *S. nigriventris* compensates by swimming upside down. In a remarkable demonstration of adaptation in response to natural selection, the coloration of this catfish is reversed. Most fish are pale in color on their ventral surface and darker on the dorsal side. Viewed from below, this color pattern blends with the bright surface of the water, making the fish less visible to predators lurking in the depths. Since getting eaten is a powerful selection pressure, fish with the reversed color pattern must have been favored in ancestral populations of this catfish. Modern populations are made up of individuals that are light on the back and dark on the belly, so they can swim upside down and not stand out against the background of shimmering water.

The arrangement of plants in this model design should be dictated by the shapes and sizes of the driftwood you select. Don't forget to place the cichlids' coconut shell where you can see it. Give the fish a sense of security by partially obscuring the shell with plants. As usual, strategically locate clumps of dense foliage to hide any unsightly equipment. Place a few plant groupings so they appear to be growing out from beneath driftwood. As I have previously mentioned, grouping three small water-worn rocks at the base of a clump of plants helps to anchor the plants to the bottom, both literally and in the aesthetic sense. You can vary the plant combinations endlessly. Try scanning pictures of aquatic plants into your computer. You can cut and paste these images into mock-ups of the aquarium you have in mind. This enables trying out different arrangements without handling, and possibly damaging, real plants. Once you have a plan worked out in your virtual tank, use it to guide you when planting the real thing.

You can also use plastic plants for this model design, in which case you won't need all the light. A single tube will suffice.

MODEL DESIGN 24   The African Butterflyfish

One of the most interesting freshwater fish I've ever kept is *Pantodon buchholzi*, the African butterflyfish. It is found in tropical western Africa, inhabiting shallow, still pools in flooded areas or at the edges of streams. Though reaching a bit over four inches in length, it gets along well with many other fish, even smaller ones. It is also hardy and easy to feed. A long, shallow tank, such as a thirty- or forty-gallon size, suits it perfectly.

Aquarium Capacity . . . . 30 or 40 gallons, long style

Water Conditions .neutral and moderately hard, or soft and slightly acidic

Optimal Temperature . . . . .75–78°F

Plants

    dwarf anubias (*Anubias barteri v. nana*) . . 1 to 3

    dwarf bacopa (*Bacopa monnieri*) . . . . 3 clumps

    green cabomba (*Cabomba caroliniana*) . . . 3 clumps

       or cabomba (*Cabomba aquatica*) . . . . 3 clumps

    Wendt's crypt (*Cryptocoryne wendtii*) . . . . 3 to 5

    crypt (*Cryptocoryne willisii*) . . . . 3 to 5

    spiral eelgrass (*Vallisneria spiralis*
       v. spiralis) . . . . 12 to 15

Other Décor . . . . .driftwood and/or roots

Background . . . . .dark brown or black

Substrate . . . . .natural gravel with added sand

Filtration . . . . .hang-on filter or canister filter

Lighting . . . . .4 fluorescent tubes, for plants

Special Requirements . . . . .none

Fish

    Pantodon buchholzi . . . . 1 mated pair

Here again, you can substitute plastic plants for the real thing and get along with less light. The remarkable butterflyfish feeds at the surface, taking into its capacious mouth all sorts of insects and worms that live in or fall into the water. It is not at all aggressive, except toward other surface-feeding fish, which it will consume if it can manage the deed. However, it generally ignores anything swimming below, so you can include bottom-feeding catfishes or any of the small schooling species mentioned elsewhere in the book.

Identifying a pair of these fish is easy. The rear edge of the male's anal fin is curved and its outermost fin rays are elongated, while the female has a small, straight-edged, unadorned anal fin. To get them to breed requires a rich diet of fresh insects, something better accomplished in an outdoor pond. So zealously will *Pantodon* pursue its prey that it may leap right out of the tank trying to catch a moth attracted to the light. Make sure the tank is well covered.

Avoid floating plants, which will prevent the butterflyfish from feeding at the surface. It will, by the way, take any sort of aquarium fare that floats; insects are not required for its survival. Otherwise, arrange plants and driftwood attractively, taking care to hide unsightly equipment. This fish looks especially good with fine-leaved plants, but don't include the *Cabomba* unless you have plenty of light. Otherwise, the plant will become straggly and lose leaves.

MODEL DESIGN 25 A Crib for Kribs

Hardy, peaceful, and colorful, the kribensis, *Pelvicachromis pulcher*, can be the focus of a small single-species tank, or form part of a larger community setup. For this model design, I've chosen a modest tank size that will fit almost anywhere in the house.

Aquarium Capacity . . . . 29 gallons

Water Conditions .neutral and moderately hard, with added salt

Optimal Temperature . . . . .75°F

Plants

    Java fern (*Microsorium pteropus*) 1

    Java moss (*Vesicularia dubyana*) . . . . 2–3 clumps

    hornwort (*Ceratophyllum demersum*). . . . . 2–3 clumps

    dwarf arrowhead (*Sagittaria graminea*). . . 3–5

Other Décor . . . . .driftwood and rocks

Background . . . . .deep green

Substrate . . . . .natural gravel with added sand

Filtration . . . . .hang-on filter

Lighting . . . . .2 fluorescent tubes, for plants

Special Requirements . . . . .2 teaspoons aquarium salt per 5 gallons

Fish

    Pelvicachromis pulcher . . . . 1 mated pair

All the plant choices tolerate brackish water well, but you could substitute plastic if you like. Because the tank is tall, I picked plants that can get along with low light. Water depth attenuates illumination. You could omit the salt; the kribs get along fine without it, but they never seem to develop their beautiful coloration to its fullest.

Why krib? An outdated name for the fish was *Pelmatochromis kribensis*. Aquarium dealers labeled them only with the species name, and it stuck. They are olive green, with purple on the belly that becomes more intense during courtship and spawning. Reaching only about four inches in length, a pair can be easily accommodated in a small tank. Make certain to provide them with one or more smooth, flat rocks. Upon one of these, they will deposit a clutch of eggs. Breeding some fish can be quite a challenge, but kribs will spawn even in a bustling community tank. Optionally, therefore, you can add other peaceful community fish to this tank.

Because of the salt, livebearers would probably make the best choice from the commonly available fish. The kribs will remain near the bottom, while the livebearers tend to swim in the middle and upper water layers.

Like other cichlids, kribs provide excellent parental care. Most books suggest leaving the fry with their parents until they are big enough to fend for themselves. If the fry are removed promptly, the parents will spawn again. Spawning too frequently saps the parents' energy and can lead to problems.

In decorating this tank, simply arrange a grouping of rocks to one side, and place driftwood with Java fern and Java moss toward the back. The fish will swim in the remaining open area, and almost certainly will spawn on one of the rocks. If you include the suggested *Sagittaria*, place it where it will receive the most light. The *Ceratophyllum* will need frequent thinning. If you choose to include livebearers, this floating plant will shelter their offspring. This setup makes a good choice for an inexperienced aquarist. It provides both ease of care and the reward of seeing fish mate and rear their young.

African Killifish

I introduced killifish earlier. Also known as egg-laying toothed carps, they have spread throughout the tropics, from South America to Southeast Asia, and beyond, even into the temperate zone. In Africa, killies occur from the Mediterranean coast to the northern portion of South Africa. Arguably, the African species are the most beautiful.

Killifish enjoy a devoted following but are rarely seen in aquarium shops. Enthusiasts, however, swap killies all the time, a practice facilitated by the spawning behavior of many of them. As a group, they are ideal choices for small species aquariums, and many make good community fish. The following model designs will give you an idea of the vast array of possible killifish tanks.

MODEL DESIGN 26 *Aphyosemion*

The lyretail, *Aphyosemion australe*, turns up from time to time in aquarium shops, so this model design makes it the focal point of a small, single-species tank. It can also be combined, however, with other fish that like the same water conditions, provided the tank is roomy enough.

Aquarium Capacity . . . . 20 gallons, long style

Water Conditions . . . . .soft, acidic

Optimal Temperature . . . . .72–74°F

Plants

    dwarf anubias (*Anubias barteri v. nana*). . . 1

    red floating fern (*Azolla filiculoides*) . . . . . 1 clump

ambulia (*Linmophila sessiliflora*)	3 clumps
African water fern (*Bolbitis heudelotii*)	3
Wendt's crypt (*Cryptocoryne wendtii*)	3 to 5
crypt (*Cryptocoryne willisi*)	3 to 5
Other Décor	driftwood and/or roots
Background	dark brown or black
Substrate	dark or black natural gravel with added sand
Filtration	hang-on filter
Lighting	2 fluorescent tubes, for plants
Special Requirements	peat or sphagnum moss on bottom
Fish	
Aphyosemion australe	1 female, 2 or 3 males

As killifish go, this fish lives a long time, about three years. Although the females are drab, the males are stunning. The anterior portion of the body has a touch of neon blue, overlain with bright red spots extending all the way back to the tip of the tail. The tail fin, which has extensions flowing from each corner, is outlined in chrome yellow, with white on the tips of the extensions. The dorsal and anal fins are marked in red, white, yellow, and blue.

Arrange the driftwood and plants in this tank to provide dense cover at the rear and sides, so the killies will be easily visible. Floating *Azolla* helps to keep the light dim and the dark bottom shows off the brilliant coloration to good effect. To mimic the debris-strewn bottom of the west African streams in which the fish naturally occurs, soak horticultural peat or long-fiber sphagnum moss in a bucket of the same water you will be using for the tank. When this material becomes sufficiently waterlogged to sink, you can place it on the bottom of the display tank.

Although the lyretail will take non-living foods such as flakes and frozen brine shrimp, live foods such as mosquito larvae and *Daphnia* will encourage them to breed. *Aphyosemion australe* is an *egg-hanger*. The eggs are deposited, about twenty per day, on the leaves of plants, probably the fine-leaved *Limnophila* in preference to the others suggested for this tank. To raise them, transfer plant stems with attached eggs to a separate small tank and maintain the same conditions as the display aquarium. They should hatch in about two weeks into rather large fry. Feed them on live brine shrimp, newly hatched, and they will grow rapidly. You can keep the most robust individuals and return them to the display tank when they are large enough to escape being eaten by their parents.

Literally dozens of species of *Aphyosemion* exist, and many of them can be obtained through exchanges among members of the American Killifish Association. Visit the AKA web site for more information.

This genus of African killifish consists of egg-hangers that seldom exceed three inches in length. Most are peaceful fish that will get along with others of similar disposition, but check references for specific recommendations. The species I have chosen is so peaceful it won't even eat its own young, as most others are inclined to do. It is found in the area of the Zaire River known as Stanley Pool.

Aquarium Capacity . . . . 20 gallons, long style

Water Conditions . . . . .moderately hard, slightly acidic

Optimal Temperature . . . . .74–78°F

Plants

    dwarf anubias (*Anubias barteri v. nana*). . . 1

    red floating fern (*Azolla filiculoides*) . . . . . floating

    African water sprite (*Ceratopteris cornuta*) 3–5

    ambulia (*Linmophila sessiliflora*) . . . . 3 clumps

Other Décor . . . . .driftwood and/or roots

Background . . . . .dark brown or black

Substrate . . . . .dark or black natural gravel with added sand

Filtration . . . . .hang-on filter

Lighting . . . . .2 fluorescent tubes, for plants

Special Requirements . . . . .added salt

Fish

    Epiplatys chevalieri. . . . . 1 female, 2 or 3 males

This killie needs two teaspoons of aquarium salt per five gallons of water. (Many other killifish benefit from a small amount of added salt, but because the family is so diverse, check more specific references before adding it.) Pearly pink overall, the fish bears glowing red dots in two rows on the upper half of the body. Below the midline of the body, the red dots converge into two parallel stripes separated by a shiny gold one. Decorate the tank heavily with roots or small pieces of driftwood, and intersperse the plants, using the *Anubias* as a centerpiece.

Spawning can often be induced by reducing the water hardness abruptly through the addition of distilled water. This simulates what happens when seasonal rains dilute the waters of *E. chevalieri's* native haunts. You can leave the eggs, which it hangs on the plant leaves, in the tank with their parents, who will ignore them. The fry must be fed tiny live foods, such as newly hatched brine shrimp, but the adults will take flakes and frozen foods. Change one-third to one-half of the water weekly, as the fish is sensitive to the build-up of pollutants. It lives about a year.

MODEL DESIGN 28 *Nothobranchius*

Our third genus of African killifish carries the seasonal spawning behavior to its ultimate conclusion. They are like annual flowers, living but a single season and making up for it with abundant eggs that wait out the dry season. *Nothobranchius* are egg-buriers, diving into the soft substrate to deposit eggs. Because they are aggressive, these killies are best suited to a single-species tank.

Aquarium Capacity . . . . 20 gallons, long style

Water Conditions . . . . .soft, slightly acidic

Optimal Temperature . . . . .70–72°F

Plants

    dwarf anubias (*Anubias barteri v. nana*). . . 1

    red floating fern (*Azolla filiculoides*) . . . . . 1 clump

    African water fern (*Bolbitis heudelotii*). . . . 3 to 5

    Java moss (*Vesicularia dubyana*) . . . . a few clumps

Other Décor . . . . .driftwood and/or roots

Background . . . . .dark brown or black

Substrate . . . . .peat moss mixed with sand

Filtration . . . . .hang-on filter

Lighting . . . . .2 fluorescent tubes, for plants

Special Requirements . . . . .peat in filter

Fish

    Nothobranchius rachovii. . . . . 1 male, 2 or 3 females

What it lacks in lifespan this killifish makes up for in coloration. Males only reach about two inches in length, but they are bright red overlain with a pattern of irisdescent blue dots and splotches arranged in more or less vertical bar patterns. The fins are blue, decorated with irregular shapes in black. The outer margin of the tail is red edged in black. Females are smaller, drab gray or brownish green.

Nothobranchius species are found in eastern Africa, unlike the others previously described, which live on the opposite side of the continent. *N. rachovii* is wide ranging, living in savannah streams all the way down to northern South Africa. It prefers cooler water than the west African killies. Because the small streams in which it lives dry up seasonally, the eggs are buried in the bottom sediment, where they remain damp and alive, awaiting the next rainy season. Spawning is encouraged by proper water conditions and a steady diet of live foods. Prepared foods alone may result in poorly developed individuals that refuse to spawn, or worse, unhealthy eggs that develop into deformed fry. These fish are not for the aquarist who is casual about caring for the tank.

After the eggs are deposited, they can be removed, substrate and all, and stored in a plastic bag. You only need enough moisture to keep the peat moss damp. They will keep this way for several months, long after the parents have passed on. When you want them to hatch, just add water. You can do a major water change on the tank using distilled water to mimic refreshing spring rains, which encourages hatching. Feed them well, and they will mature in only twelve weeks, ready to bury eggs to guarantee a new generation.

Decorating this tank should proceed as described for the other African killifish, but also place clumps of Java moss here and there on the bottom. This apparently encourages the fish to deposit eggs, and the green coloration relieves the monotony of the peat and sand layer.

Rift Lake Cichlids

Along the border between the Democratic Republic of the Congo, Zambia, and Malawi on the west, and Uganda, Rwanda, Burundi, Tanzania, and Mozambique on the east, lies Africa's Great Rift Valley, the mother lode of African aquarium fish. Split asunder by ancient tectonic movements, the long, narrow lakes along this border contain a group of cichlids so diverse they have provided material for hundreds of graduate theses as well as thousands of aquariums.

Although several smaller lakes along the great rift have interesting fish faunas, the two largest ones, Tanganyika and Malawi, supply the vast majority of African cichlids available to the aquarium hobby. Actually, they supplied the breeding stock, because most African cichlids are now tank-raised far from Africa. The cichlids of Lake Malawi are collectively known as *mbuna*, the name given to them by the humans living around the lake. These are the species most likely to be available in the average aquarium shop. The numerous (and arguably more fascinating) Lake Tanganyika species may take some searching to locate.

MODEL DESIGN 29 *Mbuna* Community Tank

When African cichlids first began to appear in the United States aquarium trade in the 1960s, just about all of the *mbuna* were originally assigned to the genera *Haplochromis* or *Pseudotropheus*. Later, ichthyologists assigned them to many new genera. As a result, older references may give different names for the species covered here. I have provided the old generic names in parentheses after the accepted names in the list below.

Anostomus anostomus (South America)

Aphyocarax anisitsi (South America)

Apistrogramma agassizii (South America)

Aplocheilus blocki (Southeast Asia)

Barbus schwanfeldi (Southeast Asia)

Barbus tetrazona (Australasia)

Barbus titteya (Southeast Asia)

Betta splendens (Southeast Asia)

Brachydanio rerio (Southeast Asia)

Carnegiella strigata (South America)

Colisa laelia (Southeast Asia)

Corydoras agassizii (South America)

Corydoras paleatus (South America)

Enneacanthus chaetodon (North America)

Exodon paradoxus (South America)

Gnathonemus petersii (Africa)

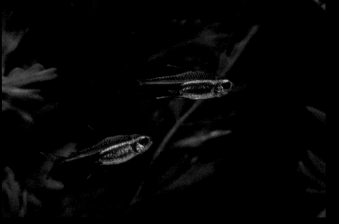

Hemigrammus erythrozonus (South America)

Hyphessobrycon erythrostigma (South America)

Hyphessobrycon flammeus (South America)

Hyphessobrycon pulchripinnis (South America)

Julidochromis marlieri (Africa)

Kryptoterus minor (Southeast Asia)

Labeotropheus trewavasae (Africa)

Macropodus opercularis (Southeast Asia)

Megalamphodus megalopterus (South America)

Melanochromis (Pseudotropheus) johanni (Africa)

Microgeophagus ramirezi (South America)

Monocirrhus polyacanthus (South America)

Nannostomus trifasciatus (South America)

Neolamprologus (Lamprologus) birchardi (Africa)

Neolamprologus (Lamprologus) leleupi (Africa)

Nothobranchius rachovii (Africa)

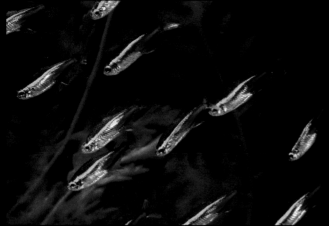
Paracheirodon innesi (South America)

Phenacogrammus interruptus (Africa)

Poecilia reticulata (Central America)

Poecilia velifera (Central America)

Rasbora borapetensis (Southeast Asia)

Pterophyllum scalare (South America)

Rasbora heteromorpha (Southeast Asia)

Semaprochilodus taeniurus (South America)

Sorubim lima (South America)

Symphysodon (South America)

Symphysodon (South America)

Synodontis nigriventris (Africa)

Tanichthys albonubes (Southeast Asia)

Telmatherina ladigesi (Australasia)

Thorichthys meeki (Central America)

Trichogaster trichopterus (Southeast Asia)

Xiphophorus helleri (Central America)

Xiphophorus maculatus (Central America)

Ceratopterus (water sprite)

Echinodorus bleheri (swordplant)

Microsporium pteropus (Java fern)

Aquarium Capacity . . . . 75 gallons

Water Conditions . . . . .moderately hard, slightly alkaline

Optimal Temperature . . . . .75°F

Plants

    none

Other Décor . . . . .rocks

Background . . . . .pale blue or gray

Substrate . . . . .light-colored natural gravel

Filtration . . . . .large canister filter, sump filter

Lighting . . . . .1 fluorescent tube

Special Requirements . . . . .African cichlid salts mix

Fish

    Labeotropheus fuelleborni . . . . 1 male, 2 or 3 females

    Labeotropheus trewavasae . . . . 1 male, 2 or 3 females

    Melanochromis (Pseudotropheus) auratus . . . 1 male, 2 or 3 females

    Melanochromis (Pseudotropheus) johanni . . . 1 male, 2 or 3 females

    Pseudotropheus socolofi . . . . 1 male, 2 or 3 females

    Pseudotropheus (Tilapia) zebra . . . . 1 male, 2 or 3 females

Early collecting activity in Lake Malawi took place close to shore. As a result, many *mbuna* now considered standards for African cichlid fanciers inhabit the shoreline. The community tank featured in this model design demonstrates several keys to keeping African cichlids successfully. First, use a large tank. The species listed mature at between four and six inches. You must have enough tank capacity to handle the large bioload. If you only have a smaller tank available, stick with only one or two species. Second, decorate the tank with plenty of rocks, arranged to provide caves, crevices, and other hiding places. All the *mbuna* live along the rocky shore of the lake. Fish that will get along just fine when plenty of hiding places are present will exhibit aggressive behavior in a bare or sparsely decorated tank. Finally, adjust the water parameters using a salt mixture designed for African cichlids.

African cichlids usually dig and nibble at plants, so an underwater garden fares poorly in their presence. Use plastic plants, or add an extra fluorescent strip light to encourage green algae to grow on the rocks. The cichlids will nibble on algae to supplement a staple diet of aquarium foods. African cichlids will take just about any available aquarium food, but do need a significant amount of plant matter. Choose prepared foods designed specifically for them or use a vegetarian formulation.

All cichlids give excellent care to the offspring, and *mbuna* are no exception. Undoubtedly, this is one reason for their ability to survive in a wide range of environments. The species listed for this aquarium are all *mouthbrooders*. After the female releases her eggs she takes them into her mouth. Males possess *egg spots* on the anal fin. During spawning, the male displays these spots to the female, who, being fooled by their appearance, tries to pick them up. In so doing, she takes in sperm released by the male, fertilizing the eggs. After spawning is complete, the male abandons his family and seeks out other females. This type of arrangement is known as a matriarchal family, and occurs only among mouthbrooders. Because the roving male must be able to recognize potential mates, distinctive color and pattern differences exist between the two sexes within a single species.

Once established, a tank of Lake Malawi cichlids can provide years of trouble-free pleasure. Make sure to perform regular water changes and feed a proper diet.

MODEL DESIGN 30 *Mbuna* Single-Species Tank I

Some Malawi cichlids grow large. To accommodate a mixed community requires a very large tank. Keeping a single-species tank affords the means to enjoy these fascinating fish in almost any home.

Aquarium Capacity . . . . 55 gallons

Water Conditions . . . . .moderately hard, slightly alkaline

Optimal Temperature . . . . .75°F

Plants

    choose hardy species such as Java fern (*Microsorium*), arrowhead (*Sagittaria*), or eelgrass (*Vallisneria*)

Other Décor . . . . .rocks, driftwood for *Microsorium*

Background . . . . .pale blue or gray

Substrate . . . . .coarse sand

Filtration . . . . .large canister filter

Lighting . . . . .2 to 4 fluorescent tubes

Special Requirements . . . . .African cichlid salts mix

Fish

    Cyrtocara (Haplochromis) moorii . . . . 1 male, 2 or 3 females

This species reaches around nine inches in length, and needs plenty of room. Both males and females are a beautiful azure blue color, and both develop a characteristic bump or hump on the forehead. The cranial bump develops in several other cichlid species, and its precise function is unclear. Possibly it plays a similar role to the antlers of deer and elk, signifying the male's robustness to choosy potential mates. In cichlids with marked sexual dimorphism, the male always has the hump, or if both have one, the male's hump is larger and more prominent.

Cyrtocara moorii lives over sandy areas of the Lake Malawi shore, hence the recommendation for a sandy substrate. Sand will also do a better job of anchoring the roots of *Sagittaria* or *Vallisneria* than will gravel. This is important, since, like most cichlids, *C. moorii* will dig and occasionally uproot plants. They won't nibble at the greenery, however, so *Microsorium*, anchored to a piece of driftwood, will escape their attentions.

Arrange the rocks along the back wall of the tank, and leave an open, sandy area toward the front. Group plantings to the sides, leaving the center of the tank open for swimming.

MODEL DESIGN 31 *Mbuna* Single-Species Tank II

This model design should suit the space and budget of nearly anyone, requiring only a small tank and minimal equipment.

Aquarium Capacity . . . . 20 gallons

Water Conditions . . . . .moderately hard, slightly alkaline

Optimal Temperature . . . . .75°F

Plants

    none

Other Décor . . . . .rocks

Background . . . . .pale blue or gray

Substrate . . . . .light colored natural gravel

Filtration . . . . .hang-on filter

Lighting . . . . .1 fluorescent tube

Special Requirements . . . . .African cichlid salts mix

Fish

    Labidochromis lividus . . . . 1 pair

This diminutive Malawi cichlid only reaches about three inches in length. While the male is a beautiful sky blue with black, white, and orange markings on the fins, the females are a drab greenish brown. Keep up with a regular schedule of water changes, and feed a varied diet that includes plenty of vegetable matter. The fish should reward you by spawning regularly. They are matriarchal mouthbrooders, a pattern described earlier, and the young are easy to raise after their mother spits them out.

Possible arrangements are somewhat limited in a twenty-gallon tank. Stack the rocks to provide at least two caves or overhangs, and keep the front of the tank clear for swimming. Although it is only about half the size of many *mbuna*, *L. lividus* also does well in a large Malawi community tank.

MODEL DESIGN 32 Tanganyika Community Tank

Lake Tanganyika's waters are harder and more alkaline than those of Lake Malawi, and it harbors a completely different cichlid fauna.

Aquarium Capacity . . . . 75 gallons

Water Conditions .moderately hard, alkaline

Optimal Temperature . . . . .75°F

Plants

    arrowhead (*Sagittaria*)or eelgrass (*Vallisneria*) or a combination   3 dozen

Other Décor . . . . .rocks

Background . . . . .pale blue or gray

Substrate . . . . .light-colored fine gravel and/or coarse sand

Filtration . . . . .large canister filter, sump filter

Lighting . . . . .4 fluorescent tubes, for plants

Special Requirements . . . . .African cichlid salts mix

Fish

    Julidochromis dickfeldi . . . . 1 pair

    Julidochromis marlieri . . . . 1 pair

    Julidochromis ornatus . . . . 1 pair

Julies, as members of the *Julidochromis* genus are called in the aquarium trade, tend to be territorial, and aggressive toward their own kind. You can maintain them in a community by providing a large tank and arranging plants strategically to subdivide the aquarium into territories. Think of the *Vallisneria* or *Sagittaria* as a hedge separating neighbors. *Julidochromis* spawn in caves, inverting themselves to deposit adhesive eggs on the ceiling. It is important, therefore, to arrange the rocks accordingly, permitting each pair to reside in a cave of its own. Otherwise, squabbles are nearly guaranteed. You can also use empty coconut shells, as described on page 112 for *Nannochromis parilus*.

To decorate the tank arrange the rocks in three groupings, each with a cave, roughly dividing the tank lengthwise into thirds. Between each rock cluster, heavily plant a row of *Sagittaria* or *Vallisneria*. Start near the back and end the row a few inches from the front glass. Stagger the plants irregularly, so they don't look like tin soldiers lined up for a drill.

Like other African cichlids, *Julidochromis* need clean, well-oxygenated water and a varied diet high in plant matter.

MODEL DESIGN 33 Julidochromis transcriptus

This fish was the first Julie with which I had experience, and it remains a favorite. Remaining under three inches, *Julidochromis transcriptus* can be kept in a twenty-gallon tank, ideal for the beginning cichlidophile.

Aquarium Capacity . . . . 20 gallons

Water Conditions .moderately hard, alkaline

Optimal Temperature . . . . .75°F

Plants

    arrowhead (*Sagittaria*) or eelgrass (*Vallisneria*) or a combination   1 dozen (optional)

Other Décor . . . . .rocks

Background . . . . .pale blue or gray

Substrate . . . . .light-colored fine gravel and/or coarse sand

Filtration . . . . .hang-on filter

Lighting . . . . .2 fluorescent tubes, for plants (if used)

Special Requirements . . . . .African cichlid salts mix

Fish

    Julidochromis transcriptus . . . . 1 pair

Neither of the plants suggested for this and other African cichlid tanks is native to Africa. They are recommended because they are inexpensive, widely available, tolerant of hard, alkaline water, and easy to grow. Feel free to substitute plastic replicas.

Julidochromis transcriptus has a pale belly and a dark upper half marked with two rows of white spots. The upper row of dots is smaller than the lower, which passes through the eye and generally follows the lateral line. The fins are yellowish, and the tail fin is delicately marked with bluish-white dots and lines, and edged in white. Like other Africans, it eats anything and everything. Make sure it gets plenty of algae or vegetable flakes.

Decorate the tank with a cairn of rocks beneath the filter, an arrangement that should hide the equipment from view. Either create a rock cave, or provide a coconut shell. In either case, the pair will use this for spawning.

Arrange plants to partially hide the entrance to the cave/coconut. To provide visual balance, group a few additional plants on the opposite side of the tank, and anchor them with three small rocks.

MODEL DESIGN 34 Birchard's *Neolamprologus*

I shall never forget the first time I saw this fish. *Neolamprologus birchardi* is a rather plain, gray color, but the elegant, flowing fins and its regal bearing make up for the chromatic deficiencies. On closer inspection, the fish will be found to have blue and green iridescence, and the edges of the fins have white pigmentation.

Aquarium Capacity . . . . 65 gallons

Water Conditions . . . . .moderately hard, alkaline

Optimal Temperature . . . . .75°F

Plants

    none

Other Décor . . . . .rocks

Background . . . . .dark blue or black

Substrate . . . . .light-colored mix of fine and coarse sand

Filtration . . . . .large canister filter

Lighting . . . . .1 fluorescent tube

Special Requirements . . . . .African cichlid salts mix

Fish

    Neolamprologus (Lamoprologus)
        brichardi. . . . . 6, including at least 1 male

Except when spawning, this species forms a shoal. Unlike more familiar shoaling species, however, it does not swim frenetically from one end of the tank to the other, but rather swims slowly, inspecting everything, as if it were the grandee of a large estate out for an afternoon stroll with the family. Once they pair up, the male and female will become more territorial, keeping the other adults away from their chosen brood site. Like many other Tanganyikan cichlids, they deposit adhesive eggs on the carefully cleaned ceiling of a rock cave. After spawning, the male patrols the territory surrounding the cave, while the female looks after the developing eggs.

Males can be distinguished from females by the shape of the doral fin, his being elongate and pointed, while hers is shorter and rounded. He will also sport much longer filamentous extensions of the tail fin than she does.

Neolamprologus brichardi provides a good example of "*stepwise breeding.*" Once a batch of fry are able to fend for themselves, the parents spawn again, abandoning the offspring they previously cared for with studious devotion. These older offspring hang around, however, and participate in the care of their younger siblings.

MODEL DESIGN 35 Shell Dwellers

Mother Nature allows nothing to go to waste. This biotope clearly demonstrates that principle. Its unique feature is a tank bottom littered with empty snail shells. Some of Lake Tanganyika's most interesting cichlids use them for homes!

Aquarium Capacity . . . . 40 gallons

Water Conditions .moderately hard, alkaline

Optimal Temperature . . . . .75°F

Plants

    none

Other Décor . . . . .rocks, large shells (see text)

Background . . . . .dark brown or gray, depending upon rock color

Substrate . . . . .light-colored fine sand

Filtration . . . . .large canister filter

Lighting . . . . .1 fluorescent tube

Special Requirements . . . . .African cichlid salts mix, live foods

Fish

    Neolamprologus multifasciatus. . . . . 5 to 7

This little fish, scarcely reaching one and one-half inches in length, lives in empty snail shells of the genus *Neothauma*. Empty shells collect in places on the lake's sandy bottom, and here *N. multifasciatus* congregates. Each fish occupies its own shell. When they pair up, the male and female continue to inhabit separate shells, but they move to a spot where they can live adjacent to each other. Quite territorial, this little fish will defend its shell against all comers, even those much larger than itself. Obviously, they are wholly dependent upon aggregations of suitable shells, and will often dig in an effort to expose additional ones that might lie buried in the sand. Although they won't eat plants, digging may uproot your aquatic garden, so I don't recommend plants for this tank. It is doubtful you will find a source of *Neothauma* snail shells. Fortunately, the empty shells of edible snails, which often are packaged together with the canned snails, are an excellent substitute. (If you don't fancy escargot, perhaps you have a friend who will welcome the canned delicacies, and you can keep the shells for your tank.)

One of the most attractive designs I have seen for this biotope employed dark colored rocks stacked on either side of the tank, with contrasting light sand in between. The sand was littered with snail shells, of course. Use a background color that more or less matches the rocks you have available, to give the impression that the rocky shore extends infinitely behind the aquarium.

Because *N. multifasciatus* feeds on planktonic organisms in the water column above its shell beds, they need live foods such as newly hatched brine shrimp, *Daphnia*, and small worms. After they become accustomed to life in your tank, they can usually be persuaded to start accepting frozen and prepared foods. Several other *Neolamprologus* species are shell dwellers, and can be maintained in this setup. However, don't mix them, or they may fight over the available shells.

MODEL DESIGN 36 Lemon Cichlid

For sheer "wow" value, few of the African cichlids can match *Neolamprologus leleupi*, the lemon cichlid. Bright yellow overall, it is relatively peaceful for a cichlid and reaches only about four inches in length.

Aquarium Capacity . . . . 45 gallons

Water Conditions .moderately hard, alkaline

Optimal Temperature . . . . .75°F

Plants

Other Décor . . . . .rocks

Background . . . . .pale blue or gray

Substrate . . . . .dark-colored fine sand

Filtration . . . . .large canister filter

Lighting . . . . .1 fluorescent tube

Special Requirements . . . . .African cichlid salts mix, live foods

Fish

    Neolamprologus leleupi . . . . 1 pair, or 1 male and 2 or 3 females

This model design makes use of an extra-tall tank, so the total fish population should be reduced to compensate for the relatively small surface-to-volume ratio. Use a large filter to ensure plenty of aeration and good water quality. If you stack the rocks from bottom to top, you will find that the fish check out and occupy caves at all levels. This helps to keep them separated in case of aggression. I suggest arranging all the rocks on one side, hiding the filtration hoses and any other equipment. Keep the opposite side open, so the fish can be easily observed when they swim out over the sandy bottom. Using a dark background and dark sand highlights the bright lemon yellow coloration of the fish.

The male may become aggressive toward females that do not meet his criteria. Accordingly, arrange the rocks to provide plenty of hiding places. This fish can be combined with other Tanganyikans, such as *Julidochromis*. Move up to a larger tank and retain the same design, and you could add *Tropheus duboisi* or *T. moorii*. They are impressive fish, reaching about four to six inches in length, that need a lot of vegetable matter in the diet. The body of either one is charcoal gray, with a contrasting blotch of color on the side about a third of the way back from the snout. Various color morphs are known, with differences corresponding to geographical regions of Lake Tanganyika. For example, some have golden bellies. In others, the side blotch has bright red in it. They are much sought after and usually command a high price in aquarium shops.

Madagascar

Pity the island nation of Madagascar. Decades of depredation by its human population has left much of this land deforested, with unhappy consequences for its unique biota, including fish as well as the forest-dwelling lemurs for which the island is famous.

MODEL DESIGN 37 A Madagascar Tank

From Madagascar's central highlands flow numerous streams that dump into the Indian Ocean. In the cooler, upland reaches of these waters live fish that only rarely appear in the aquarium trade. One such is the subject of this model design.

Aquarium Capacity . . . . 50 gallons

Water Conditions . . . . .moderately hard, alkaline

Optimal Temperature . . . . .72°F

Plants

    aponegeton (*Aponegeton boivinianus*) . . . 3

      or aponegeton (*Aponegeton ulvaceus*) 3

    dwarf arrowhead (*Sagittaria graminea*). . . 5–7

    ambulia (*Limnophila sessiliflora*) 3–5

Other Décor . . . . .water-worn rocks

Background . . . . .pale blue or gray

Substrate . . . . .dark-colored fine gravel with a little sand

Filtration . . . . .canister filter

Lighting . . . . .4 fluorescent tubes, for plants

Special Requirements . . . . .none

Fish

    Bedotia geayi 3–5

Aponegetons are some of the most beautiful aquarium plants, and this tank showcases them as much as it does the fish. I have recommended a deep tank to accommodate the tall, translucent leaves of these pale-green plants. *Aponegetons* grow from a swollen underground stem known botanically as a *corm*. This structure is usually round like a marble, but may be flattened almost to a disk in some species. The corm should be planted just below the surface of the substrate. The plants usually require a seasonal resting period, during which time growth slows or even ceases and most or all of the leaves are lost. An otherwise well-grown plant that is starting to lose leaves may simply be entering its resting phase, and should be left undisturbed until growth resumes. It is worthwhile to reduce the water temperature during this period, letting it drop to around 68°F. Since this is room temperature in many homes, you can simply disconnect the heater and let the tank cool down slowly. Because *Aponegetons* need plenty of light, I suggest a four-tube fixture for this deep tank.

One species, *Aponegeton madagascarensis*, is something of a legend in aquarium circles. It is notoriously difficult to grow. Commonly called Madagascar lace plant, it is unique in that the space between the leaf veins lacks tissue, creating the lacy appearance. Do not make the mistake of trying to grow this species with the others described in this model design. It requires soft, slightly acid, moving water that is perfectly free of fine sediment. Both sediment and algae can clog the openings in the leaves, spelling doom for the plant. Use it as the centerpiece of a soft-water show aquarium (see page 141) and keep your fingers crossed. This is not a plant for beginners.

Since *Bedotia* prefers moving water, arrange the filter outflow to create a strong, directional current. Place driftwood, a stack of rocks, or both in the path of the flow, so the current does not jostle the plants too much. Gentle movement of the leaves is fine. Locate the *Aponegetons* near the center of the tank, both to maximize the light they receive and to showcase their lovely, ruffled leaves. The *Limnophila* makes a nice backdrop for the coarser *Aponegetons*. Place the *Sagittaria* near the front, where it can form a carpet. The rainbowfish are active swimmers, and will take a wide variety of foods. You can combine them with peaceful community fish that like the same water conditions, for example, the Asian barbs mentioned in an earlier section.

CHAPTER 9

SOUTH AMERICA

More great aquarium fish come from South America than anywhere else. The majority are found in the vast Amazon River system, although other areas supply a smattering of species. In addition, some of the best aquarium plants live in South American waters. Owing to the availability of so much material, we can create a legion of aquarium designs from South American biotopes.

Amazonia

The Amazon and its tributaries form the world's largest watershed, carrying 16 percent of all the river water in the world over a 6,500-mile course from the Andean highlands to the Atlantic Ocean. Twenty percent of the world's fresh water moves through the Amazon, ten times the volume of the Mississippi River. Within the 2.5 million square miles of the Amazon Basin lives the richest biota on earth, including 500 mammals, 475 reptile species, and a third of all bird species. Hundreds of fish species live in the myriad tributaries. Some exploit the Amazon's annual floods, during which the river rises about thirty feet, flooding the rain forest for miles on either side, and producing new habitat and new food sources for aquatic life.

MODEL DESIGN 38 Basic Amazon Community Tank

Our first model design from Amazonia demonstrates the basic biotope for many of the region's most popular aquarium fish.

Aquarium Capacity . . . . 20 gallons

Water Conditions . . . . .soft, acidic

Optimal Temperature . . . . .74°F

Plants

    cabomba (*Cabomba aquatica*) . . . . 1 bunch

    pygmy chain sword plant (*Echinodorus
        tenellus*). 1 clump

    stargrass (*Heteranthera zosterifolia*) . . . . . 1 bunch

Other Décor . . . . .driftwood and/or roots

Background . . . . .deep green, brown, or black

Substrate .dark gravel with a small amount of sand added

Filtration . . . . .hang-on filter

Lighting . . . . .2 fluorescent tubes, for plants

Special Requirements . . . . .peat filtration (optional)

Fish

    Aphyocarax anisitsi 5–7

        Or *Pristella maxillarus* 5–7

        Or *Paracheirodon innesi* 12–15

    Corydoras paleatus 1–3

If you can't find the yellow *Cabomba,* substitute another species. The stargrass (*Heteranthera*) also has a fine texture. If you do not like the combination, just use one of them. It is difficult to give exact numbers for plants that are sold in a bunch, so you will need to use your own judgment. You want about six stems of each plant, or twelve if you choose to go with only one type of taller plant. More is never a problem, however. For the foreground, the pygmy chain sword (*Echinodorus*) is hard to beat, but make sure you use the dual-lamp fluorescent fixture, or it will suffer from lack of light.

Place the driftwood just left of center and arrange a backdrop of the *Cabomba* behind it. Use the stargrass in the corner to hide the filter intake. If your pygmy chain sword comes in a pot, remove it and carefully extract the potting medium before planting. Try to spread out the individual plants as much as possible, but take care not to damage the roots too much. Eventually, the pygmy sword will carpet the substrate.

If you think a school of only one species will look best in your aquarium, by all means go this route. You can successfully keep about ten to twenty one-inch fish without crowding the tank. For the armored catfish, I have recommended the typical albino variety, but you can use any species of *Corydoras* you like, as long as it stays relatively small.

The fish in this model design are quite adaptable. They may *prefer* soft, acid water, but they will probably accept your tap water. If this is your first tank, consult your dealer about the necessity for altering the tap water to meet the needs of these fish. Remember anything you do to change the condition of the water needs to be repeated for each and every partial water change.

MODEL DESIGN 39 Leaf Fish

Suppose you are a greedy, gluttonous predator with a taste for small fish. How can you get close enough to catch your prey? Equally important, how do you avoid becoming prey to a larger predator than yourself? Evolution has provided numerous answers to these two questions. The leaf fish adopts a strategy that many other fish use: camouflage. It looks incredibly similar to a dead leaf floating lazily on the current. Head tipped diagonally down, it lurks among roots and vegetation. When it drifts stealthily toward another fish, it counts on being ignored as a piece of flotsam until it is too late. When the leaf fish gets within striking range, it opens its capacious mouth and the prey disappears inside. It then resumes its normal pose, and the hunt continues.

One of many types of perch-like fishes, or *percoids*, the leaf fish inhabits slow-moving waters of the Peruvian Amazon where plenty of cover can be found. During the rainy season, when the stream swells out of its banks to flood the surrounding forest, the leaf fish patrols the swamp. The water likely will be teeming with fry, since the rainy season coincides with the breeding season for numerous species. Dead leaves are everywhere, so why should the young fish pay attention to one more?

This model design differs from the previous one only in that the fish requires more careful attention. For that reason, this tank is for a more experienced aquarist looking for something really different for a small tank.

Aquarium Capacity . . . . 20 gallons

Water Conditions .soft, acidic

Optimal Temperature . . . . .74°F

Plants

    cabomba (*Cabomba aquatica*) . . . . 1 bunch

    pygmy chain sword plant (*Echinodorus tenellus*). . . . . 1 clump

    stargrass (*Heteranthera zosterifolia*) . . . . . 1 bunch

Other Décor . . . . .driftwood and/or roots

Background . . . . .deep green, brown, or black

Substrate . . . . .dark gravel with a small amount of sand added

Filtration . . . . .hang-on filter

Lighting . . . . .2 fluorescent tubes, for plants

Special Requirements . . . . .live food, peat filtration (optional)

Fish

    Monocirrhus polyacanthus 1

Like many other species, the leaf fish adapts to water conditions within reason, although it prefers very soft water at a pH of 6.0 to 6.5. Plant this tank rather heavily and use pieces of driftwood to simulate a tangle of roots. If you would rather not grow live plants, omit them and decorate entirely with driftwood and roots. According to references I checked, this species does not like having its tank rearranged. Perhaps it becomes accustomed to a particular hunting ground, and resents changes in the terrain. On the other hand, it must cope with dramatic alterations of its natural habitat from the cycle of dry and wet seasons, so its supposed dissatisfaction with rearrangements may be apocryphal.

The leaf fish has an enormous appetite. Feed it daily with small live fish, such as feeder guppies. Small specimens will also take worms and mosquito larvae. In the hands of an aquarist with the energy and dedication to see to its food requirements, the leaf fish is a hardy and fascinating subject for a single-species tank.

MODEL DESIGN 40   Room-Temperature Amazon Tank

If you want an inexpensive, easily cared for, and simple aquarium, this model design has it all. The fish, known variously as *black widow* or *black skirt tetra* has been a staple of the aquarium trade for a long time. A peaceful schooling species found in the Rio Paraguay and Rio Guapore drainage systems, it ranks among the easiest to keep of all fish. So this model design could not be simpler. It is ideal for a child's first aquarium.

Aquarium Capacity . . . . 20 gallons

Water Conditions .anything within reason

Optimal Temperature . . . . .68–70°F

Plants

    dwarf bacopa (*Bacopa monnieri*). . . . . . . 1 bunch

    green cabomba (*Cabomba caroliniana*). . . 1 bunch

    water pest (*Egeria densa*) . . . . 1 bunch

Other Décor . . . . .driftwood (optional)

Background . . . . .deep green, brown, or black

Substrate . . . . .your choice of gravel with some added sand for the plants

Filtration . . . . .hang-on filter

Lighting . . . . .2 fluorescent tubes, for plants

Special Requirements . . . . .none

Fish

    Gymnocorymbus ternetzi. . . . . around 10

Adapting to anything from soft, acidic water to very hard and alkaline, black skirts eat anything that might be on your dealer's shelf that is small enough to swallow. Further, its preference for cooler water means it will be right at home at 68 degrees F, so you do not require a heater, unless you keep your living quarters a lot colder than I do.

Similarly, you would have trouble finding plants any sturdier than the ones recommended. All have been sold in aquarium shops for decades, and need only good light to flourish. Use any or all of them, planting small groupings here and there around the tank, and especially where they will mask equipment. The fish tend to remain out in the open, so leave a swimming area, either at one end or front and center. The décor can be relatively sparse; you don't need a lot of plants and other objects for this open-water fish.

For the ultimate in ease of care, use plastic substitutes instead of the live plants. That way you can also eliminate the larger light fixture and simply purchase a single strip light. If you skip the heater, too, this model design costs less to execute than any other in this book. All you really need is the tank, cover, and light combo, along with a modest hang-on power filter. You might even be able to pick up these simple components at a garage sale, although I recommend always checking used equipment with an extremely critical eye.

Black skirt tetras are available in a long-finned variety that is just as hardy as the normal type. Both get about two inches long. Either has but one drawback: The charming black markings of the juveniles disappear, and the fish becomes silvery gray in adulthood.

MODEL DESIGN 41   A Tale of Two Tetras

This model design is a study in both contrast and symmetry. The colors of the black neon tetra perfectly complement the luminescent orange of the glowlight tetra. The broad, pale-green leaves of the sword plants (*Echinodorus*) balance the finely divided, dark reddish-green leaves of the *Cabomba*. The dark substrate and background not only help to show off the tetras, they also contrast with the white and black catfish.

Aquarium Capacity . . . . 55 gallons

Water Conditions .soft, acidic

Optimal Temperature . . . . .74°F

Plants

Amazon sword plant (*Echinodorus amazonicus*) 9

Or ruffled sword plant (*Echinodorus martii*) 9

red cabomba (*Cabomba furcata*) . . . . . . 5 bunches

Other Décor . . . . .one large piece of driftwood or tree root

Background . . . . .black

Substrate . . . . .black gravel with a small amount of sand added

Filtration . . . . .canister filter

Lighting . . . . .4 fluorescent tubes, for plants

Special Requirements . . . . .peat filtration (optional)

Fish

Corydoras agassizii 5

Hyphessobrycon herbertaxelrodi 12

Hemigrammus erythrozonus. . . . . around 30

Choose a single large piece of driftwood carefully. It will set the stage for the rest of the model design. It is hard to give precise directions, but you want something with both asymmetry and balance. Here is an example of what I have in mind. On any sizable piece of driftwood there will usually be several smaller branches protruding from the main branch. Some of them will perhaps be broken off close to the main branch, leaving a short, jagged stub. Others may retain much of their original form, tapering to a point. The latter ones will obviously be longer, too. The relative position of the two kinds of branches provides the asymmetry; that both are part of the same larger branch provides the balance. If many branches, say, are broken and there is but a single, unscathed branch, the driftwood has the right look. Even better if the single branch curves gracefully. Study the available offerings from your local dealer, and settle on the one you think best conveys the artistic dimension for this model design. The size and shape of the driftwood will to some degree restrict its placement within the tank. As long as you avoid placing it squarely in the center, it should look just fine. Do try to place the piece so the most interesting side greets the viewer standing in front of the aquarium.

With the driftwood in position, choose a spot for a group of sword plants (*Echinodorus*). They will form a secondary focal point, helping to balance the primary focus created by the driftwood. Plant all the sword plants in a single grouping, arranging them as randomly as possible. Use the *Cabomba* to create a backdrop for everything, hiding any hoses or other visible equipment.

Because both types of tetras stay together in a school, the impact of their coloration is magnified, again emphasizing the yin and yang of this model design.

MODEL DESIGN 42 Tribute to Herbert Axelrod

Dr. Herbert Axelrod was one of the founding fathers of the modern aquarium hobby. He was also the founding publisher of the oldest American aquarium magazine still in print, *Tropical Fish Hobbyist*. Sometimes controversial, always interesting, Axelrod could claim some of the credit for introducing thousands, including myself, to the world of tropical aquarium fish. This model design features two beautiful fish that were named in Axelrod's honor. It also demonstrates how a small tank with a few well-chosen components can be a real winner.

Aquarium Capacity	30 gallons
Water Conditions	soft, acidic
Optimal Temperature	74°F
Plants	
duckweed (*Lemna minor*).	1 clump
or floating fern (*Salvinia auriculata*) . .	1 clump
Other Décor	driftwood, water-worn rocks
Background	dark brown
Substrate	natural earth-tone gravel with a small amount of sand added
Filtration	canister filter
Lighting	1 fluorescent tube
Special Requirements	peat filtration (optional)
Fish	
Corydoras pygmaeus	3
Hyphessobrycon herbertaxelrodi	7
Paracheirodon axelrodi.	15

The black neon tetra (*Hyphessobrycon*), which was also used in the previous model design, debuted in the hobby in 1960. It did not create the sensation that attended the introduction of the cardinal tetra *Paracheirodon* in 1956. Neither of these fish tolerates poor water conditions well, but neither is fussy about any other conditions. Both appreciate water movement, as they both naturally inhabit open, running waters, living at the edges of the stream where nearby trees cast shade. Both fish avoid light. Using only floating plants creates the dappled light condition they prefer. Too much light will cause them to turn pale and seek shelter. It is thought that their bright, iridescent colors help them to find each other in the darkened environment they prefer. If you use the optional peat filtration, the water itself will take on a tea color, contributing to the impression of a forest stream heavily shaded by overhanging branches.

Because the suggested plants are accustomed to shade, they will thrive under a single fluorescent lamp, and spread across the surface of the tank. If you like, use a combination of both these floating species. Use several small pieces of driftwood to suggest snags near the edge of a stream. Place smooth rocks, ideally similar in color to the gravel you have chosen, in groups near the bases of the driftwood to help anchor them visually. Bear in mind that rocks look better when they are about one-third to one-half buried in the substrate. Use pieces the size of your fist down to about the size of a half dollar.

Although popular tetras such as these two adapt to a range of water chemistry, they always do best in soft, acid water. The optimum pH is 5.8. Hardness is of particular concern. Water that is too hard may result in *calcium block*, a condition in which the tubules of the kidneys become clogged with calcium salts. Afflicted fish become bloated and soon die from kidney failure. The condition is often called *dropsy* in aquarium books. If your tap water is hard, ask your dealer for suggestions on softening it, or dilute it with distilled water from your local big-box retailer. Apart from water quality, these beautiful fish need only regular feedings. Give them a varied diet including, if possible, live foods on occasion.

MODEL DESIGN 43 Neon Dreams

If you want an impressive tank that's simple to maintain, this is the way to go—nothing can match a big tank with a large school of neons, regardless of the décor.

Once again, we take for inspiration the shady edge of a moving watercourse, in this case Rio Putumayo in eastern Peru, home of the legendary neon tetra (*Paracheirodon innesi*). Since its introduction in 1936, this beautiful little red and blue fish has been one of the staples of the aquarium trade. At one time it commanded a high price, since only wild-caught fish were available. Now, however, millions are produced in hatcheries in the Far East. If your local shop does not have neons, it is only because they were sold out the day of your visit. There is scarcely a shop on the planet that doesn't stock them. Although they prefer the soft, acid water found in their native haunts, modern strains are so adaptable they will put up with whatever you have available at the sink. Feeding them poses no problem, either. Use any of the staple flake foods, supplemented occasionally with treats, such as live brine shrimp. With proper tank maintenance they can live quite a long time for so tiny a fish, perhaps ten to fifteen years.

Aquarium Capacity . . . . .75 gallons

Water Conditions .soft, acidic

Optimal Temperature . . . . .74°F

Plants

    none

Other Décor . . . . .several large pieces of driftwood or tree root

Background . . . . .black

Substrate . . . . .fine black gravel or coarse black sand

Filtration . . . . .canister filter

Lighting . . . . .1 fluorescent tube

Special Requirements . . . . .none

Fish

    Corydoras agassizii 5

    Paracheirodon innesi 200

I developed this model design to make setup and maintenance as easy as possible. Arrange driftwood pieces to fill about two-thirds of the available space, positioning a few key pieces to hide equipment. Do not worry too much about the placement, but try to avoid regular spacing. You could even toss them in and leave them where they fall, but that would risk breaking the glass. The idea we are going for is an accumulation of wood that has been swept into the water during a flood and now lies partially buried near a bend in the stream. Locate most of the driftwood closer to the front of the aquarium, and move the light fixture as far toward the back as it will go. The neons will remain in the shelter of the driftwood, showing off their iridescent coloration. If you like, you can also add some floating plants as in the previous model design. They will help attenuate the light, which, like others of their genus, neon tetras avoid.

I have added the catfish to eat food that falls to the bottom, but you could leave them out and the tank will be just fine. With or without the catfish, make sure you siphon out accumulated debris at least once a week, and change half the water monthly. Otherwise, this tank should be trouble-free for years. That means you can sit back and watch as the school of neons flows through the driftwood maze as if it were a single organism. Beautiful, easy, big, and trouble-free: This one is the home aquarist's dream tank.

MODEL DESIGN 44   Emperor Tetra

The emperor tetra, *Nematobrycon palmeri*, should be more popular than it is. Its low fecundity provides one possible explanation for its absence from many shops. Hatcheries do not like to raise fish that only produce a few eggs per pair. The emperor tetra also tends to feed on its own eggs, further reducing the yield. Certainly the low spawning rate explains why this tetra often costs considerably more than its cousin the neon tetra.

Aquarium Capacity . . . . 40 gallons

Water Conditions . . . . .slightly acidic and soft to moderately hard

Optimal Temperature . . . . .76–78°F

Plants

    Bleher's sword plant (*Echinodorus bleheri*) 5

    horizontal sword plant (*Echinodorus horizontalis*). 7

    stargrass (*Heteranthera zosterifolia*) . . . . . 5 bunches

    Guiana hygrophila (*Hygrophila guianensis*) . . . . 3 bunches

Other Décor . . . . .2 or 3 pieces of driftwood approximately the same size

Background . . . . .light green or ochre

Substrate . . . . .dark-brown gravel with a small amount of sand added

Filtration . . . . .canister filter or sump-type filter

Lighting . . . . .4 fluorescent tubes, for plants

Special Requirements . . . . .none

Fish

    Corydoras metae 7

    Nematobrycon palmeri 15

    Otocinclus arnoldi 3

The emperor tetra likes a heavily planted tank. It is found in small coastal streams in western Colombia. Unlike the neon tetras used in several previous model designs, it does not shy away from the light. Indeed, its subtle purple-and-black coloration looks best in bright light. Separating the males from the females is easy in this tetra. Males have greatly elongated dorsal, anal, and tail fins that are edged in black. Females have smaller fins. In particular, her dorsal fin is stubby compared to his.

Position the filter return on one end of the tank to create a lengthwise current. Start decorating this tank by placing the driftwood near the back, angling it toward the front to divide the tank into crosswise segments. Make sure your spacing is not too regular or the driftwood won't look natural. Add the substrate, building it up slightly on the side of the driftwood nearest the filter. The result of this arrangement should suggest ripples on the bottom of the stream. In these deeper areas of substrate, plant the sword plants (*Echinodorus*). Group a few plants of each type at each ripple. (If you cannot find a variety of sword plants, using all of one kind will also look good.) Arrange the stargrass (*Heteranthera*) to create a curtain along the back of the tank. Place the bold-textured *Hygrophila* in a grouping on the end opposite the filter return, where it will provide balance to the delicate texture of the stargrass. Complete the look with a few small, smooth pebbles strewn along the bottom here and there.

The skunk cory cats suggested for this tank are, like the emperor tetra, found in Colombia. You can substitute any other variety of *Corydoras*. The little *Otocinclus* will help to keep the tank free of algae growth. They even clean the tough leaves of the sword plants. Numerous species of *Otocinclus* can be found in South America, but they are interchangeable for aquarium purposes, just like *Corydoras* species.

Regular feeding and maintenance are the only requirements for this tank to thrive. The delicate pink-and-lavender coloration of the fish adds a feminine feel to the overall design. This might be a good tank for a girl's room. It would also look smashing in a sunroom, almost enveloped by overflowing pots of flowers and foliage plants.

MODEL DESIGN 45 | Expert's Amazon Tank

Some fish demand more from the aquarist than others. After you gain some experience in successfully managing an aquarium for species that insist upon a particular set of water conditions, you may want try your hand at this one.

The main attractions in this model design are *blackwater* species. The blackwater stream habitat results from the leaching of tannins and other organic compounds from the abundant plant debris of the rain forest into the streams and river. The organic compounds tint the water a deep brown color, which can appear black in the right light. Hence the term *blackwater*. Other features of this habitat are moderate current, the relative absence of vegetation, and plenty of roots and snags in the water. An aquarium mimicking this habitat becomes the perfect home for pencilfishes (*Nannostomus*) and the rummynose tetra (*Hemigrammus bleheri*).

I confess a great fondness for rummynose tetras. Not only are they attractive, they are somewhat of a challenge to keep, especially if you have hard, alkaline tap water as I do. I further confess to killing several of them until I learned to use both distilled water and peat filtration to give them a proper environment. Hardness is especially critical. It should never exceed 100 parts per million, about 5 degrees on the German hardness scale often cited in aquarium literature. The pH should be around 6.0. Therefore, first make sure you can provide these water conditions. If not, choose another design.

Aquarium Capacity . . . . 33 gallons, long style

Water Conditions .very soft, slightly acidic

Optimal Temperature . . . . .76–78°F

Plants

    frogbit (*Limnobium laevigatum*) . . . . 3 clumps

Other Décor . . . . .driftwood and/or roots, water-worn pebbles

Background . . . . .dark brown

Substrate . . . . .natural earth-tone gravel

Filtration . . . . .canister filter

Lighting . . . . .2 fluorescent tubes, for plants

Special Requirements . . . . .peat filtration, live foods

Fish

    Corydoras pygmaeus 3

    Hemigrammus bleheri 5

    Nannostomus marginatus 5

    Nannostomus trifasciatus 5

    Otocinclus arnoldi 1

Select driftwood that has a vertical aspect. One piece might be a small stump, for example. Others could be roots, or branches that will stand upright like antlers. (Incidentally, if you do want to give the appearance of a stump, make sure the wood extends above the surface of the aquarium. If it is entirely below the surface, it spoils the illusion that the aquarium is part of the larger habitat that lies unseen above.)

The tank recommended is long and shallow, perfect for emulating a stream. Locate the filter return at one end to create a longitudinal current. As always, use the wood to hide the hoses from the canister filter. Arrange the driftwood along the back of the aquarium to give the impression that snags and roots protrude from an eroding stream bank. Add the gravel, sloping it from the back to the front. Scatter a few smooth pebbles of varying sizes on the gravel. The slope suggests to the viewer that the water becomes deeper as one moves away from the stream bank. Pebbles suggest the water is moving. When everything is in place, fill the tank with water of the correct hardness. Place the peat bag in the canister filter, connect up the hoses, and run the filter for about two weeks, during which time the water will take on the appearance of tea as organics are leached from the peat, precisely what happens in a real blackwater stream. Peat filtration also reduces hardness, by chemically tying up calcium and magnesium ions as insoluble compounds that precipitate from the water.

Using Peat Moss

Peat is available in aquarium shops, but I prefer to use horticultural peat moss, which is vastly less expensive. Pasteurize the peat by placing it in a fine mesh nylon bag and steaming it in a vegetable steamer for thirty minutes. Choose a mesh bag that, when filled, will fit into the canister filter you select.

Once all is in readiness, you can begin to add the living elements of the model design. Start with the frogbit (*Limnobium*), which floats on the surface and dangles hairy-looking roots into the water. Besides producing a dappled effect as the light passes through its leaves, the frogbit contributes its root structure to the hiding places so necessary to the well-being of the pencilfish (*Nannostomus*). Pencilfish remain in the shelter of underwater objects during most of the day, and emerge at dusk to feed. Without shelter, they tend to cower, refuse to feed, and eventually, of course, to starve.

Also add the cory cats and the *Otocinclus* at this stage. The latter provide the invaluable service of keeping the driftwood free of excessive algae. The former eat bits of food that make it to the bottom, but can be dispensed with if you feed judiciously. Mosquito larvae and daphnia, which should be included in the diet of the pencilfish and rummynose tetras if possible, will swim in the tank until eaten. Leave these utilitarian fish in the tank for two weeks or more before adding the rummynose tetras.

Timid little pencilfish should be added only after the rummynose have been living happily in the aquarium for a month or more. If you can only find one species, and this is the likely scenario, simply increase the number of members in the school.

Take special care to perform regular water changes. Prune the frogbit as it multiplies. You can give the offspring to aquarist friends. Try to provide live food each week. Your diligence will be rewarded with the pleasure of observing some of Nature's rare aquatic jewels.

MODEL DESIGN 46 Flying (?) Fish Tank

The fish in this model design don't actually fly, but they sure can leap a considerable distance in pursuit of a flying insect. Make sure the tank is well covered.

Aquarium Capacity . . . . 45 gallons

Water Conditions . . . . .slightly acidic and soft

Optimal Temperature . . . . .76–78°F

Plants

    Reineck's alternanthera
       (*Alternanthera reineckii*) . . . . 1 bunch

    Central American sword plant
       (*Echinodorus quadricostatus*) 5

    small-flowered sword plant
       (*Echinodorus parviflorus*) 3

Other Décor . . . . .optional

Background . . . . .green or ochre

Substrate . . . . .dark natural gravel with a small amount of sand added

Filtration . . . . .canister filter

Lighting . . . . .4 fluorescent tubes, for plants

Special Requirements . . . . .fertilizer, iron supplement, CO_2 fertilization (optional)

Fish

Carnegiella marthae. 5–7

Carnegiella strigata 5–7

Gasteropelecus sternicla 5–7

Otocinclus arnoldi 3

I suggest the tall fifty-five-gallon tank for this model design because the featured fish all swim near the surface. Hatchetfish (*Carnegiella, Gasteropelecus*) comprise a separate family closely related to the tetras included in many Amazon aquariums. They feed largely on insects that fall into the water, on aquatic insect larvae, and on occasion leap to take a flying insect from above the surface. They can fly a remarkably long distance, many times the fish's body length. Found in running water, they hang motionless in the current until they sight prey, but are capable of darting with amazing speed after a tasty morsel. Keep the water level about six inches below the cover, to lessen the likelihood that the fish will injure themselves during one of their leaping escapades.

Unlike many other model designs, driftwood is absent from this one. For one thing, driftwood tends to accumulate where the current is reduced, and these fish like a bit of water movement. The other reason is that the plants recommended need plenty of room, and driftwood might make things a bit cramped.

Of the three hatchetfish suggested, *C. marthae*, the black-winged hatchetfish, demands the most from its keeper. Soft water is a must for this species, while *C. strigata* and *Gasteropelecus* can handle moderately hard water. However, the black-winged hatchetfish is also the least likely of the three to be found in your local aquarium shop. The other two are far more common. If you cannot find all three species, just increase the number of those available. Similarly, any species of *Otocinclus* can stand in for *O. arnoldi*, as they are interchangeable for aquarium purposes.

Arrange the tall, stately *Echinodorus parviflorus* in two groups. They will be the main feature, other than the fish, in this tank. Remember not to locate them equidistant from the center of the tank, or they will look too formal. The much smaller *E. quadricostatus* should be located in the foreground, where they will form a nice stand with surprising speed when conditions are to their liking. The *Alternanthera* provides a welcome contrast to the light green swords, with its red coloration. Intersperse it with the *E. parviflorus*, leaving sufficient room between individual plants for them to grow without crowding. All these plants are vigorous and benefit from fertilization, including the use of an iron supplement. The main requirement for them, however, is light. Because the tank is twenty-four inches tall, you will need the four-tube fixture to grow them well. If that seems like too much expense, you are better off using plastic instead. With proper care, the living plants will form a lush backdrop for the fish. In fact, they will need regular pruning and thinning to keep them from crowding the tank.

I suggest allowing the plants to establish themselves for a month before adding fish. The *Otocinclus* can be added first, to help condition the tank for the eventual arrival of the hatchetfish. The tank should develop patches of algae upon which the *Otocinclus* can feed during that first month. If not, wait a while longer. You can also give them commercial food preparations designed for vegetarian species.

After introducing the hatchetfish, keep up with a regular schedule of water changes. They react quickly and negatively to declining water quality. Feed them high-quality flakes, finely chopped frozen foods, and such live foods as mosquito larvae and fruit flies. They will also relish newly hatched brine shrimp.

MODEL DESIGN 47 The Amazing Splashing Tetra

The joys of being a naturalist include learning about some of Nature's most remarkable examples of adaptation. The jumping tetra, *Copenia arnoldi*, a handsome but not strikingly colorful fish, has evolved an unusual strategy to cope with the problem of parenthood. How, if you live in one of Guyana's densely populated rain forest streams, do you provide maximum protection for your offspring? You raise them, literally, out of the water. Above the surface, they will be much safer from aquatic predators. Of course, the eggs need to remain moist.

A spawning pair of *C. arnoldi* literally jumps out of the water to deposit eggs on the underside of a leaf dangling just above the surface. The pair deposits about ten eggs every jump and makes about twenty leaps, leaving roughly two hundred eggs stuck to the bottom of the leaf. After spawning, the male remains in the water beneath the eggs, using its tail to splash them about twice a minute. Fortunately for the male, the eggs hatch in a couple of days. The fry drop into the water and are on their own from that point.

How could such an unusual adaptation have evolved? The splashing tetra, like all members of the Lebiansinidae family, lays adhesive eggs. This contrasts with other commonly kept characins, who scatter their eggs. Adhesive eggs remain in one place as a clutch, making possible the parental care characteristic of nearly all fish that lay them. Relatives of the splashing tetra lay their eggs on the bottom or on submerged leaves. The male fish guards them until they hatch, fanning them with his fins and fending off predators. Ancestors of *C. arnoldi* probably first evolved the trait of spawning on the undersurfaces of leaves; many fish spawn upside-down to place the eggs in an inconspicuous spot. The leap, if you will pardon the pun, to using terrestrial leaves is not all that enormous. Deeper water teems with both competitors for the choicest leaves and numerous predators. Plenty of vegetation overhangs the edge of the stream, often touching the surface or nearly so. The male's splashing behavior probably also developed from the egg fanning behaviors of his ancestors.

This aquarium creates a perfect spot for the splashing tetra to exhibit its uniqueness for your enjoyment.

Aquarium Capacity . . . . 77 gallons

Water Conditions .soft, acidic

Optimal Temperature . . . . .80°F

Plants

    cabomba (*Cabomba aquatica*) . . . . 1 bunch

    pygmy chain sword plant
        (*Echinodorus tenellus*) . . . . 1 clump

    terrestrial plants . . . . several, depending upon their size

Other Décor . . . . .driftwood and/or roots

Background . . . . .light green

Substrate . . . . .light-colored gravel with a small amount of sand added
                                         large smooth pebbles, such as quartz, about an inch in
                                         diameter
                                         long-fiber sphagnum moss

Filtration . . . . .canister filter

Lighting . . . . .4 fluorescent tubes, for plants

Special Requirements . . . . .peat filtration

Fish

    Copenia arnoldi. 5–7

The aquarium is only going to be filled halfway, so choose a canister filter with sufficient lifting power to pump water up and over the side of the tank. Since we want the intake as close to the bottom as possible, and the tank is twenty-four inches in height, you need a pump that can handle two feet of head. Your dealer should be able to help with this.

Start constructing the aquarium by installing a retaining wall to separate the terrestrial portion from the aquatic side of the tank. Have a piece of quarter-inch-thick plate glass cut to fit across the tank at the bottom, about one foot in height. Have the glass shop polish the edges, so you won't cut your fingers. Make sure they know the dimension you want is *after* the edges are polished. It should fit snugly, but not tight enough to stand up without support. There should be a one-sixteenth inch (or less) gap. Place this pane about two feet toward the center from either end, dividing the tank into a smaller terrestrial side and a larger aquatic side. With the help of a friend, mark its position on the outside of the tank, using a felt-tipped marker. Move the tank to a well-ventilated area. Using the mark as a guide, run a bead of silicone down the sides and across the bottom of the tank. Set the pane in place and have your helper hold it while you caulk the joint on both sides with more silicone. Wear plastic gloves to prevent getting silicone on your skin. Moisten your forefinger and use it to smooth the silicone into a seal resembling those with which the tank is assembled. Use a couple of bricks on each side to keep the new partition from tipping until the silicone sets. Set two bricks a short distance back from the glass so you don't end up gluing the bricks to the tank with the silicone. Place the other bricks on top, offsetting them so they touch the glass, holding it in place. Wait at least forty-eight hours before proceeding.

The next step is to paint the background a leafy green color. Be sure to mask off anything you don't want painted. I find the seam where the partition meets the front glass objectionable. My solution is to paint this section of the front glass black, masking the rest of the front. This results in a two-tiered view. When the paint is dry, carefully clean the tank inside and out. Use a mixture of one cup of vinegar in a gallon of water. Take care not to scratch the paint. Rinse it well with tap water. The tank can now be placed in its permanent position.

Begin building the terrestrial side of the paludarium by placing a two-inch layer of large pebbles behind the partition. This will provide drainage, essential to the well being of the plants you will soon add. Cut a piece of plastic screen to fit over the top of the pebbles to prevent planting mix from filling in the spaces. Add another eight inches or so of sterile potting mix, or any growing medium suitable for the plants you have chosen. You can also leave the plants in their plastic nursery containers, but I find this restrains my ability to place them exactly as I want them. The choice of plants is up to you, so long as you make sure to provide some foliage that overhangs the partition. The ubiquitous houseplant, *Philodendron scandens*, or trailing philodendron, serves this purpose well and is darn near indestructible. It also happens to be a South American native. Choose a taller plant to add interest to the rear corner. Spathe lily, *Spathphyllum wallisi*, is a bog plant often sold as Brazilian sword plant in aquarium shops, though it does not last long when grown fully submerged. Its glossy, dark green, sword-like leaves atop a strong stem form a tight clump. Periodically, it produces fragrant white flowers. It is another ideal choice for this paludarium. You will no doubt find other possible selections in the tropical department of your local garden center. For the most natural look, stick with only a few kinds in this small space. Once the plants are in place, cover any exposed potting medium (or the rims of pots, if you use them) with long-fiber sphagnum moss, also available from a good garden center.

To aquascape the wet side of the tank, first place a two-inch layer of substrate on the bottom. Install the intake for the canister filter just above the substrate and parallel to it, attaching it to the back glass with suction cups. Use driftwood to obscure the partition, giving the illusion of an eroded bank with roots exposed to the water. Partially fill this area with water to make planting easier. Plant the sword plants toward the front of the tank, where they will eventually cover a good portion of the substrate. Use the *Cabomba* toward the back to hide hoses. Running the filter hoses behind the terrestrial plants makes them less conspicuous. If you like, you can use water-worn rocks to build up a small waterfall where the partition meets the back glass. Directing the return hose over them can suggest a tiny rivulet flowing into the stream. Wait a month before adding the fish, to give the plants time to become established.

If you expect the splashing tetras to spawn, you will need to provide them with the correct water conditions. As with many other species, soft, slightly acidic water is important if they are to thrive. Offer live foods, such as brine shrimp, mosquito larvae, and fruit flies, regularly.

MODEL DESIGN 48 | Amazon Tank for Big-Fish Enthusiasts

Not all Amazonian fish are dainty little tetras. For those who like a tank with a few larger fish, this model design will fill the bill. And it's no trouble to maintain, either.

Aquarium Capacity . . . . .75 gallons

Water Conditions . . . . .soft to moderately hard, slightly acidic to neutral

Optimal Temperature . . . . .75°F

Plants

>   none, or use plastic

Other Décor . . . . .driftwood and/or roots, large water-worn rocks

Background . . . . .deep green, brown, or black

Substrate . . . . .medium earth-tone gravel

Filtration . . . . .canister filter

Lighting . . . . .2 fluorescent tubes

Special Requirements . . . . .none

Fish

>   *Anostomus anostomus*. 7–9
>
>   *Leporinus fasciatus* 1
>
>   *Semaprochilodus taeniurus* 1–3
>
>   *Sorubim lima* 1

All the fish for this tank except the catfish (*Sorubim*) eat plants, so live plants are out. These species also like a moderately strong current. Choose a canister filter that will deliver plenty of flow, not only to provide current, but also to ensure that you have efficient filtration. Big fish produce a lot of waste. All of these fish reach six inches or more in length, so you may eventually need to move them to a larger tank.

Anostomus anostomus is known as the *striped headstander* for its habit of swimming with its head dipped about 30 degrees toward the bottom. They spend most of their time in vertical rock crevices feeding on algae. They can be acclimated to a diet of aquarium foods made for vegetarians. The bright illumination is recommended to encourage algae growth. When shopping for rocks with which to decorate this tank, choose pieces that will lend themselves to an arrangement that provides the vertical crevices the headstander prefers. Like many characins, it does best in a school. Closely related *Leporinus fasciatus*, though it reaches an impressive ten inches in length, remains peaceful. It also feeds on just about any aquarium food suitable for vegetarians.

Another big characin, *Semaprochilodus taeniurus*, known in the aquarium trade as the flag-tailed prochilodus, also feeds on plants. It grows to about a foot in length. The common name reflects the fact that this species was once called *Prochilodus taeniurus*. Ichthyologists changed the generic name but the old one stuck with the aquarium trade.

The shovel-nose catfish, *Sorubim lima*, tops ten inches at maturity, too. It lies in wait under cover of rocks or roots to ambush prey. Anything that will fit into its capacious mouth is fair game, so it is best kept in such company as the peaceful large vegetarians suggested for this model design. As you might expect, it eats all sorts of meaty foods, including feeder fish and frozen carnivore diets.

Decorating for these species is straightforward. Arrange large to medium rocks to provide an ample number of vertical crevices for the headstanders. Fill the remaining space with well-chosen driftwood, to provide cover for the catfish. Both the *Leporinus* and the flag-tailed prochilodus will remain out in the open, so you should leave swimming space for them toward the front of the tank. If, after you place the rocks and driftwood, you think the tank needs a touch of green, very good plastic reproductions of Amazonian sword plants can be found in any aquarium shop.

Install the filter return near one rear corner of the tank and direct its flow toward the farthest front corner. This should produce a strong diagonal current. You could add an extra powerhead in the corner near the filter return if you wish. The fish will love the additional water movement. Maintenance for this system involves weekly water changes, to keep the water in good condition.

MODEL DESIGN 49 Terror on the Amazon

Piranha, despite their legendary status as a feared predator, make rather uninteresting aquarium fish except at feeding time. The other suggestions for this model design are vicious predators equal to the piranha, but more active when not devouring some hapless prey. Do not try to combine these species in the same tank, as someone will feed on someone else.

Aquarium Capacity . . . . 75 gallons

Water Conditions .soft to moderately hard, slightly acidic to neutral

Optimal Temperature . . . . .75°F

Plants

    none, or use plastic

Other Décor . . . . .driftwood and/or roots, large water-worn rocks

Background . . . . .deep brown or black

Substrate . . . . .dark gravel

Filtration . . . . .canister filter

Lighting . . . . .1 fluorescent tube

Special Requirements . . . . .none

Fish

    Chalceus macrolepidotus 1

        Or *Exodon paradoxus*. 12–15

        Or *Serrasalmus nattereri* 3–5

Set this tank up just like the previous model design. You could use the smaller tank for the pink-tailed chalceus (*Chalceus*), although it will grow to about a foot in length. A single piranha (*Serrasalmus*) could also be given a thirty-eight-gallon tank of its own. Give the school of bucktoothed tetras (*Exodon*) the larger aquarium to prevent them from nipping each other. You could also substitute any of the other species of piranha for the *S. nattereri*. Mild winter areas of the country may prohibit the importation of piranha, due to fears that they could become established in local waters.

Any of these fish will tear to shreds whatever meaty aquarium food you might have available. Feeder fish, either guppies or goldfish depending upon the size of the predator, are always preferred. Remove uneaten food promptly and carry out a weekly water change.

While none of these predators will damage live plants, you really don't want to use them. Plants require regular pruning and other care involving putting your hands into the tank. This increases the likelihood that you will be bitten. Piranha are especially dangerous. A large one can remove a chunk the size of a quarter from your hand. If you happen to be a fan of Nature's mayhem, one of these variations may appeal to you. Obviously, a tank like this should not be accessible to small children.

MODEL DESIGN 50   Ultimate Amazon Tank

My first serious aquarium could serve as the prototype for this one. The design remains a favorite of mine. The abundance of tetra varieties in the many streams of the Amazon region make possible a beautiful community tank consisting only of them. In the aquarium trade, almost any characin might be called a tetra. The ichthyological definition is somewhat more precise. Found throughout Central and South America, in most of sub-Saharan Africa, and even in Texas, at least 1,200 species of characins have been described, and many more undoubtedly await discovery. The group is divided into several families, together constituting the Order Characiformes. About the only characteristic they have in common that you might notice is the presence of an adipose fin. It is a tiny, much reduced fin located behind the dorsal fin. Otherwise, characins exhibit lifestyles as varied as those of the vegetarian *Semaprochilodus* and *Leporinus* to the famously carnivorous piranha. Aquarists usually reserve the term *tetra* for the small schooling species comprising the Tetragonopteridae family of characins. The family name approximately translates to *four rear wings*, a reference to the frequently four-fold symmetry of the dorsal and anal fins and the two lobes of the caudal fin. Although notable exceptions exist, the *true* tetras are interchangeable for aquarium purposes, so feel free to mix and match among the species recommended for this tank. Always keep them in groups of five or more.

Aquarium Capacity . . . . 125 gallons

Water Conditions .soft, slightly acidic

Optimal Temperature . . . . .75°F

Plants

    Reineck's alternanthera (*Alternanthera reineckii*) . . . . 1 bunch

    dwarf bacopa (*Bacopa monnieri*). . . . . . . 3–5 bunches

    red cabomba (*Cabomba furcata*) . . . . . . 3–5 bunches

    Amazon sword plant (*Echinodorus amazonicus*) . . . . (see text)

    Bleher's sword plant (*Echinodorus bleheri*) . . . . (see text)

    horizontal sword plant (*Echinodorus horizontalis*). . . . . (see text)

    red sword plant (*Echinodorus osiris*) . . . . . (see text)

    Central American sword plant (*Echinodorus quadricostatus*) . . . . (see text)

    Honduran sword plant (*Echinodorus radicans*) . . . . (see text)

    spiral eelgrass (*Vallisneria spiralis v. spiralis*) 15–18

Other Décor .driftwood and/or roots, large water-worn rocks

Background . . . . .dark brown or black

Substrate . . . . .dark gravel with a small amount of sand added

Filtration . . . . .sump filter or large canister filter

Lighting . . . . .3 150-watt metal halide lamps (preferred) or 4–6 fluorescent tubes

Special Requirements . . . . .peat filtration (optional)

Fish

Hasemania nana (silvertip tetra)

Hemigrammus caudovittatus (Buenos Aires tetra)

Hemigrammus erythrozonus (glowlight tetra)

Hemigrammus ocellifer (head-and-taillight tetra)

Hyphessobrycon bentosi (Roberts' tetra)

Hyphessobrycon callistus (callistus tetra)

Hyphessobrycon erythrostigma (bleeding heart tetra)

Hyphessobrycon flammeus (flame tetra)

Hyphessobrycon herbertaxelrodi (black neon tetra)

Hyphessobrycon heterorhabdus (flag tetra)

Hyphessobrycon loretoensis (loreto tetra)

Hyphessobrycon pulchripinnis (lemon tetra)

Megalamphodus megalopterus (black phantom tetra)

Megalamphodus sweglesi (red phantom tetra)

Moenkhausia sanctaefilomenae (yellow-banded moenkhausia)

Paracheirodon axelrodi (cardinal tetra)

Paracheirodon innesi (neon tetra)

Pristella maxillarus (X-ray tetra)

Thayeria oblique (penguin tetra)

Ancistrus dolichopterus

   Or *Farlowella gracilis*

   Or *Hypostomus punctatus*

Search out an unusually large piece of driftwood for the centerpiece of this tank, and locate it where its most attractive side will be visible. Behind it, create a curtain of *Vallisneria*, planting them densely where you want to hide equipment. The *Alternanthera*, *Cabomba,* and *Echinodorus osiris* all have red foliage. They all need plenty of light to show this coloration to best advantage. Each will tend to attract attention. You may want to select only one of them to plant as a focal point a foot or so to one side of the center of the tank. The red sword plant, *E. osiris*, if you can find it, makes an impressive centerpiece. All the other *Echinodorus* species have bold foliage. Choose one to three of the species listed to create a large stand positioned where it will balance the red foliage of the centerpiece. Use small clumps of the *Bacopa* to provide contrasting, more finely textured foliage as a counterpoint to the sword plants. Once the tank is planted, leave it alone for a month to allow the plants to become established before you add the fish.

As mentioned in the introductory paragraph, you can select any of the tetras in the list. At least five individuals of any species should be added. Larger schools are fine, as long as you don't overcrowd the tank. About one hundred adult fish should be the goal, perhaps a few more if you choose only the smaller species. Keep in mind the ideas of contrast, color harmony, and balance when choosing. For example, the flashy silvertip tetra, an active species, strikes a good balance with the penguin tetra, more subtly colored and inclined to remain motionless for long periods. Good red coloration is found in several of these species. Take care not to choose too many red fish, or the effect is diminished. The bleeding heart looks better combined with the lemon tetra, for example, than with the callistus tetra, because the latter looks more like the bleeding heart. I suggest limiting yourself to five species, but this kind of restraint may be hard to practice with a large, well-planted tank.

The non-tetras listed all feed on filamentous algae. Known in the trade as *plecostomus*, *Hypostomus punctatus* has been the standard aquarium algae eater for years. Though extremely durable, it does grow to a considerable size, often as much as ten inches, in captivity. In a tank with lots of small fish, a behemoth like this looks out of place. Better choices lie with the other two species of loricarid catfishes on the list. *Ancistrus dolichopterus* goes by *bristlenose catfish* in the aquarium trade. It remains small, around six inches, and the sensory appendages on the snout, more elaborate in males than in females, give it a more interesting appearance. My personal favorite, however, is the whiptail catfish, *Farlowella gracilis*. Thin as a pencil and up to eight inches long, *Farlowella* does its best to look like a stick as it scours the tank for algae. It will delicately clean the leaves of the sword plants without damaging them. Keep only one, or you may not have enough algae to satisfy its constant grazing. The other two cats will eat prepared foods such as pellets, but *Farlowella* insists on a fresh crop of algae. Driftwood may be important for the health of all these members of the family Loricariidae, in that the bits of wood rasped from its surface by the fish's teeth provide fiber that the soft algae lacks.

Sturdy sword plants reach for the light. A school of iridescent tetras weaves in and out among the stems. Done on a grand scale as in this model design, the ultimate Amazon tank represents the ideal freshwater aquarium for many aquarists, both beginner and expert.

South American Killifish

Just about all the South American killifish in the aquarium trade are annual species that inhabit temporary ponds. These fish deposit eggs in the soft bottom debris, where they survive the dry season to continue the family line after the parents have perished in the drought.

Aquarium Capacity . . . . 20 gallons

Water Conditions . . . . .soft, slightly acidic

Optimal Temperature . . . . .68°F

Plants

    water pest (*Egeria densa*) . . . . 1 bunch

    floating fern (*Salvinia auriculata*) . . . . 1 clump

Other Décor . . . . .none

Background . . . . .dark brown or black

Substrate . . . . .soft, fine sand with a layer of peat on top

Filtration . . . . .hang-on filter

Lighting . . . . .1 fluorescent tube

Special Requirements . . . . .peat filtration (optional)

Fish

    Cynolebias bellotti . . . . 1 male, 2 females

The peat layer on the bottom is important for the deposition of eggs. Sterilize the peat and place a layer about an inch and a half in depth over the sand after planting the *Egeria*. Because this killifish prefers cool water, we must also use plants that do not require warmth.

Properly fed with both prepared and live foods, the fish should spawn in the peat layer. Remove the parents to another tank after spawning, where they will complete their brief lifespan of less than a year. The peat with its eggs should be kept dry for about four months, whereupon it can be placed in a small tank and remoistened with distilled water to promote hatching.

Because of the specialized life cycle, annual killifish are not for every aquarist.

South American Cichlids

Although the African cichlids have a large following in the aquarium world, the South American cichlids were hugely popular even before the Africans were first imported.

Cichlids in general are known for their aggressive behavior and ability to grow to a large size in the aquarium. However, the genus *Apistogramma* contains numerous small, attractive species that are at home in a community tank.

Aquarium Capacity . . . . 20 gallons

Water Conditions . . . . .soft to moderately hard, slightly acidic

Optimal Temperature . . . . .75°F

Plants

    red cabomba (*Cabomba furcata*) . . . . 1 bunch

    stargrass (*Heteranthera zosterifolia*) . . . . . 1 bunch

    Central American sword plant
       (*Echinodorus quadricostatus*) 3

Other Décor . . . . .driftwood, water-worn flat rocks, pebbles

Background . . . . .dark brown or black

Substrate . . . . .dark natural gravel with a small amount of added sand

Filtration . . . . .hang-on filter

Lighting . . . . .2 fluorescent tubes

Special Requirements . . . . .none

Fish

    Apistogramma agassizii . . . . 1 male, 2 females

    Any small tetra species 5–7

    Corydoras paleatus 2

Dwarf cichlids, as the *Apistogramma* clan is known, become territorial only when spawning. This makes them suitable for a mixed community tank. The choice of tetra species does not matter, although I suggest choosing one of the red ones, such as *Megalamphodus sweglesi*. It will provide a nice contrast to the mostly blue *Apistogramma*. You can also substitute any small *Corydoras* species.

Living as they do in heavily vegetated areas, dwarf cichlids appreciate a well-planted aquarium. Use the sword plant as a centerpiece. Arrange the *Cabomba* and stargrass (*Heteranthera*) in two stands, leaving room on one side or the other for a cave to be constructed from the flat rocks. To make the sides of the cave, do not place rocks on edge; this looks unnatural. Instead, stack several pieces like pancakes in two stacks about three inches apart. Then place a larger piece across the top for the roof. Also place one or two smaller pieces of the same type of rock nearby in the gravel, so the cave will not look out of place. Place the driftwood so it provides some additional shelter near the mouth of the cave, but without blocking or obscuring the cave from view. The dwarf cichlids will spawn on the roof of the cave, and are exceptional parents.

You can substitute another species of *Apistogramma* for the one suggested. They do not turn up often in aquarium shops.

MODEL DESIGN 53 Butterfly Cichlid

Once considered one of the *Apistogramma* species, *Microgeophagus ramirezi* has been in the aquarium trade since the '40s. It never fails to attract attention with its blue-and-yellow coloration accented with black. Both males and females have elongated, colorful fins that earned this fish the common name, *butterfly cichlid*. Many shops call them *dwarf rams*. This is a shortened version of the species name, of course, but *butterfly cichlid* makes them sound more attractive, in my view.

Aquarium Capacity . . . . 20 gallons

Water Conditions . . . . soft, neutral

Optimal Temperature . . . . 75°F

Plants

    sword plants (*Echinodorus*, any species) . . . 5

    Java moss (*Vesicularia dubyana*) . . . . 1 clump

Other Décor . . . . driftwood, smooth rocks

Background . . . . dark brown or black

Substrate . . . . soft, fine sand with a layer of peat on top

Filtration . . . . hang-on filter

Lighting . . . . 2 fluorescent tubes

Special Requirements . . . . peat filtration (optional)

Fish

    Microgeophagus ramirezi . . . . 1 male, 1 female

    Any small tetra species 5–7

    Corydoras paleatus 2

This model design is basically the same as the previous one, with the exception that no cave is needed. The butterfly cichlid spawns either on a rock or in a pit excavated from the substrate. They spawn readily in captivity, which is why the fish is much more widely available than the other dwarf cichlid species. Unfortunately, their lifespan is only about three years, but they are so beautiful you will want them anyway. Make sure you choose robust individuals with healthy coloration and no evidence of disease, as they are sensitive to mishandling.

MODEL DESIGN 54 Angelfish

This fish may well have converted more casual enthusiasts to serious aquarium hobbyists than any other. The color pattern, silver with black bars, shows up on many kinds of fish, probably because it provides effective camouflage. The long, trailing fins give the angelfish its appeal, and when coupled with its graceful swimming pattern, make it one of the most elegant fish you can keep. Over the years, several varieties have been developed from the wild type. All require the same care.

Aquarium Capacity . . . . 55 gallons

Water Conditions .soft, slightly acidic

Optimal Temperature . . . . .68°F

Plants

     sword plants (*Echinodorus*, any species) . . . 7–15

     dwarf arrowhead (*Sagittaria graminea*) . . . 12–15

Other Décor . . . . .none

Background . . . . .medium green or brown

Substrate . . . . .dark natural gravel with a small amount of added sand

Filtration . . . . .canister filter

Lighting . . . . .4 fluorescent tubes

Special Requirements . . . . .none

Fish

     Pterophyllum scalare. . . . . 5 juveniles (see text)

You could certainly add other fish to this model design, because unlike many large cichlids, the angelfish remains peaceful toward fish too large to swallow.

I prefer to showcase them in a tank by themselves. Arrange the sword plants (*Echinodorus*) around the perimeter of the aquarium, leaving the center open. The angelfish will spend their time out in the open, often motionless for long periods, affording the maximum opportunity for observation. You can add other decorative items if you like, but why detract from the angelfish?

Start out with juveniles about the size of a half dollar. They will form a school at this stage. The sexes are nearly impossible to distinguish except at breeding time. As they grow, hopefully two will take a fancy to each other and you will have a pair. When this happens, I prefer to remove the other fish and leave the pair to themselves, but this is not necessary, as they will simply select a particular spot and keep the other fish at bay. Spawning usually occurs on the upper surface of a large leaf, and any of the taller species of *Echinodorus* provides an ideal surface. Feed them a varied diet. Add food sparingly, as they tend to gorge themselves when food is abundant, to the detriment of their health.

MODEL DESIGN 55 Discus

Sometimes called the *king of the aquarium*, discus require a specific set of conditions to do well, and are not for the armchair enthusiast.

Aquarium Capacity . . . . 75 gallons

Water Conditions . . . . .soft, slightly acidic

Optimal Temperature . . . . .80–85°F

Plants

    sword plants (*Echinodorus*, any species) . . . 15

    dwarf arrowhead (*Sagittaria graminea*) . . . 12–15

    spiral eelgrass (*Vallisneria spiralis*
      v. spiralis) 35

Other Décor . . . . .driftwood, water-worn rocks

Background . . . . .deep green or brown

Substrate . . . . .fine, dark natural gravel with added sand

Filtration . . . . .sump filter

Lighting . . . . .4 fluorescent tubes or 2 x 150-watt metal halide lamps

Special Requirements . . . . .peat filtration

Fish

    Symphysodon aequifasciatus . . . . 5 juveniles (see text)

The model design for discus mimics the previous model design for angelfish. The main differences include more space and a larger capacity filtration system. Discus do not appreciate a decline in water quality, but they live in a much wider range of water parameters than was once thought. Being something of a wild-type snob, I have given water preferences for breeding the beautiful blue-and-gold wild form of *S. aequifasciatus*. If breeding them holds no interest, they will do well across a range of water conditions, from a pH of 5 to 8, in moderately hard water. Hard, alkaline water leads to poor breeding success, however. Regardless of the conditions you supply, avoid dramatic fluctuations in water conditions, which can seriously harm, or even kill, your discus.

Wide ranging in the Amazon region, discus generally inhabit flooded forests or the heavily vegetated margins of lakes or rivers. Like the angelfish, they look their best in a well-planted tank, with perhaps a particularly shapely piece of driftwood as a focal point. You can always use plastic plants if you want to avoid the additional effort live plants require.

Place the substrate in the tank, sloping it from one end to the other, with the greatest depth on the end near the filter intake. We want to give the impression of a cross-sectional view of the river near one bank. Starting near the filter intake, plant your stand of *Echinodorus* in the deep area of the gravel. Sword plants grow and flower above the water level during the dry season, so you would expect them to be most abundant in shallower water. Carefully placing a few pebbles here and there around the bases of the plants helps to give the impression that they grew there naturally. Try to find pebbles that vary in size and repeat the general color scheme of the gravel. Away from the bank, in deeper water, we will plant a grassy area using the dwarf *Sagittaria* in the foreground, and the tall *Vallisneria* along the back and across the end. If you want to avoid the expense of the sword plants, this tank would be just as impressive with only a heavy planting of *Vallisneria* surrounding an open area dominated by the *Sagittaria*.

You needn't bother with encouraging your discus to spawn if your aquarium serves a purely decorative purpose. They get along amiably in a school, and it is hard to beat the display produced by their color, their regal bearing, and their slow, deliberate way of swimming, as if carefully considering each move before undertaking it. When you learn about their breeding behavior, however, you may want to encourage them to raise a family in your tank. Like the angelfish, discus show no outward signs of their gender. Obtaining a pair usually means keeping a group of juveniles together, raising them to maturity, and letting them pair off naturally. At breeding time the pair becomes territorial. In the tank this will be indicated by two individuals keeping the others away from a preferred spot. They carefully clean a rock or leaf on which to deposit a few hundred eggs. Both parents guard the eggs, keeping them free of debris and picking off and discarding any that are non-viable. Discus carry parental care to perhaps the greatest extreme among all fish. Not only do they conscientiously guard the eggs and fry, but also after the fry become free-swimming they feed off a secretion produced by the parents' skin. This adaptation, not unlike the production of milk by mammalian mothers, no doubt improves the chances of survival for the fry. Interestingly, I have read that the young are not above munching on their parents' scales and skin if other food sources are not present. This can actually lead to the parents' death.

Routine care is straightforward. Feed regularly, keep the tank clean, and do those weekly water changes. No doubt wild discus eat all sorts of small invertebrates along with the algae that comprise most of their diet, but they can be harmed by too much animal food. In a brightly illuminated aquarium natural algae growth will provide some food. Also, feed twice daily with high-quality prepared foods. You can also give them occasional treats, such as blackworms. You can find discus food recipes in magazines and on the Internet.

Although their care requirements and the need for ample space mean that discus will not appeal to every aquarist, few things surpass a healthy tank with one or two pairs of adults.

CHAPTER 10

CENTRAL AMERICA

C entral America has scarcely contributed the abundance of species to the aquarium trade that South America has. Nevertheless, the region has offered up some of the most popular, durable, and extensively hybridized fish, including the legendary guppy.

Livebearers

Although the majority of fish species lay eggs, some give birth to live young. The ultimate in parental caregiving, sheltering the fertilized eggs within the mother's body during larval development secures a better chance that the baby fish will survive when expelled into the world of predator and prey. The larvae of egg-layers may scarcely be able to do anything other than drift at the whim of the currents until their yolk sacs are absorbed. Baby livebearers arrive as fully formed miniatures of their parents, ready both to dart to safety and to attack planktonic food.

MODEL DESIGN 56 | Guppies

Livebearing fish clearly evolved from killifish. The vast number of varieties and hybrids that have been bred by aquarists over the years testifies to the large amount of inherent variation present in their genes. Most livebearers occupy hard, alkaline waters, including brackish estuarine habitats. The popular aquarium species, such as the guppy—nearly synonymous with aquarium—have been around since the early twentieth century. One possible reason for their initial popularity could be their tolerance of cooler temperatures, thus requiring no heater. Plus, they can thrive under a wide range of conditions. Keeping them is a good way to introduce children to aquariums.

Shops typically offer two types of guppies. *Common* guppies seldom exceed an inch and a half in length, but nevertheless come in a variety of colors and fin patterns. *Fancy* guppies may be twice as large. They have been as carefully selected for their color and finnage as pedigreed dogs are selected for their coat and bone structure. The fancy varieties, predictably, fare less well than their plebian relatives if neglected, but nevertheless pose few challenges in reasonably capable hands.

Aquarium Capacity . . . . 20 gallons

Water Conditions . . . . .anything within reason

Optimal Temperature . . . . .70°F

Plants

    hornwort (*Ceratophyllum demersum*). . . . . 1 clump

    water pest (*Egeria densa*) . . . . 1 bunch

    corkscrew eelgrass (*Vallisneria*
       americana biwaensis). . . . . 1 bunch

Other Décor . . . . .smooth, water-worn rocks

Background . . . . .deep green, brown, or black

Substrate . . . . .dark gravel with a small amount of sand added

Filtration . . . . .hang-on filter

Lighting . . . . .2 fluorescent tubes, for plants

Special Requirements . . . . .none

Fish

    Poecilia reticulata. 3–9

Because guppies inhabit moving waters that lack heavy vegetation, you can skip the plants altogether and simply decorate with rocks and driftwood. However, if you want babies, you should at least provide a wad of floating hornwort (*Ceratophyllum*). The newborn guppies can hide among its finely divided foliage and so escape predation by their cannibalistic parents. All the plants suggested for this model design tolerate hard water and cool temperatures well.

Select a hang-on filter that will provide a moderate current. Use the dark-green, bushy foliage of *Egeria densa* (usually identified as *Elodea* in aquarium shops) to hide the equipment. The pale-green hornwort contrasts nicely with *Egeria*. It merely floats on the surface, never producing roots. The *Vallisneria*, which you will find labeled *corkscrew val*, twists attractively as it grows upward, giving a whimsical effect that a kid might enjoy. You could simplify this tank by using either the *Egeria* or the *Vallisneria*, but not both. Simply increase the number of plants.

Add the guppies as trios of one male and two females. If you maintain a one-to-one ratio, the females will be harassed to exhaustion by the overly romantic males. The sexes may be identified easily: Males are smaller, more colorful, and have the pelvic fins formed into the gonopodium, by which sperm is introduced into the female.

Feeding and maintenance are basic. Guppies will thrive on any and all aquarium foods, and should have the water changed partially every week. If you skip a water change now and then, they are not likely to suffer any ill effects. You will need to prune the plants regularly. Remove the outer tips of the hornwort together with six inches or so of the older portion. Discard the rest and return the tips to the tank. *Egeria* needs similar treatment, although you should remove cuttings about six inches long from the growing tip of the plant. Take off about an inch of leaves at the bottom and bury the stem in the gravel. Soon they will root and resume growth. *Vallisneria* produces new plants on runners, which need to be thinned out from time to time. None of these plants fares well in poor light, so you can certainly substitute plastic.

Because guppies have been bred in captivity for so long, the offspring seldom bear the fabulous coloration and beautiful fins of their parents. Breeders must cull ruthlessly to maintain a particular line. The culls are sold as feeder guppies, destined for the gullet of larger fish, such as cichlids. For the lowest cost aquarium possible, you can find among the feeders males that are colorful enough to attract the attention of anyone who is not themselves an aquarist.

MODEL DESIGN 57　The Wonderful World of Platies

Although I have kept my share of guppies, I don't go ga-ga over the fancy, inbred types. Platies, on the other hand, come in just about any color combination possible within the restrictions of their genetic makeup, and I like them all. No doubt, the reason lies with my first experience with tropical fish, in 1957. For my birthday, I received a paper carton, the type Chinese take-out food comes in, with the little wire bail. This was the preferred way of transporting aquarium fish before plastic bags became commonplace. Inside my carton was a strand of hornwort, and swimming in the pint of water was a bright orange platy. To this day, I remember exactly that first glimpse into the carton. Although I did not realize it then, that little orange fish hooked me for good.

The name *platy* derives from an outdated generic name for these fish, *Platypoecilus*. The aquarium industry has a way of clinging to fish names long after they are deemed incorrect by ichthyologists. The prefix *platy* means *flat*, and refers to the much deeper body of these fish compared to the thinner, more elongated members of the livebearer clan. All the livebearers are lumped into a single family, the Poecillidae, and are clearly closely related. Besides the aquarium species, several others occur in the waters of Mexico, Central America, and northern South America. The genetic variability of the platy clan is evident from the astonishing number of color varieties that have been developed over the years. These types have been given equally colorful names. Wag platies, for example, have black on the fins and tail, with the remainder of the body a solid red, orange, or gold color. Tuxedo types have black on the flanks with colorful fins and a lighter body color. Mirror platies have a patch of light, iridescent scales on each side. There is even a Mickey Mouse platy with a pale yellow-orange body and the famous round head with two ears emblazoned in black on the tail. Add to these variations in the size of the fins and the possible combinations become numerous indeed.

The idea with this model design is to exhibit as many of these different types as you like. The larger the tank, of course, the more varieties you can keep. One of my personal favorites is the sunset type of *X. variatus*, aptly named for its color combination of golden yellow and bright orange. You will enjoy the constant movement and the riot of color without the need for any but the most basic maintenance.

Aquarium Capacity . . . . 20–75 gallons

Water Conditions . . . . .not critical, but neutral and hard preferred

Optimal Temperature . . . . .68–70°F

Plants

    none

Other Décor . . . . .water-worn rocks

Background . . . . .pale gray-blue

Substrate . . . . .light gravel of varying sizes, including larger pebbles

Filtration . . . . .canister filter

Lighting . . . . .fluorescent (see text)

Special Requirements . . . . .none

Fish

    Xiphophorus maculatus . . . . (see text)

    Xiphophorus variatus . . . . (see text)

Although these two platies do fine together or in a mixed community tank, they actually come from different habitats. From the eastern Mexican coast through Guatemala and into northern Honduras comes *X. maculatus*, also known as *moonfish* or *moon platy*. The variatus platy naturally occurs only in southern Mexico. (I realize Mexico is part of North America, but for our purposes it makes sense to consider Mexican species along with Central American ones.) Both tolerate a wide range of water conditions, although preferring hard water of neutral to alkaline pH. The moon platy lives in slow-moving streams, canals, and ditches with weedy banks, while the variatus platy lives in spring runs with heavy vegetation. Both do well in cooler water, so the tank can be maintained at room temperature. A cool temperature will also slow down reproduction, though not much. You will need to remove the offspring periodically to keep the aquarium population in check, although in this aquarium without plants the majority of the babies will be eaten by their parents.

I omit plants from this tank for simplicity's sake and to showcase the colorful fish. If you wish to include greenery, choose tolerant, cool-water varieties such as *Sagittaria* and *Vesicularia*, or use plastic reproductions.

With or without live plants, bright illumination will not only show off the colors, but also will encourage plenty of algae growth. Algae forms an important part of the diet of these, and most other, livebearers.

Install a filter that will produce a moderate current and provide a turnover rate of at least two tank volumes per hour. If possible, install the filter on one end of the tank, creating a lengthwise current. If your situation makes this impractical, locate the filter on the back of the tank near the left end and direct its output toward the right front corner. Slope the substrate from left to right along the length of the tank. Build up a grouping of larger rocks on the left, and add pebbles on top of the substrate. Use progressively smaller pebbles as you move toward the right side. Try various arrangements until you achieve a look of random placement. The look you are aiming for is that of a small downstream pool protected by rocks on the upstream side. Using a pale background and substrate lends a bright, almost sparkling, look to the aquarium, the perfect foil for the intense coloration of the fish. Plenty of illumination enhances this effect. If you wish, you can include a few dark-toned rocks for balance, or a group of three to five dark rocks can be placed to create a focal point.

With a good crop of algae growing on the rocks, you can leave for two weeks on vacation and the fish will be just fine. Do make a partial water change, about a third, at least once a month. Besides algae, platies eat any of the available aquarium foods. Give them a variety, and be sure to include prepared foods labeled as containing color enhancers to help keep the reds and oranges at maximum intensity.

MODEL DESIGN 58 Swordtails

Closely related to platies, the swordtails also come in many color types. Found in running water from southern Mexico to Guatemala, *Xiphophorus helleri* normally blends in with its background. Aquarium types, on the other hand, run the gamut of riotous color.

Aquarium Capacity . . . . 30 gallons

Water Conditions .not critical, but neutral and hard preferred

Optimal Temperature . . . . .72°F

Plants

    hornwort (*Ceratophyllum demersum*). . . . . 1 clump

    arrowhead (*Sagittaria species*) 12–15

    eelgrass (*Vallisneria species*) 12–15

Other Décor . . . . .water-worn rocks and pebbles

Background . . . . .pale green

Substrate . . . . .fine, light gravel mixed with river sand

Filtration . . . . .canister filter

Lighting . . . . .2 fluorescent tubes, for plants

Special Requirements . . . . .none

Fish

   Xiphophorus helleri. . . . . 1 male, 5–7 females

   Other community fish (see text)

Reaching about three inches in length, some variation of the orange-red swordtail will be available in any pet shop. Males have a greatly elongated lower lobe of the tail fin. Outlined in black with a bright yellow center, this *sword* probably serves to announce the possessor as a better mate, or perhaps a better defender of territory. Two males in the same tank often squabble.

Use the hornwort (*Ceratophyllum*) only if you want to protect the fry from being eaten. Otherwise, spread the substrate and shape it with your hands to give the impression of ripple marks in a sandy bottom. The ripple marks should be deepest on the downstream side. Direct the outflow from the filter appropriately, so the rooted plants will stream in the proper direction. The *Vallisneria* and *Sagittaria* should be planted in randomly placed small clumps.

Care for this tank is the same as in the previous model design, as are the feeding instructions. If you prefer more variety, good candidates would include many of the Asian barbs described in Chapter six. You could also include any species of *Corydoras* catfish. Avoid fish that do best in soft, acidic water.

Mollies

Mollies (from their old genus name, "*Mollinesia*") are a special subgroup of livebearing fishes, at least in terms of their aquarium care. Beginners often kill this fish because they do not understand its requirements. However, under the conditions given, it thrives: added salt, no temperature fluctuations, and a diet rich in vegetable matter.

One seldom sees the wild type these days. Almost all the mollies in aquarium shops are black. In good health, the black molly looks as though covered in black velvet. Without synthetic sea salt in the water and plenty of algae in the diet, this fish will not do well, and often suffers from infestations of the common parasite, *ich*. (See page 67.)

Three years is a long time for one of these fish to live in captivity. It makes up for its short lifespan by producing an unusually large number of offspring. You can easily raise the young on prepared foods. Protect them from their parents by floating hornwort, real or plastic, on top of the tank to provide hiding places.

Although keeping mollies may sound like a lot of maintenance, a well-developed male sporting his colorfully dotted, much enlarged dorsal fin supplies ample reward for your time.

MODEL DESIGN 59 Mollies I

Mollies offer yet another variation on the basic livebearer body. They require more care on the part of the aquarist, but they also have a lot to offer. This model design features one of two basic molly types.

Aquarium Capacity . . . . 20 gallons

Water Conditions . . . . .hard, alkaline, and slightly brackish

Optimal Temperature . . . . .75°F

Plants

    plastic, one variety 12–15

Other Décor . . . . .none

Background . . . . .light tan

Substrate . . . . .light gravel of varying sizes, including larger pebbles

Filtration . . . . .hang-on filter

Lighting . . . . .fluorescent (see text)

Special Requirements . . . . .add 2–5 percent seawater

Fish

    Poecilia sphenops . . . . 1 male, 3–5 females

Decorate for the molly as I suggested for the swordtail, although using plastic plants. Purchase a good heater to guard against temperature swings, which the much-inbred black molly does not tolerate well.

The species also comes in a pearl-and-charcoal-marbled variety. It requires the same care as the all-black form. Aquarium shops love mollies because they do not have a naturally long lifespan, making it likely that the customer will return for more.

MODEL DESIGN 60 Mollies II

Still more challenging to keep is the other wild molly type, the sailfin. Two species, *Poecilia velifera* and *P. latipinna,* occur in the wild. Aquarium varieties, including hybrids between these two species, have more brilliant coloration than the wild types. These, usually called "green sailfin" mollies, show up now and then in aquarium shops.

Aquarium Capacity . . . . 30–55 gallons

Water Conditions . . . . .hard, alkaline, and brackish

Optimal Temperature . . . . .70°F

Plants

    plastic, one to three varieties . . . . 7–15 of each

Other Décor . . . . .a few pebbles

Background . . . . .light tan or blue

Substrate . . . . .fine gravel and/or coarse river sand

Filtration . . . . .canister filter

Lighting . . . . .fluorescent (see text)

Special Requirements . . . . .add 5–10 percent seawater

Fish

    Poecilia latipinna . . . . 1 male, 3–5 females

        Or *Poecilia velifera*. . . . . 1 male, 3–5 females

        Or Hybrid sailfin molly . . . . 1 male, 3–5 females

The sailfin mollies can reach six inches under aquarium conditions. They have the same requirements as *P. sphenops* in the previous model design, though they like more salt. By doing 10-percent water changes with full strength seawater, these fish can be acclimated to saltwater. They can then be placed in an aquarium with other marine species. In this model design, we have them in a tidal creek environment.

Use the same basic design as in the previous tank, but combine multiple plant varieties to suggest a heavily vegetated backwater area. I have seined up beautiful sailfin mollies that probably escaped from grow-out ponds, living in creeks in Florida. They need plenty of space, the proper water conditions, and a largely vegetarian diet to thrive. Sailfin varieties seldom reproduce without special attention from the aquarist and the addition of live foods, such as mosquito larvae, to the diet. Therefore little need exists for hiding places for the offspring. For that reason, I suggest using plastic reproductions of rooted plants only. If possible, install a two-tube fluorescent fixture to encourage the growth of algae, supplementing the standard diet of vegetables and prepared foods intended for plant eaters.

Central American Cichlids

As with the livebearers, the cichlids of Central America include some of the most popular and hardy aquarium varieties. Another similarity is their preference for hard, alkaline water, although they are extremely tolerant.

Ichthyologists always seem to be quibbling over the names of fishes. This one has been known under various generic names. The old name you are most likely to see in aquarium books is *Cichlasoma*. This genus was once used as a sort of catch-all for many Central American cichlid species.

The common name is clearly suggested by the pale gray body with eight or ten black bars. Its behavior might also be characterized as thuggish. For example, a pair can demolish a tank of plants in an afternoon, eating some and uprooting nearly all of them. Plastic plants are merely uprooted. They seldom tolerate other fish in the tank. Here again, some are eaten, if they are small enough. Larger ones will be harassed to the point of exhaustion, subsequently developing disease problems.

Unlike many cichlids, such as the angelfish and discus, juvenile convicts quickly form pairs and start families. When courting, tending eggs, or herding their offspring around the tank, their aggressive tendencies become greatly magnified. Parents may butt or bite your hand, for example. A six-incher can chomp rather painfully, to which I can personally attest. Ease of breeding has made this fish a favorite of hatcheries, and the cute two-inch juveniles frequently tempt novice aquarists into adding them to a community tank. As time passes, the foolhardiness of this decision becomes increasingly apparent. If the fish appeals to you, be prepared to give it a large tank to itself.

Aquarium Capacity . . . . 55 gallons

Water Conditions .not critical, but neutral and hard preferred

Optimal Temperature . . . . .70°F

Plants

    none, or plastic reproductions

Other Décor . . . . .water-worn rocks, driftwood

Background . . . . .charcoal gray

Substrate . . . . .dark natural gravel of varying sizes, including larger pebbles

Filtration . . . . .canister filter

Lighting . . . . .1 fluorescent tube

Special Requirements . . . . .none

Fish

    Archocentrus nigrofasciatum . . . . 1 pair

You could have a lot of fun with the aquarium by masking the front glass and painting prison bars on the outside. Such a novelty tank might be right for a tavern or game room.

Decoration for the convict tank must necessarily be bare bones. Greenery of any sort is out. Live plants, as I said, will quickly be eaten. You will spend hours replanting the plastic ones as the convicts repeatedly uproot them. One hobbyist I know attempted to solve this problem by gluing the bases of plastic plants to the bottom of his tank with silicone. The cichlids simply tore them to pieces, though it took longer than it might have otherwise. As you arrange rocks to simulate a river bed, place one to three larger ones, up to the size of a grapefruit, say, slightly to one side of the center of the tank. One of these will likely serve the fish as a place to deposit a clutch of eggs. Convicts, like cichlids generally, provide care to the eggs and fry until the offspring reach about a quarter inch in length. Studies have shown that the babies respond to communication from the parents, in the form of movements and perhaps other means. Such obedience has obvious adaptive value in a river full of hungry mouths.

MODEL DESIGN 62 Mexican Firemouth

No, Mexican firemouth is not something you get when the chili is too spicy. Undeniably one of the most beautiful Central American cichlids, its name refers to the cherry-red lower jaw of the male. This color intensifies and spreads to the belly during spawning season.

The firemouth lives in Mexico, Guatemala, and Belize, in moving water over sandy bottoms. It favors shallow margins with plenty of vegetation. Its habitat is easy to replicate in a tank.

Aquarium Capacity . . . . 30 gallons

Water Conditions . . . . .not critical, but neutral and medium hard preferred

Optimal Temperature . . . . .72–74°F

Plants

    dwarf sword plant
      (*Echinodorus latifolius*) 3

    radicans sword plant
      (*Echinodorus cordifolius*) 1

    creeping ludwigia (*Ludwigia repens*) . . . . 2 bunches

Other Décor . . . . .driftwood

Background . . . . .deep green or dark mud brown

Substrate . . . . .river sand, not too coarse

Filtration . . . . .canister filter

Lighting . . . . .1 fluorescent tube, for plants, or metal halide

Special Requirements . . . . .none

Fish

   Thorichthys meeki. . . . . 1 pair

Select driftwood for a centerpiece. A piece that appears to project from the rear of the tank toward the viewer looks intriguing. Locate a piece and cut off the large end so it fits flat against the rear glass. A piece that arches downward as it tapers to a point most resembles a protruding root. To get the correct position, you may need to cut it at an angle. Glue it to the back glass with silicone. Allow the silicone to cure at least a week before filling the aquarium.

The driftwood will provide shelter for the fish and they will likely spawn on a smooth rock placed in the sand underneath. Place the big *Echinodorus cordifolius* to one side of the driftwood. This plant, known in the aquarium trade as *radicans* sword plant, has tough, spoon-shaped leaves and can stand up to the excavations of the firemouth pair. They often dig a pit here and another one over there before settling on just the proper place for bedding down a clutch of fry for the evening. On subsequent days, they will move the fry to another pit. This behavior probably serves to confuse predators. A predator that finds food in a particular spot today may be smart enough to return tomorrow. Relocating overnight foils this hunting strategy. Firemouth may dig up shallow-rooted plants, but *E. cordifolius*, if allowed a month or more to become established before the fish decide to begin digging, will resist their efforts. Firemouth do not eat plants, and only dig when preparing to spawn. Leave the area surrounding the driftwood open and arrange a grouping of *E. latifolius* on the side opposite the other sword, in the foreground where it will eventually form a turf. Place groups of *Ludwigia* stems toward the back, and use them also to hide equipment from the viewer. As they grow, prune and replant the top portions. *Ludwigia glandulosa* has colored foliage, and would make a pretty substitute for *L. repens*.

Rather docile as cichlids go, the firemouth nevertheless becomes aggressive when parenting. It is therefore best to give them a tank of their own. If you want tank mates, large swordtails might work, but no guarantee.

Feeding this fish is easy, as it needs plenty of vegetable matter and occasional treats of animal protein. Most types of prepared foods are fine, provided they contain a high proportion of algae. A great source of healthy food for this and other cichlids is sheets of the *nori* seaweed used by sushi chefs to wrap *maki* rolls. You can find it in many supermarkets and specialty markets. Inexpensive and highly nutritious, it keeps six months in an airtight container. Live blackworms are gobbled up greedily.

One nice thing about cichlids: They don't jump as much as smaller schooling fish do. You can leave the tank open. If you do so, and use the optional metal halide lighting, the firemouth tank becomes a paludarium of sorts. The sword plants grow fully submerged only part of the time, and produce tall shoots that extend above the surface. Flowers, also, are borne up in the air, where they are accessible to pollinating insects. Bright illumination will encourage this. For that reason, a pendant-type metal halide fixture will work better for this model design than a unit that sits directly on top of the tank. You could, of course, use a taller tank and lower the water level.

In another of the seemingly endless variations on the cichlid lifestyle, the yellow-belly cichlid inhabits rivers. Hiding among vegetation, rocks, and roots to ambush small crustaceans and fish, *Cichlasoma salvini* can be combined with plants in the aquarium.

Aquarium Capacity . . . . 40 gallons

Water Conditions . . . . .not critical, but neutral and hard preferred

Optimal Temperature . . . . .75°F

Plants

    Echinodorus cordifolius. 5

    Cabomba caroliniana. . . . . .5 bunches

Other Décor . . . . .driftwood and/or roots, water-worn rocks

Background . . . . .deep green

Substrate . . . . .dark gravel of varying sizes, including larger pebbles

Filtration . . . . .canister filter

Lighting . . . . .4 fluorescent tubes, for plants

Special Requirements . . . . .none

Fish

    Cichlasoma salvini. . . . . 1 pair

Select a spot for the driftwood, and place it where you want the fish to spend time. They are likely to use it for shelter. Add the substrate, leaving a slight depression near the center. Leave this space open so the fish will swim there. Use the dark-green, feathery *Cabomba* toward the rear of the tank, hiding the filter equipment. For the background, choose a color that closely resembles the leaves of the *Cabomba*, to give the impression that a huge stand of plants stretches into the distance. Against this backdrop place the sword plants, grouping three toward one end of the tank and two toward the opposite end. If you place them toward the foreground, the tank will appear deeper, just what we want. The cichlid has found a primo piece of real estate ideally suited for ambush. Use larger pebbles in clusters around the bases of the sword plants. Place a group of larger stones between the sword plants and the *Cabomba*, further enhancing the false perspective we are trying to achieve.

Like most cichlids, the yellow-belly takes care of its eggs and young with extreme devotion to duty. Like the convict, they will bite, especially when brooding young. Their aggressive nature plus a tendency to eat anything small enough to swallow makes them most suitable for a single-species tank. Mixing them with large barbs might work. Increase the size of the tank appropriately if you want to try adding other fish, as this one reaches six inches. Two of them, especially given their appetite, is about it for a forty-gallon tank.

MODEL DESIGN 64 Jack Dempsey

I've seen countless dorm tanks with a single individual of this fish. True to its common name, the Jack Dempsey is a heckuva fighter, so it is one pair, at most, to a customer. The only way to avoid them spawning in any sort of reasonably maintained aquarium is to keep only a single specimen. A spawning will raise the issue of what to do with the babies. Like other cichlids, Dempseys are good parents and produce many off-spring per pair. Shops in your area may take a few, but your supply will far outstrip demand. They are hardy and easy to rear. Unless you are prepared to use the offspring as feeder fish, you may want to think twice about encouraging Dempsey's to start a family.

Aquarium Capacity . . . . 40 gallons (minimum)

Water Conditions .not critical, but neutral and hard preferred

Optimal Temperature . . . . .75°F

Plants

    none

Other Décor . . . . .driftwood and/or roots, water-worn rocks, bamboo canes

Background . . . . .deep green

Substrate . . . . .coarse river sand

Filtration . . . . .canister filter

Lighting . . . . .1 fluorescent tube

Special Requirements . . . . .none

Fish

    Cichlasoma octofasciatum . . . . 1 pair, or a single individual

Not only does this fish fight with other fish (or else swallow them), it apparently fights with plants, too. It will uproot and eat anything you try to grow, so don't even bother. Décor for this aquarium will necessarily be determined by the shape and size of the rocks and driftwood you select.

You have no doubt noticed that among the different cichlids we have considered, each exploits a particular biotope. The firemouth prefers areas of heavy vegetation, while the convict is found farther away from the bank, in swifter waters. The Jack Dempsey exploits sluggish swamps, bog ponds, and man-made canals and ditches over weedy, muddy bottoms. This propensity toward waters of low oxygen content probably explains why it adapts readily to aquarium life.

The idea of a swamp suggests a lot of submerged deadwood, so choose several smaller pieces of driftwood that can be placed, points up, to suggest it has been inundated. Sharp stubs sticking out of the sand can be placed in the foreground. Toward the back you could have a piece that extends all the way to the surface. As I described in another model design, lengths of bamboo cane that extend above the water line effectively suggest a reedy swamp. For this forty-gallon tank, use pieces about the diameter of your little finger, making the Jack Dempsey look even bigger. Arrange them randomly in the sand, clustering them into groups of five to seven closely spaced canes. With luck, the fish will leave them alone. Placing a single large, smooth stone in the tank will encourage breeding, if that's what you want. The pair will use it to deposit eggs. The urge to spawn is so strong in this species, though, that they will use almost any smooth surface available.

The green, gold, and blue iridescence of the Jack Dempsey's scales render it an undeniably beautiful species. Living as it does in the swamp, it makes do with whatever swims by or falls in. Feed a wide variety of foods, including live fish and crustaceans from time to time. The coloration will absolutely glow. This hardy, tolerant cichlid is at home in a trouble-free tank that needs only regular maintenance to keep the fish in excellent condition. Jack Dempsey will keep you entertained for a minimal investment of time and money. It's time for this fish to move out of the dorm room and into the living room.

MODEL DESIGN 65 Blue Acara

At last, we have a larger cichlid that gets along well with tank mates. It will, of course, swallow small fishes whole, but anything not likely to be eaten will be tolerated. Neither will they eat or uproot plants.

Aquarium Capacity . . . . 120 gallons

Water Conditions .not critical, but neutral and hard preferred

Optimal Temperature . . . . .72°F

Plants

    Central American sword plant
        (*Echinodorus cordifolius*) 15

    green cabomba (*Cabomba caroliniana*). . . 5 bunches

        or dwarf arrowhead
           (*Sagittaria graminea*) 24

        or corkscrew eelgrass
           (*Vallisneria spiralis biwaensis*) 24

Other Décor . . . . .driftwood and/or roots, water-worn rocks

Background . . . . .deep green

Substrate . . . . .coarse river sand, with a few pebbles

Filtration . . . . .sump filter

Lighting . . . . .2 150-watt metal halide

Special Requirements . . . . .none

Fish

    Aequidens pulcher . . . . 1 pair, or a single individual

    Xiphophorus helleri. . . . . 1 male, 7–12 females

The basic concept here is to have an open, grassy area above which the swordtails will swim, with an area of taller vegetation closer to the riverbank, where the blue acara should feel very much at home. Because of the left-to-right asymmetry of this model design, decide which end you want the riverbank to be and order the tank with the overflow for the filter installed on that end. After placing a deep layer of coarse sand on the bottom, plant the sword plants on the end you have chosen, where they will hide the overflow. Plant them with the crowns about four inches apart, to create a dense stand. You could also plant fewer, larger specimens of any large sword plant. Because the tank is two feet tall, they won't outgrow it. Stop planting sword plants before you have filled one third of the length of the tank. The remainder of the tank should be densely planted with the *Cabomba* or grasses. Adjust the number of plants until you have most of this space covered. After the tank is planted, I recommend running it for at least a month to allow the plants to grow some new roots before you add fish.

To render the possibility of aggression reasonably remote, add the swordtails all at the same time, and leave them to themselves for a month. Pick the largest swordtails you can find. When the appropriate time comes, try to get a smaller acara; it will eventually reach seven or eight inches in length. The hope here (though I make no guarantee) is that the big cichlid will become accustomed to the bright orange swordtails. It will regard them as a normal part of its environment; only something completely new will be eaten. I have seen this phenomenon repeatedly in captive predatory fish. Typically, one feeder fish, say a small goldfish, escapes being eaten and hides in the plants. Wary enough to avoid capture, the fish need only survive for a day or two before the big predator decides to ignore it. Thereafter, this particular fish will not be eaten, although the predator will consume similar fish added later.

You can add more of the carpeting plants for the open area initially, but it is better to let them grow in by themselves. This produces the most natural look.

Once again, as in the case of the cichlids of Africa, described in Chapter eight, and those of South America, covered in Chapter nine, the Central American cichlid species have their own unique personalities and lifestyles. Because of their aggressive nature, it is usually necessary to give them a tank to themselves. With a large tank, plenty of cover, and the acclimatization process I described, you should be able to enjoy a really large fish in the company of smaller tank mates. The color combination of the orange swordtails with the turquoise, charcoal, and hints of ochre in the acara's pigment pattern makes a striking impression, while the side-to-side planting scheme lends a feeling of expansiveness.

Mexican Cave Fish

All sorts of critters populate caves. In the case of this tetra, the resulting changes in its body have been similar to those observed in other cave-dwelling species.

MODEL DESIGN 66 Mexican Cave Tetra

Pale pink in color, *Astayanax mexicanus* was originally restricted to the Nueces, lower Rio Grande, and the lower Pecos River drainages in Texas, but now is established elsewhere in Texas, New Mexico, and in eastern and central Mexico. Inhabiting rocky and sandy pools and backwaters of creeks, rivers, and springs, its diet consists mostly of insects, crustaceans, and worms.

Aquarium Capacity . . . . 30 gallons

Water Conditions .not critical, but neutral and hard preferred

Optimal Temperature . . . . .75°F

Plants

    none

Other Décor . . . . .slab rocks and water-worn rocks

Background . . . . .black

Substrate . . . . .dark gravel of varying sizes, including larger pebbles

Filtration . . . . .canister filter

Lighting . . . . .fluorescent and/or incandescent (see text)

Special Requirements . . . . .none

Fish

    Astayanax mexicanus 10

Lacking eyes, the Mexican cave tetra has no need of lighting. The concept of this model design is to fool the viewer into thinking they are looking into a cave. The fish is easy to keep, feeding well on a variety of readily available foods. Routine maintenance keeps the aquarium in top shape, and need only be done every two weeks. Because this fish adapts well to the aquarium, this model design should be trouble free. You can combine this fish with other community species, as it is not aggressive, but the others would not be comfortable in the setup described here.

Cover the ends and back of the tank with background paint in flat black. If you want, you can get creative with this background. First, use an artist's brush to paint a few narrow, horizontal strokes in medium gray along the back glass. After the gray dries, mask the tank and spray paint with the flat black. The effect should be to suggest layers of rock in the walls of the cave. You can practice on a scrap of glass or clear plastic. The trick with this faux painting technique is to have neither too few nor too many of the gray strata lines. Experiment on paper. Try to match the vertical distance between gray lines to the thickness of the real rocks you have available.

Creating a convincing cave habitat requires shopping carefully for rocks. You need some stackable ones to create both the front frame and the backdrop. Small, rectangular slabs in a dark color would be ideal. Build up walls of rocks on both sides of the front, about two inches back from the glass. Along the rear glass, build another long wall to serve as a backdrop. Try to avoid stacking the rocks like bricks, or you will not wind up with a natural-looking cave. Stack the pieces so one or two project out from the others, creating a jagged appearance. Lay them flat, never on edge as props, both for safety's sake and because you want to imitate the natural position of rock strata. These rock formations do not have to reach all the way to the surface; merely suggesting the craggy interior of the cave is enough. The dark background and low light level will complete the illusion.

Lighting for this tank should be subdued. Blue *actinic* lamps sold for use on marine aquariums will produce an eerie effect. You could also use a red fluorescent lamp. With either color of fluorescent lighting, installing an incandescent spotlight above the tank gives you additional lighting options. For example, the spotlight could be on during a party, producing a dramatic-looking shaft of light with the tetras swimming in and out. The spotlight also serves to allow you to see when working in the tank.

Because little algae growth will occur under the low light, the time normally spent cleaning glass can be used for other purposes. Specifically, you should be careful to maintain a schedule of weekly water changes, since there will not be much plant life to help absorb nitrogenous wastes. Feeding the cave tetra poses no problem, as it eats a variety of small invertebrates. Frozen, prepared, or live foods should be offered in variety.

CHAPTER 11

NORTH AMERICA

North America hosts an impressive fish fauna. From colorful sunfishes to the stickleback, North American native species have been aquarium subjects for many years. The temperate climate of most of North America imposes special demands upon aquarium designs based on native biotopes. Keeping the tank cool enough poses the biggest challenge. The fun and excitement of collecting aquarium fish from your local waters, however, will more than make up for the added effort and expense. You can even enjoy some North American native species without having to collect your own. Several frequently appear in aquarium shops.

Focusing on the Southeast United States

It would be a great insult to my ichthyological colleagues for me to claim aquarium expertise regarding the native fishes of the United States. The greater proportion of my hands-on aquarium experience has been with exotic tropical species. On the other hand, I have had some wonderful opportunities to observe North American fishes in their natural habitat, and in the aquariums of friends doing research. I know from these experiences that many of our native species make great aquarium subjects. In this chapter, I will be focusing primarily on southeastern species, not because good aquarium fish cannot be found elsewhere in North America, but because of the following reasons:

1. I grew up in the Southeast, specifically Tennessee, and have trekked alongside and into the streams and rivers of this region for as long as I can remember.

2. During and for several years after college, I worked with a cadre of professional ichthyologists and students headed up by Dr. David Etnier at the University of Tennessee. With this group, I spent twenty years of weekends traveling from Florida to Texas on field trips, possibly being bitten by more kinds of mosquitoes than any human who has lived to tell the tale. What I do know about collecting and aquarium care of the fishes of North America is limited to the species found in the southeast United States.

3. Fishes native to the southeast United States exhibit a wide range of diversity. Tennessee and Georgia, for example, each has more than 300 species of native freshwater fish. High diversity means more choices for different types of aquariums, and a greater range of possibilities for community aquarium groupings. Although many rare species occur in the South, some of the best aquarium choices come from among the commoner species, such as sunfishes.

4. From a practical standpoint, the mild climate provides still another reason for choosing southeastern fish for aquarium subjects over those living in higher latitudes. Fish whose natural waters can reach temperatures in the 80s during summertime can tolerate lower dissolved oxygen levels than species restricted to cold water. Lowered oxygen can occur in the aquarium when, for example, a power outage reduces the amount of aeration. Fish from warm-water environments are less likely to suffer damage under such conditions, so the aquarium has a margin for error. Further, you are relieved of the necessity for refrigerating the tank to accommodate cool-water species.

5. A final reason for this focus is that many southeastern natives have been included on the lists of tropical fish wholesalers for decades. Florida flagfish and the black color morph of the sailfin molly are but two examples.

Why Native Fish?

With so many intriguing and attractive tropical fish to select from, why go to the additional trouble required to maintain common local species? To provide an adequate answer, allow me to share some anecdotes. During college and for many years thereafter, I had the privilege of going on field trips in the company of the foremost ichthyologists in the United States. Looking over the shoulders of these giants gave me the opportunity to observe aspects of the aquatic world only seen by a lucky few. For many species, field studies provide valuable information, but only by observing the fish in the aquarium can certain life history details be brought to light. My colleagues observed, for example, darter spawning behavior not previously witnessed by humans. Small, secretive species present special difficulties to the would-be observer in the field. The same traits of size and behavior, however, may make them ideally suited to aquarium culture.

Aquariums have also played a central role in the success of Conservation Fisheries, the only fish hatchery in the United States devoted to producing rare and endangered species of native North American freshwater fish. Rearing native fish in aquariums for eventual reintroduction into their natural habitat has proved an invaluable tool in restoring depleted populations.

The owners of home aquariums devoted to native fish species can contribute to the pool of information about them. Aquarium observations can easily be shared on the Internet, via both text and images. In designing aquariums for research, professional aquarists often use information from home aquarium sources. You do not have to be maintaining a rare species to make a valuable contribution. Sometimes just sharing a simple tip helps a lot.

Conservation Issues

More than 2,500 species of fish swim in the waters of North America, both marine and fresh. The United States Fish and Wildlife Service lists around 100 as endangered or threatened. Aquarists must take care that their collecting does not harm local fish populations. All states have fishing regulations. Federal statutes protect endangered fish. Before you head out with your net, make sure you have complied with all regulations, including obtaining a fishing license or permit where required.

Never release collected fish into waters they do not naturally inhabit. By the same token, do not release any aquarium fish, regardless of its origin, into natural waters. Many kinds of aquarium fish have become pests in the warmer portions of the United States. The Oscar (*Astronotus ocellatus*), a popular South American cichlid, is a common sight in Everglades National Park, for example. Bold and aggressive, it competes with native species for food and breeding sites, and preys on their offspring. Even in cool-water habitats, some exotic aquarium species have become threats to the local fish population.

Non-native plants also pose threats to indigenous plants. Anyone cultivating aquarium plants should avoid discarding unwanted specimens where they might find their way into a native stream. Aquarists in warmer regions should take care with all tropical aquatics, while in cooler parts of the country only species able to survive winter pose problems.

Collecting and Transport Techniques

Collecting fish for the aquarium requires not only nets and/or seines, but also a suitable method of transport. Keeping the fish alive between the stream and the tank requires additional equipment, depending upon how far into the wild you plan to venture. If you are taking specimens from within a short drive of your home, then an insulated picnic cooler will probably suffice. For a weekend excursion you will need more than one cooler, a battery-powered air pump for each cooler, and extra batteries for the air pumps.

Wild fish experience considerable stress during capture and transport. Stress contributes to the majority of health problems in captive fish. Techniques for minimizing stress include:

- Keeping temperature fluctuations to a minimum by using insulated coolers to carry fish
- On long trips reducing oxygen depletion by aerating the water in the coolers
- Minimizing accumulation of pollutants in the transport water with daily water changes from the source stream
- Having the aquarium ready to receive the targets of your collecting trip a couple of weeks before you depart
- Acclimating the fish carefully to their new environment
- Having a source of live foods, at least until your specimens adapt to a diet of prepared foods

The best way to assure the success of a fish-collecting trip is to plan carefully. Have a specific objective in mind, either in terms of the species you want or a particular stream. Advance planning also includes setting up a proper aquarium, ready to receive the fish when you get them home.

Different habitats may call for different collecting methods. Trapping, dip netting, seining, and angling are the most widely used. Each of these may be subject to regulation, depending upon your local laws. Always check with the responsible agency in your state before collecting live fish by any method.

Fish should be transferred as gently as possible from the collecting device to a perforated container that allows water from the surrounding stream to flow through. Once you are ready to travel, move the catch to an insulated picnic cooler containing stream water. Aerate the water in the cooler using a battery-operated air pump, or one that can be plugged into the dashboard of your car. If the fish will be in the cooler for less than an hour and you take care not to crowd specimens together, aeration may not be needed.

Upon arrival home, use plastic bags or plastic food storage containers to scoop the fish out of the cooler. Netting them removes the slime coat and can damage skin. Avoid using the net to reduce the chances of an infection and lessen the fish's stress level. Float the fish in their containers in the aquarium until the temperature is equalized. Presumably, you have prepared the tank with water appropriate to the species you collected. Release your captives into their new home and leave the lights off until the next day, when you should begin offering live food.

Modifications to the Aquarium System

The need for cooler temperatures often complicates the design of aquariums for temperate North American fishes. Coupled with low water turnover, warm temperatures reduce the oxygen available in the aquarium and permit carbon dioxide to build up.

If you undertake to maintain species that require cool water, you have two options. Either air condition the room, or chill the water in the tank. For built-in designs, it may be possible to air condition the closet-like work space behind the tank. For a free-standing tank, it is usually either too costly or too uncomfortable to air condition the entire room, and a chiller becomes the best option. For a large tank, a chiller can cost as much as a new refrigerator. Nevertheless, maintaining some species of darters, for example, usually requires cooling the water. Chiller capacity is rated both by the performance of the unit's compressor and the rate of water flow through its heat exchanger. Rather than attempting the complicated math, follow your dealer's advice regarding the correct chiller for your application.

Providing robust water turnover poses less of a problem than temperature control. Simply install a larger pump. For smaller tanks, this may mean simply choosing a larger hang-on or canister filter. For larger installations, many pump choices exist. Consult your dealer for specific recommendations for your application.

In the model designs that follow, I have chosen species that adapt well to captivity. I indicate those with more exacting requirements where appropriate.

Lazy Rivers

The aquatic habitats of the Southeast region's Atlantic and Gulf coastal plains differ markedly from those of its mountainous interior. Tidal creeks, sluggish streams, canals, rivers, and lakes; Florida, the Gulf Coast, and the southeastern Atlantic coast provide varied and abundant aquatic habitats for fish to exploit. Clear, slowly-moving water with abundant vegetation and a mild climate characterize the preferred habitats of some of our most beautiful native candidates for the home aquarium. From this region we also have a good selection of aquarium plants.

MODEL DESIGN 67 Southeastern U.S. Swamp

Areas that remain flooded for long periods often contain large stands of plants that grow well both in and out of water. Ponds that contain permanent water through the dry season harbor water lilies and related plants. Among their stems and leaves, the blue-spotted sunfish lurks to await its prey.

Aquarium Capacity . . . . 30 gallons

Water Conditions .neutral with moderate hardness

Optimal Temperature . . . . .65–70°F

Plants

   creeping ludwigia (*Ludwigia repens*) . . . . 3 bunches

   dwarf arrowhead (*Sagittaria graminea*). . . 15 individual plants

Other Décor . . . . .driftwood, pebbles

Background . . . . .light green to tan

Substrate . . . . .river sand with some added gravel

Filtration . . . . .hang-on filter

Lighting . . . . .2 fluorescent tubes, for plants

Special Requirements . . . . .none

Fish

   Enneacanthus gloriosus 1 male, or a mated pair

Spangled with neon blue dots over a background of dark gray bars, the blue-spotted sunfish is one of our prettiest native fish. Reaching only about four inches in length, it is both attractive and hardy enough to serve as the perfect introduction to native-fish aquarium keeping.

Start setting up the tank by deciding on which end you want the filter. With the background and equipment in place, create a bi-level planting area by building up the area in front of the filter to a height of four to six inches with the river sand substrate. Working toward the opposite end of the tank, shape the sand into a plateau, then slope down sharply to about one and a half inches in depth. The angle of the slope will depend upon how willing the sand is to remain in place. If necessary, use a driftwood log as a retaining wall. Continue placing the layer of substrate, sloping much more gradually to about an inch in depth when you reach the glass.

Plant the *Sagittaria* on top of the sandy plateau. Here it receives plenty of light by being closer to the surface. Its compact growth will help hide the filter equipment, and it should grow toward the center of the tank, toward the edge of the slope and beyond, its roots holding the sand in place. At the foot of the slope, plant a stand of the *Ludwigia*. Any species will do, if you cannot find the green variety recommended. This plant is found all along the U.S. coast, and the genus reaches Virginia. The tall stems of the *Ludwigia*, together with its dark-green, rounded leaves, contrast well with the brighter green and stiff, squat growth habit of the *Sagittaria*. Separate the bunches of *Ludwigia* stems and space them so the tips of the leaves of adjacent plants barely touch. This should ensure they have room to grow. You will need to prune and thin them periodically, because the plant is vigorous under favorable growth conditions. If you are unwilling to spend the extra money for a two-lamp light fixture, you can substitute plastic.

The blue-spotted sunfish should spend time swimming in the open area of the tank beyond the stand of plants, as well as waiting among the stems for food. Start newly collected specimens with a variety of live foods, such as grass shrimp, mosquito larvae, and small feeder fish. They soon adapt to frozen and prepared foods.

Sunfish comprise the Family Centrarchidae, and are the temperate ecological equivalents of the mostly tropical cichlid family. In the case of *E. gloriosus*, the males become territorial during courtship. If you want to try breeding them, giving the male his choice of several females, a method also used for pairing cichlids, should give the desired results. Remove other fish when you observe that two have paired up. The male will dig a shallow pit in the sand into which the female deposits a clutch of adhesive eggs. After spawning, only the male defends the eggs. He does so with such enthusiasm that removing the female may be the best strategy to prevent her from being damaged. By the time the fry reach the free-swimming stage, the male will have lost interest. As with cichlids, the primary problem in breeding is finding homes for all the resulting offspring. For this reason, you may find keeping a single male makes the most sense.

MODEL DESIGN 68 Southeastern U.S. Pond or Lake

In drainages hugging the coast from New Jersey to Florida and river systems flowing westward into central Georgia, the black-banded sunfish inhabits vegetated lakes, ponds, quiet pools, and backwaters of creeks, and small to medium rivers. Filled with still-water aquatic plants, such habitats lend themselves to duplication in the aquarium.

Aquarium Capacity	30 gallons
Water Conditions	neutral with moderate hardness
Optimal Temperature	60–70°F
Plants	
"banana" plant (*Nymphoides aquatica*)	15 individual plants
American frogsbit (*Limnobium spongia*)	3 clumps
Other Décor	pebbles
Background	(dark green, brown, or black)
Substrate	river sand with some added gravel
Filtration	hang-on filter
Lighting	2 fluorescent tubes, for plants
Special Requirements	peat filtration (optional), lily mud (optional)
Fish	

Enneacanthus chaetodon 1 male, or a mated pair

Peat is suggested for this model design only because it will tint the water a pale yellow-brown, like the water often is in the habitat of *E. chaetodon*. The black-banded sunfish turns up almost anywhere the fish hunter is likely to dip a net, including roadside ditches and canals. Owing to its adaptability over a wide geographic range, the fish tolerates a range of aquarium conditions.

The plants recommended adapt to aquarium conditions as readily as does the black-banded sunfish. For the most vigorous growth and possible blooming, spread a layer of *lily mud* on the bottom of the tank. Bagged, the mixture of clay and fine sand is sold for potting water lilies. You can leave out the mud, but the banana plants (*Nymphoides*), being relatives of the water lily, appreciate its addition. Banana plants are so named because the fleshy roots look like a bunch of bananas. On top of the layer of clay or directly on the bottom of the tank, add a three- to four-inch-deep layer of river sand. It should be more or less level, sloping slightly from the back of the tank toward the front. Here and there as randomly as possible, plant just the tips of the banana plants' roots in the substrate. Bury them only enough to secure them in place. Smaller roots will soon grow to anchor them. The frogbit (*Limnobium*) simply floats on the surface, dangling its fibrous roots into the water. It grows rapidly during the warmer months, sending out short runners at the tips of which rosettes of heart-shaped leaves develop on short, horizontal stems. Before adding it, run the tank for a while with only the banana plants. This allows them to settle in and begin to extend their floating leaves on long stems all the way to the surface. The banana-like clusters of roots and the narrow, round stems form a maze where the sunfish stalks its food. Once the banana plants have several leaves floating on the surface, you can add the frogbit. Thin out the runners regularly to maintain roughly the same number you started with. The surface of the tank should be partially covered with leaves, producing a dappled lighting effect deeper in the water.

With only a slight modification, this model design can show off the interesting flowers of the two plants. Use a forty-five-gallon tank, which has the same footprint as the thirty-gallon suggested above but is twenty-four inches deep. Keep the water level six to eight inches below the top of the tank, providing room for the bloom stems to emerge above the water.

All sunfish feed on whatever small fish and invertebrates they can catch, and will take most living aquarium foods greedily. After they have acclimated to captivity, they will accept frozen foods and small pieces of fish from the grocery store.

Black-banded sunfish can be bred in captivity with ease. Courtship and mating are like that described for *E. gloriosus*.

Do not be alarmed if your banana plants begin to die back after about six months of growth. They pass the winter in a dormant state when the water cools down. Because the sunfish also responds to cold weather with reduced activity and feeding, you could maintain this aquarium in an unheated garage or sunroom. Never place a glass tank, of course, in any location where it might freeze.

MODEL DESIGN 69 Everglades

Here is a small aquarium that can include plants or not. It is intended to invoke the river of grass that extends from Lake Okechobee to the southern tip of Florida, known as the Everglades. However, you could use the same design to display pygmy sunfish from another part of the Southeast.

The Everglades pygmy sunfish is one of six pygmy sunfish species found in the southeastern United States. The pygmy sunfish family, Elassomatidae, was at one time considered to be part of the sunfish family, Centrarchidae, but anatomical differences led ichthyologists to give them a family of their own. Unlike centrarchids, some of which can live many years, the lifespan of pygmy sunfishes is at most only about three years. Nevertheless, they adapt well to a small tank devoted to their particular needs, such as the one described here.

Aquarium Capacity . . . . 20 gallons

Water Conditions .neutral with moderate hardness

Optimal Temperature . . . . .65–70°F

Plants

    none (see text)

        or pondweed (*Potamogeton* species). . . 3 clumps

        or arrowhead (*Sagittaria* species) 5–7

Other Décor . . . . .bamboo canes, plus driftwood or a few smooth rocks

Background . . . . .light green to tan

Substrate . . . . .fine river sand with some added gravel

Filtration . . . . .hang-on filter

Lighting . . . . .2 fluorescent tubes, for plants if used

Special Requirements . . . . .none

Fish

Elassoma evergladei 1 or 2 males, 2 or 3 females

As we have done with other designs, for this one we will cut several lengths of bamboo canes and stick them in the substrate to mimic a stand of reedy plants emerging from the water. If you use plenty of bamboo, you need not add additional plants, but live water moss (*Fontinalis*), pondweeds (*Potamogeton*), or arrowhead (*Sagittaria*) will be at home in this aquarium. Both the fish and plants will benefit from a cool period in the winter, when the water temperature can be allowed to drop into the 40s. Over one hundred species of pondweeds live in North and Central America. You can probably collect some cuttings along with the pygmy sunfish. Given cool water, they will adapt well to the aquarium in strong light, though like many temperate plants they require a winter rest. One variety that grows near my home in Tennessee has transparent green leaves that grow in a spiral shape, arranged in rosettes around the stem. It looks quite beautiful in the aquarium, but will not live with continuous warmth.

It is possible to keep two pairs in the same tank. Use some large rocks or a piece or two of driftwood to divide the tank roughly in half, so each male can set up his territory. After an elaborate mating ritual, he and his mate will lay eggs among plants on their side of the fence, and guard the clutch. If you use plants in this model design, confine the bamboo to the back wall of the tank, and locate a stand of arrowhead or pondweed on each end, leaving an open area in the middle. If you opt for a single pair, with a planted tank to themselves, you should have no trouble observing their spawning behavior, which takes place during early spring.

A larger and longer-lived species than *E. evergladei* is *E. zonatum*, the banded pygmy sunfish. It occurs from North Carolina south and west all the way to Texas, and up the Mississippi River Valley as far as Illinois. It is therefore accessible to many more collectors than its more restricted cousin. It lives about three years, compared to half that for *E. evergladei*, and reaches two inches in length, a giant among its family. All members of the pygmy sunfish family feed on insects, worms, and crustaceans and need live foods. From the aquarist's point of view, they are much like tropical killifish, being small, short-lived, and often finicky.

The idea of duplicating a man-made environment in the aquarium struck me as pointless until I saw the huge tank representing Nickajack Reservoir at the Tennessee Aquarium in Chattanooga.

Aquarium Capacity . . . . 50–90 gallons

Water Conditions .neutral with moderate hardness

Optimal Temperature . . . . .65–70°F

Plants

  none (see text)

Other Décor . . . . .driftwood, rocks, and pebbles

Background . . . . .light gray or blue

Substrate . . . . .river sand with some added gravel

Filtration . . . . .canister filter

Lighting . . . . .1 fluorescent tube

Special Requirements . . . . .none

Fish

  Lepomis, any species 1 male

This model design has much in common with a big cichlid tank. Sunfish, with several species found throughout the eastern United States, are scrappy, grow large, and eat anything. They also tolerate any reasonable set of water conditions. They are excellent candidates, therefore, for a big tank with one big fish.

Farm ponds sometimes are built by damming a small creek. Barren of plants except at the edges, a broad expanse of still water with a bit of through-flow from the creek makes the perfect place for many sunfish to thrive. Indeed, they are often stocked in large ponds to provide forage for game fish, such as largemouth bass, also stocked by the farmer. Reservoirs constructed by damming a river usually fill up a canyon cut when the river was free-flowing. Like the pond derived from a creek, the shores of the reservoir will be a jumble of rocks and snags derived from inundated trees. Irregular pieces of sandstone or slate, together with chunks of driftwood, can be used to simulate this man-made environment on a small scale.

Arrange slab rocks in layers to mimic strata, placing them along one end of the tank. Choose pieces that do not quite reach the front glass. By building up a stack across one corner of the aquarium, you suggest to the viewer they are looking along a line parallel to the rugged shore. It is not necessary that this rock formation reach the surface. Making a stack that tall might be too much weight for the tank. Top off the stack with a larger slab placed like a table top to separate the tank into two zones, shallow and deep. Rock strata sometimes form this kind of stairstep structure beneath the surface of a dammed-up river. Cover the bottom of the tank with a shallow layer of river sand, mixed with pebbles of varying sizes. Install a large canister filter that will create plenty of water movement and trap the debris resulting from the fish's big appetite.

For sunfish species, you have plenty of choices. The redbreast, *Lepomis auritus*, usually hunts alone and likes moving water. It grows to nearly a foot in length, and is found all along the Atlantic coast from Maine to Florida. The green sunfish, *L. cyanellus*, inhabits the Mississippi Valley. Widely introduced outside its natural range, this is one of the most durable species of freshwater fish and can be recommended to any beginning native fish enthusiast. It gets about a foot long, as does the warmouth, *L. gulosus*, which is found throughout the central and southern United States. Smaller, and arguably much more attractive than any other *Lepomis*, is *L. megalotis*. Its range includes Quebec and extends through the central portion of the United States, southwestward to Texas. It does not naturally occur east of the Appalachians, but it has been introduced far and wide. The body of this sunfish is deep orange, overlain with spots, lines, and squiggles in brilliant sky blue. The elongated gill cover, the fish's *long ear* is blue with a double outline, first jet black, then enamel white. It lives among snags or aquatic vegetation, where it lies in ambush for various invertebrates and smaller fishes. It is a popular sport fish and puts up quite a fight when hooked. Catching it with a barbless hook is one way to collect a specimen for the aquarium.

If you choose, you could elaborate this tank into a paludarium. Use a ninety-gallon tank to give you more height to work with. Build up the rock structure in one corner as just described, but hide a large plastic pot behind it. Fill the pot with a mixture of coarse sand and peat with a little added clay. Use any variety of *Sagittaria* in the pot. Grassleaf arrowhead, *S. graminea*, is recommended here because it stays relatively small. You could also plant *S. latifolia*, the duck potato, or *S. australis*, southern arrowhead. Both reach up to a meter in height, so plan accordingly. If you only fill the tank halfway, either of the larger arrowheads will grow out the top. This may be desirable, however, as their glossy, tropical-looking foliage is attractive.

An alternative planting for this tank would be dwarf cattail, *Typha minima*. It is native to Europe and Asia, and is widely sold for garden ponds. Reaching only two feet in height, it produces the familiar strap-like foliage and cylindrical flower spikes so characteristic of pond margins. Cattails grow naturally in mud, and should be potted in bagged water-lily growing medium for use in the paludarium. Keep the water level just at the soil line in the container, around a foot.

Give both the longear sunfish and the arrowhead or cattail plants a cool winter rest. One aquarist of my acquaintance used to build his sunfish aquarium in the spring, stocking it with both fish and plants from his own farm pond. The tank served as an eye-catching decoration for his roadside produce market during warm weather, and the fish and plants were returned to the pond by autumn.

MODEL DESIGN 71 Southeastern U.S. Spring Run

All over the southeastern coastal plain, clear spring water erupts from underground and forms creeks or *runs* that carry it, eventually, to the sea. Spring runs and other moving, well-oxygenated waters are populated by shiners, many of which make hardy and attractive aquarium fish.

Aquarium Capacity . . . . 30 gallons

Water Conditions .neutral with moderate hardness

Optimal Temperature . . . . .65–70°F

Plants

    creeping ludwigia (*Ludwigia repens*) . . . . 5 bunches

Other Décor . . . . .driftwood, water-worn rocks, pebbles

Background . . . . .dark brown or green

Substrate . . . . .river sand with some added gravel

Filtration . . . . .hang-on filter

Lighting . . . . .1 fluorescent tube

Special Requirements . . . . .none

Fish

    Pteronotropis, any species 5–7

The genus *Pteronotropis* contains some of the most colorful of our native cyprinids. Males of *P. hubbsi*, the bluehead shiner, and *P. welaka*, the bluenosed shiner, sport metallic blue coloration during the breeding season. These and the related sailfin shiner, *P. hypselopterus*, and flagfin shiner, *P. signipinnis*, adapt well to the aquarium. The genus name prefix, *ptero*, or *wing*, makes reference to the enlarged dorsal and anal fins which add to the appeal of the group. These fish are restricted to the Southeast.

A simple aquarium design with a curtain of *Ludwigia* across the back shows off the impressive finnage and coloration of these fish. Place two inches of river sand in the tank, sloping it gently from back to front. Plant individual stems of *Ludwigia* randomly, beginning near the back glass and extending in a band about four inches forward. Scatter a few pebbles on the surface of the sand near the front to add interest and reinforce the deception that the viewer is looking from the middle of the run toward its vegetated bank. You could also add a piece of driftwood, but take care to keep the overall design simple in this small tank.

Feeding *Pteronotropis* poses no challenge, as they readily take a variety of foods. As with any native fish, starting them off with live food is a good idea. Blackworms, mosquito larvae, and *Daphnia* make a good combination. Gradually shift the bulk of the diet to prepared and frozen foods.

MODEL DESIGN 72 Tidal Creek

From Maine, all along the eastern coast, down and around the Florida peninsula and along the gulf shore to Texas, the sheepshead minnow inhabits tidal creeks. Scarcely have I gone out with a seine along the Atlantic or Gulf without catching several of these pupfish.

Aquarium Capacity . . . . 30 gallons

Water Conditions . . . . .hard, alkaline, and brackish

Optimal Temperature . . . . .65–70°F

Plants

    dwarf arrowhead (*Sagittaria graminea*) . . 15 individual plants

    crystalworts (*Nitella, Chara*) . . . . (see text)

    mangrove (*Rhizophora mangle*) (optional, see text)

Other Décor . . . . .sandstone, smooth pebbles, broken seashells

Background . . . . .light green to tan

Substrate . . . . .river sand with some added shell fragments

Filtration . . . . .hang-on filter

Lighting . . . . .2 fluorescent tubes, for plants

Special Requirements . . . . .none

Fish

    Cyprinodon variegatus 1 male, 3–5 females

Pupfish are close relatives of the killifish and share with them not only bright color patterns but also a tendency for the males to be pugnacious toward potential competitors. Reaching about three inches in length, the males become iridescent blue during the breeding season. Females are olive. Both sexes have darker bars on the sides and yellow bellies. Non-breeding males can be recognized by the black edging on the tail fin.

Cyprinodon species in general are among the most tolerant fishes known. The sheepshead lives quite well when trapped in a muddy pool by the receding tide. Water temperature in the pool can climb into the 90s, causing evaporation and a dramatic rise in salinity. Unperturbed, the sheepshead continues feeding on the mosquito larvae and algae trapped with it in the pool. When the tide returns to inundate the pool, the fish can move about freely again.

Needless to say, the sheepshead is a tough cookie in the aquarium. It does, however, tend to harass tank mates, and should be maintained in a single-species tank. Males will not tolerate each other, and only females ready to breed are accepted by the male during the breeding season.

A tank for the sheepshead minnow can be decorated with sandstone alone to provide vertical relief, or you can plant the sandy substrate with arrowhead (*Sagittaria*) and reduce the amount of salt in the water. The fish tolerates pure fresh water as well as seawater up to several times ocean salinity.

In addition to arrowhead, coastal waters are often home to a remarkable group of algae, the Characeae. Their brittle stems are reinforced with mineral salts extracted from the water. One genus, *Chara*, resembles the familiar hornwort (*Ceratophyllum*). A tolerant species widely sold for the aquarium is *Nitella*. It resembles a moss. These large algae grow well in cool, brackish water and make good additions to any tidal creek tank design.

MODEL DESIGN 73 Rally Round the Flagfish

A relative of the wide-ranging sheepshead minnow, the flagfish is restricted to the Florida peninsula. It has long been available, and in my view underappreciated, in the aquarium trade.

Aquarium Capacity . . . . 20 gallons

Water Conditions . . . . neutral, moderately hard

Optimal Temperature . . . . .65–70°F

Plants

    giant bacopa (*Bacopa caroliniana*) . . . . . 3 bunches

        or green cabomba (*Cabomba caroliniana*) . . . . 3 bunches

        or creeping ludwigia (*Ludwigia repens*) . . . . 3 bunches

    crystalwort (*Nitella flexilis*). . . . . 1 clump

    dwarf arrowhead (*Sagittaria graminea*). . . 5 individual plants

Other Décor . . . . .pebbles or worn seashell fragments

Background . . . . .dark green, brown, or black

Substrate . . . . .river sand with some added gravel

Filtration . . . . .hang-on filter

Lighting . . . . .2 fluorescent tubes, for plants

Special Requirements . . . . .none

Fish

    Jordanella floridae 1 male, several females

Ideal in a small tank, the Florida flagfish only reaches a length of two to three inches. It offers no special challenges to the aquarist, adapting well to a range of water conditions. It is found in quiet, shallow water in lakes, ponds, and ditches in Florida from about Gainesville south. Its preferred haunts usually bear abundant vegetation. Keeping them in a heavily planted tank allows the females to seek shelter from the male, who may become aggressive during the breeding season from April to August. Spawning takes place either in a pit in the sand or over a mat of plants. In the aquarium, *Nitella* makes an ideal spawning substrate. The pugnacious male remains with the clutch of eggs, guarding them against all comers until the fry become free-swimming.

This aquarium can be planted with any of the commonly available bunched plants that will grow in cool water. Though the flagfish may sometimes enter brackish streams, for the benefit of the plants leave out the salt when setting up this design. Choose only one type of bunch plant to cover the back of the tank, planting the individual stems in a random pattern to create a leafy curtain. Group the arrowheads (*Sagittaria*) at one end of the tank, leaving the other end open for swimming. Place some pebbles or shell fragments around the bases of the arrowheads, and scatter a few on the sand. Aquarists who wish to avoid live plants can use plastic substitutes in this display.

The common name for *Jordanella, flagfish,* refers to the supposed resemblance of the color pattern to the American flag. Near the top of the head behind the eye, males have a patch of dark turquoise that becomes light blue along the base of the dorsal fin. Below this region, the pale olive body color is overlain by cherry-red stripes. Viewed in bright light, the iridescent color pattern can be seen as a convincingly rendered image of the Stars and Stripes.

MODEL DESIGN 74 Primitive Fishes

Approximately where the Mississippi rolls lazily past Memphis on its eternal trek to the Gulf of Mexico, in small, sluggish tributaries and in the Big Muddy itself, one finds representatives of four primitive freshwater fish groups. Few places on earth can offer up so many examples of these ancient groups living in such close proximity. Two of them, more demanding in their needs, should be left to the professionals at public aquariums. The Mississippi paddlefish (*Polyodon*) grows to over six feet. It is the sole North American representative of its primitive family, Polyodontidae, with a single related species found in China. It feeds by swimming with its huge mouth held open, straining planktonic invertebrates from the water. Sturgeons, such as the shovelnose sturgeon (*Schaphirynchus*), comprise another primitive family, Acipenseridae, closely related to the paddlefish. Most of them reach huge size and consume enormous quantities of mollusks and crustaceans that they seek on sandy and muddy bottoms of large to medium rivers.

The two primitive fish that are suitable for a large home tank, the bowfin (*Amia*) and spotted gar (*Lepisosteus*), both inhabit sluggish to stagnant backwaters with plenty of plants.

Aquarium Capacity . . . . 150 gallons

Water Conditions . . . . .neutral with moderate hardness

Optimal Temperature . . . . .65–70°F

Plants

      giant bacopa (*Bacopa caroliniana*) . . . . . 7–15 bunches

      green cabomba (*Cabomba caroliniana*). . . 7–15 bunches

      creeping ludwigia (*Ludwigia repens*) . . . . 7–15 bunches

      common water lily (*Nymphaea* species). . . 1 plant

      dwarf arrowhead (*Sagittaria graminea*). . . 15 individual plants

Other Décor . . . . .driftwood, roots

Background . . . . .medium brown to black

Substrate . . . . .river sand with some added gravel

Filtration . . . . .sump-type filter

Lighting . . . . .2 150-watt metal halide lamps, for plants

Special Requirements . . . . .see text

Fish

      Amia calva 1

      Lepisosteus oculatus 3

These two can be exhibited together if the individuals are approximately the same size when placed in the aquarium. The bowfin (*Amia*) and the spotted gar (*Lepisosteus*) both feed exclusively by predation and both sport a mouthful of sharp teeth, so there is no guarantee they will not look upon a tank mate as dinner. Either can deliver a serious bite to the aquarist, also. Gars will tolerate each other well, but the bowfin is territorial and aggressive, although not inclined to bother fish not of its own species.

If you can find an unusually large piece of driftwood that looks attractive, use it for a focal point in this aquarium. Plant the rootstock of the water lily (*Nymphaea*) a short distance to one side of the center of the tank. Its exact placement will depend on the shape of the big piece of driftwood. Aim for the eye-catching effect of the lily's stem twining upward through the branches of the driftwood.

A word about water lilies: Look for dwarf, tropical varieties sold in garden pond specialty shops and through catalogs. Standard water lilies grow much too large even for an aquarium of the size recommended here, with a footprint of six by one and one half feet. The tropical varieties will be just fine if you keep the aquarium cool to cold during the winter months and allow it to warm up with the change of seasons. An unheated sunporch would provide the ideal location for this large, impressive display, or indeed any aquarium based on the habitats of the Southeast.

Arrange the bunch plants in stands of one species, placing the stand of fine-leaved *Cabomba* where it will receive the most light and the round-leaved *Bacopa* and *Ludwigia* toward the ends and back of the tank.

Topminnows

North America has its share of killifish relatives, and like their exotic counterparts many make fine aquarium fish. They remain small, tolerate low levels of water movement, and are often brightly colored. The thirty-plus North American species all belong to Family Fundulidae, commonly called *topminnows* instead of killifish. Although they range north all the way to Newfoundland, the best topminnows for the aquarium are those from the southeastern coastal plain and the Mississippi Valley.

MODEL DESIGN 75 Golden Topminnow Species Tank

I will never forget the first time I saw this fish. It was during a field trip to Reelfoot Lake in northwestern Tennessee. The lake has an interesting history. It was formed as a result of the great New Madrid earthquake early in the nineteenth century. The land subsided and the Mississippi River ran backward, filling the lake. To a modern observer, placid Reelfoot, dotted with cypress trees and emergent plants, gives no hint of its violent birth. Along with millions of gallons of water, the Mississippi brought to Reelfoot the ancestors of the golden topminnows found there today.

Aquarium Capacity . . . . 20 gallons

Water Conditions .neutral with moderate hardness

Optimal Temperature . . . . .65–70°F

Plants

    dwarf ludwigia (*Ludwigia repens*) . . . . . . 5 bunches

        or green cabomba (*Cabomba caroliniana*) . . . . 5 bunches

    dwarf arrowhead (*Sagittaria graminea*). . . 5 individual plants

Other Décor . . . . .cypress knees (see text)

Background . . . . .light green or blue

Substrate . . . . .coarse river sand with some added gravel

Filtration . . . . .hang-on filter

Lighting . . . . .2 fluorescent tubes, for plants

Special Requirements . . . . .none

Fish

    Fundulus chrysotus 2 males, 3 to 5 females

Fundulus chrysotus was a popular aquarium fish in the early days of home aquariums. As it is content at normal indoor temperatures and sluggish water, it could be kept without much equipment beyond the tank itself. Once heaters, pumps, and the other accoutrements of modern aquarium keeping made it easy to maintain the exotic tropical species, native fish such as this one lost much of their appeal.

So beautiful a fish deserves to be rediscovered by aquarium enthusiasts. It has the typical elongate body of the cyprinodont clan, with the rounded dorsal and anal fins set well back from the head. One notable feature is the unusually large eye, half the width of the head. Males and females carry the same pale bluish-green background scales. In the male, the tail, dorsal, and anal fins, and the dorsal body surface are a brassy, golden color that intensifies during the breeding season. The rear third of the body is decorated with brilliant red dots, as if the fish had been spattered with paint. Females tend toward pale greenish blue, with a few golden highlights here and there, and a scattering of red dots similar to those of the male but less distinct. Both sexes grow to about three inches.

Set up a tank for the golden topminnow that reflects a quiet Reelfoot Lake backwater area. Locate the filter on one end of the tank, hanging from the back glass. Obscure the view of the filter with a cypress knee. This is a structure produced from the roots of the tree, which often grows partially submerged in swamps and marshy areas at the edges of lakes. Sticking up above the surface, the knee absorbs atmospheric oxygen, a task the roots are unable to perform when waterlogged. Cypress wood is extremely durable and will not rot in the aquarium. You may find cypress knees offered for sale in souvenir shops on the Gulf Coast. Stripped of its bark and sanded smooth, the wood is very decorative. For aquarium purposes, cypress could be called instant driftwood. If you cannot find a piece of cypress, select a chunk of driftwood that convincingly resembles a stump, and place it in the aquarium. Behind the cypress or driftwood and along the back and far end of the aquarium, distribute the stems of the bunched plants to form a lush curtain of growth. Group the arrowheads (*Sagittaria*) near the end opposite the wood. Avoid placing them in a spot exactly corresponding to the wood's position, or the resulting look will be too symmetrical and formal. As with any heavily planted aquarium, if possible allow the plants to become established for a month to six weeks before you begin introducing fish.

The golden topminnows relish all types of small live foods, including mosquito larvae, blackworms, *Daphnia,* and brine shrimp. They readily adapt to frozen and prepared aquarium foods.

Another fish found in Reelfoot Lake deserves mention. The banded pygmy sunfish, *Elassoma zonatum*, is a handsome species that lives among heavy vegetation in lakes, swamps, and sluggish streams from southern Illinois down the Mississippi to the Gulf and across to the Atlantic Coast as far north as North Carolina. Patterned in black dots on a white body, it remains under two inches in length and could be maintained in the same tank with *Fundulus chrysotus*. Males have been observed defending territories among plants, and displaying to females by bobbing up and down and signaling with fins held erect. This fish feeds on many types of foods and adapts well to aquarium life.

Here is another small, colorful species of *Fundulus* that readily adapts to aquarium life.

Aquarium Capacity . . . . 45 gallons

Water Conditions . . . . .neutral with moderate hardness

Optimal Temperature . . . . .65–70°F

Plants

    creeping ludwigia (*Ludwigia repens*) . . . . 3 bunches

    common water lily (*Nymphaea* variety). . . 1 (see text)

    dwarf arrowhead (*Sagittaria graminea*). . . 5 individual plants

Other Décor . . . . .none

Background .light green to tan

Substrate . . . . .river sand with some added gravel

Filtration . . . . .hang-on filter

Lighting . . . . .2 fluorescent tubes, for plants

Special Requirements . . . . .none

Fish

    Fundulus notatus 7–12

      Or *Fundulus olivaceus* 7–12

This model design employs a tall tank to facilitate observing the fish from below. As one might infer from the common name, *topminnow*, *Fundulus* tend to remain near the surface. Both species suggested above are olive green on the back and pale on the belly, with a dark longitudinal stripe. *Fundulus notatus* has more numerous and darker black dots on the back, and lives primarily in slackwater areas, while *Fundulus olivaceus* is less strikingly patterned and favors more water movement.

Although aquarium setup and care for either of these fish is quite similar, my personal favorite is the black-spotted topminnow, for its interesting feeding strategy. The top of the head bears a light-colored, reflective patch of scales. When the fish congregate at the water surface, it is hypothesized that sunlight reflecting from these spots creates a sparkling light show that attracts insects. The fish are quick to grab hapless insects that may fall into the water. Because of their effectiveness in controlling mosquito larvae, either of these topminnows is a good choice for summering outdoors in a garden pond. You can net out a few individuals in late fall to stock the aquarium for indoor enjoyment during the winter.

If you want to include a water lily in this aquarium, try to locate a tropical dwarf variety. Most garden pond water lily varieties grow far too large to accommodate in the aquarium, at least for long. Position your selection as the centerpiece of the tank. If you want to try for flowers, keep the water level about four inches below the rim of the aquarium. A good substitute for a water lily is the closely related banana plant, *Nymphoides aquatica*. Plant just the tips of the bananas in the substrate, and the plant should readily grow, floating surface leaves on long stems.

Frame the water lily or banana plant with *Ludwigia* on both sides and toward the back, leaving the front of the tank open. To produce a sense of enclosure of this underwater scene, plant a grouping of all the *Sagittaria* near either the left or right side.

If you place this tank on a stand of normal height (about thirty-two inches) it will look especially good when viewed from a seated position. You will see light passing through the mottled, translucent leaves of the water lily, and the darting and hovering movements of the topminnows. Carry out weekly partial water changes on this tank, and feed the topminnows with floating prepared foods as well as regular supplements of mosquito larvae, fruit flies, or blackworms. These fish will live around three years. If you keep some outdoors as suggested above, they will breed readily and keep you continuously supplied.

MODEL DESIGN 77 Bluefin Topminnow

Our coverage of tank designs for North American killifish ends with another species common in Florida and along the Gulf Coast. *Lucania goodei*, the bluefin topminnow, inhabits the weedy margins of lakes, ponds, and streams. It shows a marked preference for the clear, cool waters of spring runs. A diminutive native killifish that adapts well to captivity, the bluefin topminnow is also one of the most beautiful species.

Aquarium Capacity . . . . 20 gallons

Water Conditions .slightly acidic with moderate hardness

Optimal Temperature . . . . .50–70°F (see text)

Plants

    dwarf bacopa (*Bacopa* monnieri). . . . . . . 5 bunches

       or creeping ludwigia (*Ludwigia repens*) . . . . 5 bunches

    Java moss (*Vesicularia dubyana*) . . . . 1 clump (see text)

    floating fern (*Salvinia auriculata*) . . . . 1 clump

       or duckweed (*Lemna minor*) . . . . 1 clump

Other Décor . . . . .roots

Background . . . . .dark brown

Substrate . . . . .river sand with some added gravel

Filtration . . . . .hang-on filter

Lighting . . . . .2 fluorescent tubes, for plants

Special Requirements . . . . .none

Fish

    Lucania goodei 5–7

Cover the bottom of the aquarium with a uniform two-inch-deep layer of river sand. Embed the base of a tangled tree root or a piece of driftwood on one end of the tank toward the rear. Secure some strands of *Vesicularia* to the wood or root, using monofilament fishing line. Separate the bunched plants into individual stems and plant them in randomly placed groups of three to five stems spaced about an inch apart. Add the floating plants to create dappled light. Remember that they will need to be thinned frequently to avoid obstructing the light too much and depriving the rooted plants below.

The bluefin topminnow requires cool temperatures to thrive, as might be deduced from its preference for cool spring runs. During the summer, a comfortable 70 degrees F in an air conditioned room should be about right. In the winter, these fish need cooler temperatures, around 50–55 degrees F. Installing an aquarium chiller may be the best option for achieving control of the temperature. With its steel-gray body, black midline, and diamond-shaped scale pattern on the back, this fish would command attention even if it were not also brightly colored. The base of the tail fin bears a splash of blood-red pigment. The large, rounded dorsal and anal fins are outlined in black, which surrounds broad patches of cerulean blue. Patches of red-orange on the fins call further attention to the male during his elaborate courtship display.

Bluefin topminnows feed enthusiastically on many types of live foods, but are especially fond of mosquito larvae. They also take frozen and flake foods.

Inland Waters

Moving inland from the coastal plain brings changes in the kinds of aquatic habitats we encounter. New habitats and new species give us some additional options for aquarium designs.

MODEL DESIGN 78   Texas Cichlid

Head west into Texas from the Mississippi River delta region until you reach the Rio Grande, and you will encounter the habitat of the Texas cichlid. This species is the only native representative of its family found in the United States, though other cichlids have been introduced from elsewhere.

This model design would work well in a setting where high visual impact and low maintenance are priorities, such as in an office or waiting area.

Aquarium Capacity . . . . 55 gallons

Water Conditions . . . . .neutral with moderate hardness

Optimal Temperature . . . . .68–70°F

Plants

Other Décor . . . . .roots, large rocks, pebbles

Background . . . . .deep green, brown, or black

Substrate . . . . .river gravel

Filtration . . . . .canister filter

Lighting . . . . .1 fluorescent tube

Special Requirements . . . . .none

Fish

    Cichlasoma cyanoguttatum 1 male, or a mated pair

This cichlid requires a simple tank design because, while it is typically found in sluggish, heavily vegetated waters, in the aquarium it will uproot plants and generally make a mess of things. It also appreciates water movement.

Arrange rocks and roots along the back glass and at one end of the aquarium, to suggest a pool in a nook at the edge of a stream. Start by positioning a large root or other piece of driftwood on one end of the tank. A piece large enough to protrude slightly above the water surface would be ideal. Decide on which end to install the filter return, and position the wood where it will hide the hose. Direct the return stream onto the wood near the water surface to create turbulence. You should see some air bubbles from the surface agitation. Group some rocks at the base of the driftwood, and place pebbles here and there on the gravel. Along the back of the tank, arrange more rocks, forming a backdrop for the fish. Try to find dark-colored rocks to make a backdrop for the bright turquoise-blue dot pattern that decorates the Texas cichlid's body.

Easily reaching ten inches in length in the aquarium, the Texas cichlid, like so many of its relatives, is best as a single large specimen in a tank by itself. Feeding readily on all types of aquarium foods, the fish grows rapidly. It is intolerant of tank mates, though a mated pair can be maintained in a large aquarium. It may dig in the gravel for no apparent reason, like other large cichlids. This actually helps to prevent the accumulation of debris, although it may frustrate your efforts to maintain a tidy look to the tank. With regular partial water changes and filter maintenance to keep the tank clear and clean, the Texas cichlid will live for years, making few other demands.

For longer than twenty years, a certain big riffle in the Little River, Blount County, Tennessee, has served to introduce beginning ichthyology students and interested onlookers to the diversity of freshwater species in the Tennessee River drainage system. I have many fond memories of that riffle, wading in the chilly water, either helping to tow a seine or doing the shuffle-and-kick step march we performed to dislodge rocks and drive fish from their hiding places toward the nets waiting downstream.

With a large, well-model designed aquarium, it is possible to duplicate one of North America's most interesting aquatic biotopes, the fast-running water of a clear, rocky stream. While the shiners, dace, and darters are not for beginning aquarists, they will reward a dedicated and careful enthusiast with engaging behavior and coloration seldom seen on cold-water fish.

I have chosen the Little River as an inspiration for a design that can be used to exhibit a number of fishes native to the central South and Mississippi Valley. Several good reasons can be cited for using the Little River as an archetype for a native stream biotope tank. The Little River is the largest watershed in the Smoky Mountains, its headwaters arising on the slopes of Clingman's Dome, the highest peak in Great Smoky Mountains National Park. Flowing northwest across the park boundary into Blount County, it joins the French Broad River near Maryville, Tennessee. Unlike most other rivers in the Tennessee system, the Little has escaped being dammed. Free-running and fed by dozens of mountain tributaries, it is home to over forty species of fish. Large riffles, which are accumulations of rocks and boulders where water movement is brisk, can sometimes yield up a dozen species in a single pass of the seine.

The tank I have suggested for this model design could of course be scaled down considerably. You could keep a broadly representative selection of North American stream fishes in this tank, however, and it would be a sensational design feature for a vacation home in the mountains.

Aquarium Capacity . . . . 180 gallons

Water Conditions . . . . .neutral with moderate hardness

Optimal Temperature . . . . .50–70°F

Plants

    none

Other Décor . . . . .large to medium water-worn rocks, pebbles

Background . . . . .deep green, brown, or black

Substrate . . . . .river gravel and coarse sand

Filtration . . . . .sump-type filter

Lighting . . . . .1 fluorescent tube or metal halide

Special Requirements . . . . .none

Fish

    (see text)

Install a pump that will provide three to five times the tank volume per hour in flow rate. Also install a chiller with sufficient cooling capacity to keep the aquarium in the correct temperature range.

The aquascape for this aquarium is quite simple; on one end of the tank lies a deep pool with a sandy bottom. Dividing the pool from the rest of the tank is a row of large to medium rocks, lying between the front and back glass panels. Build up with larger rocks to about eight inches in height before adding a one-inch layer of sand on either side of the riffle. The arrangement will look more natural if the riffle is to one side or the other of the tank's center. You can make the depth appear somewhat greater by angling the row of rocks back slightly, rather than keeping it perpendicular to the back glass. This gives the viewer the impression of looking toward the riffle from a short distance out in the stream. Finish the rocky biotope by spreading one to two inches of gravel on top of the sand on the downstream side of the riffle, opposite the pool. The substrate for this area should be of varied sizes, ranging from gravel about $\frac{1}{16}$ inch in diameter up to pebbles the size of a walnut.

The return pipe from the filter system should dump into the pool end of the tank. Aim the flow of water just under the surface and in the direction of the riffle to create the maximum amount of turbulence. The more tightly directed the flow, the more turbulence you will get. You should see plenty of bubbles of entrapped air.

Other than filamentous algae, the only vegetation likely to be found in a stream habitat such as this are sturdy emergent plants such as river cane and water willow. You could simulate their presence by inserting thin bamboo canes toward the rear of the tank and allowing them to extend above the surface. This technique has been used in other designs to suggest the stream bank. The actual native plants grow too large for use in this display. They also need a period of cold dormancy in the winter. You could also omit any reference to emergent plants from the design, without sacrificing any of its authenticity. If you absolutely require a touch of green, the water moss, *Vesicularia*, widely available for aquariums, can be tucked here and there between the rocks. You may also be able to locate *Fontinalis*, or a similar cold-water species of moss. Sometimes a collecting trip for fish will also turn up a mossy rock that can be placed in the tank.

This aquarium can be populated with a community of fish taken from any number of locations in the greater Mississippi Valley region. Several freshwater stream fish are protected by state and federal laws, so be certain of both your identification and local regulations before you collect. The following examples I have chosen all can be found in the Little River itself, and I have listed some other good species that could be included, depending upon where you choose to go collecting.

- Perhaps the most widespread species in all the streams of the region, the central stoneroller, *Campostoma anomalum*, is found throughout the eastern and central United States and adapts well to an aquarium with cool, moving water. It can reach about a foot but is commonly caught at a much smaller size. Stonerollers are the functional equivalent of tropical algae-eating cyprinids, such as *Epalzeorhynchus* (see page 82). While snorkeling, I have often observed them in a large school busily scouring the rocks at the very base of the riffle, where it seemed impossible they could swim against the surging current. They use their underslung mouth to scrape algae, detritus, diatoms, and anything that becomes entangled in the algal mat, from rock surfaces and the stream bottom. Half a dozen stonerollers would make a good scavenging team for the aquarium.

● Tropical aquarists usually think of catfishes as the main bottom-dwelling species to include as scavengers, but our most common native catfishes all grow too large to be trusted with smaller, more colorful species. One group, the madtoms, usually grow to less than five inches in length, and so are suitable aquarium subjects. As a rule, madtoms are secretive, and many are quite rare. The most widespread species is the brindled madtom, *Noturus miurus*, a yellowish-tan species with black blotches that lives in silty pools from the southern Great Lakes region all the way to Louisiana. Madtoms are opportunistic feeders and will take a variety of worms, crustaceans, and fish fry, typically under cover of darkness. They are cave spawners, and presumably spend the daylight hours hiding in crevices and under rocks. Madtoms are considered difficult to collect because of their habit of hiding during the day; if you do happen to acquire a specimen, though, they will adapt to aquarium life well provided the water does not get too warm.

● Another bottom-dwelling group that adapts to captivity without too much trouble is the sculpins, Family Cottidae. In the Little River, the mottled sculpin, *Cottus bairdi*, is a likely catch. Other cottids can be found throughout North America in marine, brackish, and freshwater habitats. The approximately twenty-five freshwater sculpins have large heads and capacious mouths with plenty of tiny teeth. They lack a swim bladder, and have generally flattened bodies with wing-like pectoral fins. These anatomical features ideally suit them for a life on the bottom, where their cryptic, earth-tone coloration keeps them hidden from both predators and potential prey. They lie in wait, facing upstream. The water rushing past assists them in remaining stationary on the bottom and carries with it the potential meal. Sculpins can swallow prey approaching the size of the sculpin itself. Like the bottom-dwelling madtoms, they are cave spawners, nesting under slab rocks with the eggs being guarded by the male. They are durable and interesting aquarium fish, though not brightly colored. Owing to their predatory habits, sculpins cannot be included in tanks with fish small enough for them to eat.

● For bright coloration, we must seek out aquarium specimens from the carp (cyprinids) and perch (percinids) clans. Among the most abundant fishes in our native streams, cyprinids can be well-represented in your aquarium. One attractive and hardy choice is *Luxilus coccogenis*, the warpaint shiner. They grow to just over four inches in length and live about five years. Breeding males have shiny silver scales and wear warpaint. The lips are orange-red, and a bar of the same color marks the gill cover behind the eye. A red blotch also colors the forward portion of the dorsal fin. The dorsal also has a prominent black blotch, and traces of orange and black appear on the tail. This and other species of shiners are a common sight in cool, clear streams with rocky bottoms. They feed opportunistically. I have been followed by warpaint shiners while snorkeling. They were feeding greedily on insects and other invertebrates stirred up by my movements along the stream bottom. Many shiners, including *L. coccogenis*, use nests built by other, larger cyprinids for spawning. Presumably, the eggs and fry of the nest borrowers benefit from the attention paid by the actual builder of the nest. A common nest host is *Nocomis micropogon*, the creek chub.

- Redbelly dace, comprising the genus *Phoxinus*, provide some of the most brilliant coloration you'll find in coldwater stream fish. The southern redbelly dace, *P. erythrogaster*, does not occur in the Little River, but would feel right at home in the tank in this design. It reaches about three inches in length, and lives three years, much like many tropical cyprinids. It is found from western Pennsylvania to the Great Plains, in spring runs and smaller streams with cool, clear water over rocks. A close relative, the northern redbelly dace, *P. eos*, is smaller, and occurs in bog ponds as well as small streams and brooks. In the Little River drainage, the uncommon Tennessee dace, *P. tennessensis*, would be found in small woodland streams, but not in the river proper.

  Any of these redbelly dace species is marked with a dark stripe on the back, a much darker mid-lateral stripe, and a cream-colored or light-brown stripe in between. Below the mid-lateral stripe the belly is red. The fins are generally colorless. During the breeding season, the color of the males intensifies, the underbelly becoming fiery red-orange and the fins taking on a yellow hue. The pectoral and anal fins may become lemon yellow. The dark stripes also intensify, changing from deep brown to shiny, enameled-looking black.

  Redbelly dace inhabit shallow pools, often over gravel and sand. They feed mainly on algae, occasionally ingesting small invertebrates in the course of grazing. Some researchers have suggested that the sand they consume by accident helps to break apart the plant matter that provides their nourishment, much like stones in a chicken's gizzard help to grind grain.

- Of all the many fish species found in Little River, no group is more consistently colorful and interesting than the darters. I admit to being prejudiced in their favor, however, because my ichthyological mentor, Dave Etnier, is one of the foremost authorities on darter biology, not to mention discoverer of the famed snail darter (*Percina tanasi*). The snail darter became synonymous with environment versus development issues in the 1970s when its discovery halted construction of the billion-dollar Tellico Dam project on the Little Tennessee River. Congress eventually acted to exempt the Tellico project from the Endangered Species Act, and when the dam was closed in 1979, the Little Tennessee became the last river of the Tennessee drainage to be impounded. Though they survive in other streams than the Little Tennessee, the snail darter remains categorized as a species threatened with extinction. While no snail darters will be recommended for our native stream tank aquarium, they have numerous cousins that make splendid choices when the water is kept reliably cool and well-oxygenated. I will briefly describe some small, colorful, and relatively common examples from the Little River and elsewhere. If you live east of the Mississippi, chances are colorful darters can be collected near you. Bottom dwellers, darters lack a swim bladder and have sturdy pelvic fins that help them navigate the substrate in areas of strong water movement.

- The greenside darter, *Etheostoma blennioides*, is widespread over the central portion of the country, from the Great Lakes south to northern Georgia and Alabama. Both males and females are tan to greenish brown in color, with a series of U-shaped black blotches along the sides. During the breeding season from early spring to summer, males darken and become intensely green or blue-green on the sides and head. The first dorsal fin (darters have a pair of dorsal fins) develops a bright green margin with an inner band of red-orange. These handsome fish feed on aquatic insect larvae and snails, and have proven amenable to aquarium care.

- *Etheostoma flabellare*, the fantail darter, never attains the brilliant breeding colors of some other species, but its pattern of black dots and spots overlain on a tan to golden background color is nevertheless attractive. The yellowish tail is marked in curving parallel rows of small black ovals that appear to blend together, forming wavy lines. Reaching three inches in length, it feeds mostly on insect larvae and tiny crustaceans.

- Redline darters, *Etheostoma rufilineatum*, win my vote for the prettiest member of the genus to be found in the Little River. The sides have a checkerboard appearance, marked in dark brown, light tan, and deep brick red. Males have red lines following the margin of the fins, a red belly, and a bright red backwards-C shape on the tail fin. The outer edges of the tail, second dorsal, and anal fins are further decorated with a thin line of blue pigment. It prefers swift, shallow riffles over rocks in small streams to large rivers. Like many other darters, it feeds on insect larvae.

- No mention of the river-dwelling darter clan should end without a reference to the logperch, *Percina caprodes*. Although tan in color marked with irregular greenish stripes from behind the gill cover to the base of the tail, the logperch makes up for its somewhat drab appearance with its interesting feeding behavior. It uses its slightly elongated snout to flip over small rocks to get at the invertebrates hiding underneath. The top of the snout has a fleshy patch to help protect it during this procedure. Widespread from Canada to the Gulf, the logperch adapts well to a properly designed aquarium. Its life history has been thoroughly studied, owing to its extensive geographic range and adaptability. It reaches a length of about six inches. Several other species of logperch occur in the upper South, but they are restricted to a few areas and are not likely to be encountered by the average aquarist.

The foregoing has been but an introduction to the native fishes of North America. I hope it has captured your interest, and that you will endeavor to learn more about the fishes in your own backyard. Much of our aquatic heritage is under threat from development, pollution, and the introduction of non-native species. Even if you never keep an aquarium of darters or dace, I urge you to support efforts to conserve these jewels of our rivers and streams for the enjoyment and edification of future generations.

CHAPTER 12

PURELY ARTISTIC DESIGNS

Throughout this book I have based the aquarium model designs on grouping fish and plants from the same geographic area. Often, I have narrowed the focus to a single river system or a specific biotope. A systematic review of aquarium possibilities, which is what I hope to accomplish, is easily organized according to geography. I should also confess my personal preference for biotope aquariums. The design suggestions I make are drawn from many years of thinking about fish in regard to their natural habitats.

That said, one should never make the mistake of thinking that biotopically, or even regionally, inspired aquariums are the only ones possible. With such a variety of fish and plants from which to select, the possible combinations for successful aquariums multiply almost infinitely. Whatever your application, if you are thinking about an aquarium as *living art*, plenty of styles exist to suit any taste or décor.

Purely Plants

A well-done planted aquarium enhances a room even without fish. If you have a sunroom or similar space with lots of terrestrial plants, consider adding a tank of aquatic plants. Located where it will receive indirect sun, a well-established plant tank thrives without much care beyond pruning. And you don't have to water!

MODEL DESIGN 80 Dutch-Style Plant Aquarium

You cannot have failed to notice that I am fond of living plants in aquariums. I am, in fact, fond of living plants in all sorts of situations, and my house and garden overflow with many different varieties, well over 300 kinds of plants. It should come as no surprise, then, that my first choice for an aquarium designed for maximum decorative effect should be an all-plant tank in which the fish are almost an afterthought.

Aquarium Capacity . . . . 150 gallons

Water Conditions .neutral to slightly acidic with low to moderate hardness

Optimal Temperature . . . . .75°F

Plants

    common crypt (*Cryptocoryne willisii*) 15

    Thai crypt (*Cryptocoryne balansae*) 7

    Wendt's crypt (*Cryptocoryne wendtii*) 15

    radicans sword plant
        (*Echinodorus cordifolius*) 1

    ruffled sword plant (*Echinodorus martii*) . . . 3

    pygmy chain sword plant
        (*Echinodorus tenellus*) 7–15

    stargrass (*Heteranthera zosterifolia*) . . . . . 12 bunches

    giant red rotala (*Rotala macrandra*) . . . . . 7 bunches

    Reineck's alternanthera
        (*Alternanthera reineckii*) . . . . 7 bunches

Other Décor .driftwood, roots

Background . . . . .medium brown to black

Substrate . . . . .river sand with some added gravel

Filtration . . . . .sump-type filter

Lighting . . . . .3 150-watt metal halide lamps, for plants

Special Requirements . . . . .carbon dioxide fertilization, peat filtration

Fish

    Paracheirodon innesi . . . . ±200

My concept for this aquarium has a large stump, finally eroded from the sandy stream bank, toppling into the water amid lush, tropical vegetation. I have chosen plants for either their adaptability or a preference for the water conditions I can most easily provide. For other circumstances, different varieties of plants could be substituted. I have found that the great majority of aquarium plants adapt to different aquarium conditions, so long as the water hardness remains in the one hundred ppm range or less. I would flesh out the design of this tank based on the selection of driftwood available to fill the role of the fallen stump. It should have plenty of roots or snags sticking out, in order to be convincing. A tank this large should have two overflows feeding the sump, and the obvious location is in each rear corner. You should arrange the driftwood piece to help hide one of them, and use a dense stand of stargrass (*Heteranthera*) to obscure the other one. Placing three tall *Cryptocoryne balanse*, with its interesting seersucker leaf pattern, near the base of the driftwood piece, one plant on one side and two on the other, should distract the viewer from noticing the equipment lurking behind them. I would use the other *Cryptocoryne* plants in mixed stands toward either end of the tank, since lower light levels will prevail there. The pygmy chain sword plant (*Echinodorus tenellus*) should go in the center foreground, where it always looks best. It will take a while for the seven to fifteen plants suggested above to grow into a lush carpet that blends on either edge with the darker, broader-leaved *Cryptocorynes*.

With this frame of plants in place, you can proceed to devote the center of the tank to a riotous jungle of red and green foliage. The bright green, substantial leaves of *Echinodorus martii* will stand out beautifully against a backdrop of the deep red tones of *Rotala* and *Alternanthera*. Plant the bunch plants by separating them into individual stems and inserting groups of stems, with each about an inch apart in the group, into the sand. Start with the *Rotala* near the stargrass area, plant toward the center of the tank, and continue with *Alternanthera* when you run out of stems of the first plant. As you go, building up a background planting of red color, place the sword plants toward the front of the tank, making sure you leave room for their eventual growth. For a durable and dependably striking centerpiece, plant the *Echinodorus cordifolius* so that its leaves gracefully drape over the submerged wood. The aquascape should have an open space for this plant to grow into, as if the existing vegetation had been leveled by the falling log. I would allow this aquarium to grow and develop for a month or more with only the plants before adding the neon tetras. You could, of course, use any small, colorful fish as a substitute for the neons.

Trouble-Free Tanks

Some people like the idea of an aquarium, but not the notion of maintaining it rigorously. The designs in this section emphasize ease of care by including hardy species that can tolerate a missed water change or two. No aquarium, of course, can get along forever without maintenance, but these two will accept the bare minimum.

MODEL DESIGN 81 Miniature Aquarium

I am not, as a rule, favorable toward unusually small aquarium tanks, because they can so easily become table-top disasters. Compact units that come with everything built in and a decent lighting system have appeared on the market in response to the interests of saltwater minireef enthusiasts. I would use one of these micro-tanks for a freshwater design that would remain on my desk, trouble free, without the effort and expense of a saltwater system.

If you are going to go small, I strongly recommend choosing one of the complete miniature aquariums now available, rather than trying to cobble one together yourself from scratch. It is critical that all the components work well and look good together, since the aquarium will be in full view from all sides as it sits on your desk or credenza. The challenge with an aquarium this small is to convince the viewer that the space is much larger than it actually is. Each element must be considered carefully, because mistakes are magnified in a small design. Working with small aquariums taught me much about gardening in a confined space, and vice versa. Please review the design principles discussed on pages 14–15. Executing this aquarium design provides a good way to practice for a larger tank.

Aquarium Capacity . . . . 8 gallons

Water Conditions .neutral with moderate hardness

Optimal Temperature . . . . .65–70°F

Plants

    Java moss (*Vesicularia dubyana*) . . . . 1 clump

Other Décor . . . . .medium to small water-worn rocks and pebbles, small piece of driftwood

Background . . . . .medium brown to black

Substrate . . . . .river sand with some added gravel

Filtration . . . . .built-in filter

Lighting . . . . .as supplied with the tank

Special Requirements . . . . .see text

Fish

    Tanichthys albonubes 5

One of the chief difficulties in growing plants in small containers stems (if I may say so) from the disproportionately large leaves of most readily available varieties. A plant with large, sturdy leaves sitting in a small tank looks uncomfortably crowded. What is needed are plants with tiny individual leaves, no matter how large the entire clump might eventually grow. Mosses stand out as an obvious selection, and *Vesicularia* is a tough, widely available variety that adapts to many circumstances. It looks particularly decorative when attached to something. For this tank to look really smashing, you could start by attaching some of the moss to a rock or piece of driftwood, using a piece of monofilament fishing line. Place this in a container in a sunny location; even a bucket of clean, aerated water will do. Just drop a diffuser in the bucket and connect it to a small air pump. A white polypropylene bucket, the kind that many products are packaged in, is perfect, provided it is completely clean. Just enough light passes through the sides of the bucket to allow the moss to grow lushly and quickly attach itself to the rock or wood, after which time the fishing line can be cut away and the piece transferred to the aquarium for display. The same trick, by the way, can also be used to grow a specimen aquatic plant in a pot for subsequent transfer to the display aquarium.

Set up the tank according to the manufacturer's directions, add the substrate and water, and install your pre-planted mossy driftwood. Arrange a grouping of pebbles and a single large stone to form, with the driftwood, a triangle with unequal sides. If the large stone is nearest the viewer and the driftwood is farther away, the space will appear larger. From the opposite side, the space will look even smaller. Wait a few days and add two of the White Cloud mountain minnows. After a week, add the other three.

Small tanks allow you very little room for error. Be sure to carry out a 50 percent water change every week. Avoid overfeeding.

Paludariums

I like paludariums. Combining both aquatic and terrestrial species in one display really conveys the feeling of a complete ecosystem. You can combine any plants that like a warm, humid environment, rather than choosing species from only one biotope or region. Make sure your selections won't outgrow the tank, or plan to keep them pruned.

MODEL DESIGN 82 Killifish Paludarium

Unless the tank is unusually tall, a paludarium will not have room for much water, since you have to leave headroom for the terrestrial portion. Therefore, in order to include fish in the aquatic portion, they have to be tolerant of a confined swimming space besides being colorful and interesting. Many killifish species fit this description perfectly.

Aquarium Capacity . . . . 65 gallons

Water Conditions . . . . .soft, acidic

Optimal Temperature . . . . .72°F

Plants

    floating fern (*Salvinia auriculata*) . . . . 1 clump

    water hyacinth (*Eichornia crassipes*) . . . . . 1 plant

    terrestrial plants (see text)

Other Décor . . . . .roots

Background . . . . .deep green

Substrate . . . . .river sand with peat

Filtration . . . . .canister filter

Lighting . . . . .4 fluorescent tubes, for plants

Special Requirements . . . . .see text

Fish

    see text

The big challenge in designing a paludarium is having enough room. For that reason, I prefer one that is at least eighteen inches deep and twenty-four inches tall, regardless of length. Thus, the size choices are sixty-five and ninety gallons, or anything larger. The greater the depth of the tank, the more room you have to elevate the terrestrial portion without blocking the front glass. If you simply pile up material on one end of the tank, from front to back, the viewer is treated to a cross-section of the substrate, rocks, or whatever you have placed underneath the terrestrial portion.

Because the tank in this design is eighteen inches deep, you can install a one-foot-wide planting container six inches back from the front glass. The ideal planting container for this purpose would be lightweight, waterproof, and dark in color. A textured surface resembling stone would be ideal. Check your local garden center for candidates in plastic or molded resin. Once you have the perfect container, install it in the tank using black silicone sealant to secure it in place. Place it at least six inches in from one end of the tank. Paint the tank background a close match to the color of the planting container, to help make it disappear when water and aquatic plants are added.

The scene we want for this paludarium is of a narrow spit of land, represented by the planting container, jutting out into a pond and surrounded by water on three sides. Try to find roots or a piece of driftwood that you can use to help obscure the front of the planting container from view. The sides will not matter so much, as they will be difficult to see once the tank is filled. Place the river sand on the bottom of the aquatic portion of the tank, keeping it uniformly about an inch deep. Place a layer of pebbles about two inches deep in the bottom of the planting container and fill it with potting mix.

Plenty of choices for terrestrial plants exist. An easily grown favorite is *Syngonium*, which you can find in any garden shop. It has arrowhead-shaped leaves on stems about a foot tall. Many horticultural varieties exist. The foliage is very tropical looking and will lean attractively over the water. You might fill in the space around the base of the plant with a *Selaginella*, or spikemoss. It is a creeping groundcover that will grow more rapidly than true moss, filling the available space quickly.

Fill the tank with water up to the top of the terrestrial plant container. Spread a thin layer of well-soaked horticultural peat on top of the sand substrate. Add the floating plants, then allow them to grow undisturbed for about two weeks before you add the tropical killifish of your choice. Be sure to choose a species that does well in peaty, acidic water. The *Salvinia* and water hyacinth (*Eichornia*), both undemanding, will grow rapidly and require regular thinning. The long, black roots of the water hyacinth provide all the underwater interest.

MODEL DESIGN 83 Orchid Paludarium

I came up with this model design when a friend gave me the aquarium tank. It is tall enough to have a terrestrial area above the water, but the depth is so small you cannot really have an attractive planting space. I solved this dilemma with plants that don't need to be grown in soil.

Aquarium Capacity . . . . 77 gallons

Water Conditions .acidic to neutral with low to moderate hardness

Optimal Temperature . . . . .74°F

Plants

    common crypt (*Cryptocoryne willisii*) . . . . 7–15 plants

    pygmy chain sword plant (*Echinodorus tenellus*)   15 plants

Other Décor . . . . .big piece of driftwood (see text)

Background . . . . .dull yellow green

Substrate . . . . .river sand with some added gravel

Filtration . . . . .canister filter

Lighting . . . . .4 fluorescent tubes, for plants

Special Requirements . . . . .see text

Fish

    Brachydanio rerio 12

    Hyphessobrycon erythrostigma 7

    Corydoras, any species 3

Pulling this off hinges entirely on finding the right piece of driftwood. Look for a piece that projects upward about a foot before bending approximately ninety degrees, with a long branch after the bend. You want to have a portion of the wood submerged in the foot of water you will place in the tank, with a branch projecting out of the water and parallel to the surface. On the projecting branch, you will attach small orchids or bromeliads with pieces of nylon monofilament fishing line. Place this piece near one end of the tank, so the branch with its attached orchids is positioned where you want it. Add the sand in a layer about two inches deep. Fill the tank about half full, then plant the *Cryptocoryne* plants in a stand clustered around the driftwood's base. In the open space on the opposite end of the tank, plant the pygmy chain sword plants (*Echinodorus*).

Gradually add the fish over a period of weeks after the tank is set up. The danios (*Brachydanio*) will spend most of their time near the top, the bleeding hearts (*Hyphessobrycon*) will forage in midwater, and the catfish (*Corydoras*) will patrol the bottom. All these are hardy species that will thrive on a varied diet of commonly available foods. Change one third to one half of the water weekly.

You can make the aerial branch more interesting and decorative by adding, in addition to orchids and/or bromeliads, small epiphytic ferns and mosses. Any of these will in time attach itself to the branch, and the fishing line can be removed. You could also use more than one piece of driftwood, with plants growing on the emergent portions of each.

For the person who wants a few large, colorful fish that are easy to care for, here is your tank.

Aquarium Capacity . . . . 75 gallons

Water Conditions .neutral with moderate hardness

Optimal Temperature . . . . .65–70°F

Plants

    none

Other Décor . . . . .driftwood, water-worn rocks

Background . . . . .medium brown or blue, or black

Substrate . . . . .natural gravel

Filtration . . . . .canister filter

Lighting . . . . .1 fluorescent tube

Special Requirements . . . . .see text

Fish

    Chromobotia macracanthus. 1

    Danio aequipinnatus. 7

    Trichogaster trichopterus 5

    Cichlasoma salvini 1

You will not be able to do much creative aquascaping with this tank, other than arrange the rocks and wood so as to provide hiding places. The yellow-belly cichlid (*Cichlasoma*) and clown loach (*Chromobotia*) should each have its own territory. The danios (*Danio*) and gouramis (*Trichogaster*) will remain out in the open most of the time. You should have few problems with this aquarium. Make sure to carry out those weekly water changes!

The Non-Traditional Tank

Traditional aquariums take on the informal look of a cottage garden. Such a design can be out of place in a room with ultramodern décor and a plasma television, just as a blowsy, blossoming cottage garden might look out of place surrounding a contemporary-style house. Stripping the aquarium down to its essentials and choosing colors and finishes carefully produces a modern look.

MODEL DESIGN 85 A Black-and-White Aquarium

This model design has a minimalist influence that many people would think appropriate in a contemporary home. It would look especially hi-tech with a cabinet and light enclosure in stainless steel or gray laminate.

Aquarium Capacity . . . . 55 gallons

Water Conditions .neutral with moderate hardness

Optimal Temperature . . . . .65–70°F

Plants

    see text

Other Décor . . . . .large pebbles to match gravel

Background . . . . .pale gray

Substrate . . . . .white sand

Filtration . . . . .canister filter

Lighting . . . . .1 fluorescent tube

Special Requirements . . . . .added salt

Fish

    Poecilia sphenops 15

For an aquarium that is all about contrast, you need five large pieces of water-worn white quartz. Place the sand on the bottom and arrange the rocks in two groups, one with three pieces and one with the other two. You may find it helpful to look at some pictures of Japanese dry gardens that feature only rocks and raked sand, in order to get ideas for placement in the aquarium. Once you have an arrangement you like, fill the tank. Add the black mollies three at a time for five weeks, to allow the filter system to establish itself. Make sure to add salt, a tablespoon per gallon, at the beginning and to the replacement water during water changes. Use synthetic seawater salt mix from the aquarium store. To keep everything stark white, you may need to periodically remove the rocks and sand, clean them in bleach solution (one cup liquid bleach per five-gallon bucket of water) and return them to the tank. The bleach works fast, so you can transfer the mollies to a separate holding container with some of the tank water during the cleanup.

Community Tanks

When someone says "aquarium," most of us think of a community tank, filled with a variety of colorful fish. A community tank can include species from different parts of the world, so long as they all like the same water conditions. Whether large or small, a community tank with plastic plants will be easier to care for than one with live plants. You don't need a fancy lighting system, either.

MODEL DESIGN 86 Basic Community Tank

Here is a good-looking community of fish that should get along with each other easily. Plastic plants make setup and care a cinch.

Aquarium Capacity . . . . 55 gallons

Water Conditions .neutral with moderate hardness

Optimal Temperature . . . . .72–74°F

Plants

    plastic

Other Décor . . . . .driftwood or water-worn rocks

Background . . . . .medium brown to black

Substrate . . . . .natural gravel

Filtration . . . . .canister filter

Lighting . . . . .1 fluorescent tube

Special Requirements . . . . .none

Fish

    Trichogaster leeri . . . . 1 pair

    Pterophyllum scalare. 3

    Xiphophorus maculatus 5

    Corydoras paleatus 3

    Hyphessobrycon callistus. 12

I would recommend this community of fish for any beginner with a reasonably large tank. The group includes top, mid, and bottom swimmers, and every one is hardy and easy to feed. You could do all kinds of substitutions, of course. Blue gouramis could stand in for the pearl gouramis (*Trichogaster*), or just about any other species of *Corydoras* or *Hyphessobrycon* for the ones suggested. Similarly, variatus platies could stand in for the moon platies (*Xiphophorus*).

Since you do not have to worry about the care requirements for plastic plants, I suggest choosing three types. One should be tall with narrow, straplike leaves, such as *Vallisneria*. Another should be of medium height, with bolder foliage, such as a sword plant or *Aponogeton*. The third should have fine-textured foliage. Good possibilities for the third type would include *Cabomba*, *Limnophila*, and *Ceratophyllum*. Quality plastic reproductions of all of these come in several sizes. Remember that it is better to have a lot of plants of a few types than only a few individuals of many types. Keeping the finely textured plants to the ends and back of the tank helps to make it look larger. Always keep plants in stands of one variety, rather than intermingling the different types all over the tank. In a large tank such as this one, two stands of the same plant, located some distance apart, would be fine.

Remember to arrange plants so they hide equipment from view. You will find the aquascape easier to arrange if you use either larger stones or driftwood, but not both. Too many varied elements will make the tank look cluttered. A beginner blessed with a large tank such as this may be tempted to add one of everything. This usually results in a jumble rather than a design.

MODEL DESIGN 87 | Basic Small Community Tank

This limited community of fish will do well in a small starter tank. Plastic plants are recommended again, to keep maintenance simple and easy.

Aquarium Capacity . . . . 20 gallons

Water Conditions . . . . .neutral with moderate hardness

Optimal Temperature . . . . .72–74°F

Plants

    plastic

Other Décor . . . . .water-worn rocks

Background . . . . .medium brown to black

Substrate . . . . .natural gravel

Filtration . . . . .hang-on filter

Lighting . . . . .1 fluorescent tube

Special Requirements . . . . .none

Fish

   Barbus titteya. 5

   Hasemania nana 7

   Hemigrammus ocellifer 7

   Synodontis nigriventris 1

Trust me on this idea for plastic plants: pick up about a dozen of one type, such as *Vallisneria*, and use only these to cover part of the rear glass and part of one end. Arrange the plants in a semicircle, beginning near the corner where you have placed the filter. You should end up with a stand of plants fanning out toward the viewer. Toward the opposite front corner, group the rocks. Add the fish over a period of about three weeks to a month.

Part IV

THE APPENDIXES

FRESHWATER FISH AND PLANTS

E very aquarium book, it seems, must have its compendium of fish and plants. Only a limited number of ways exist of expressing this information in a useful manner. For example, fish are usually grouped taxonomically, often preceded by an outline of the taxonomy of the entire fishy class. This works well for aquarists with some prior knowledge of ichthyology, but leaves everyone else mystified. Aquarists may find other cataloging criteria more useful. Software makes cross-referencing, once quite a labor, a simple task. For aquarium purposes, you do not need to know that one fish belongs to the Poecillinae and the other to the Tetragonopteridae. You want to know if they like the same pH. The following collection of lists is an attempt to improve upon the way fish catalogs are presented to aquarium enthusiasts. Please consider it a starting place only. I make no pretense that it is comprehensive. The species I have included are among the most popular, based on my experience as an aquarium retailer. (Neither do I pretend that the taxonomy reflects the most recent, cutting-edge research.)

Fish

Freshwater fish exhibit astounding diversity. Thousands of species have been identified, and many more undoubtedly lie undiscovered. Since I have chosen to base most of my suggested designs on combining species from the same geographic region, a sort of the species described in this book by locality comprises the first list.

List 1: Cross Reference of Fish Species by Locality

Genus	Species	Common Name(s)	Range
Aphyosemion	australe	African killifish	Africa
Nothobranchius	rachovii	annual killifish	Africa
Ancistrus	dolichopterus	bristle-nosed plecostomus	Amazonia
Anostomus	anostomus	striped headstander	Amazonia
Apistogramma	agassizii	dwarf cichlid	Amazonia
Chalceus	macrolepidotus	pink-tailed chalceus	Amazonia
Farlowella	gracilis	whiptail catfish	Amazonia
Hyphessobrycon	callistus	none	Amazonia
Hyphessobrycon	erythrostigma	bleeding heart tetra	Amazonia
Hyphessobrycon	heterorhabdus	flag tetra	Amazonia
Hyphessobrycon	loretoensis	loreto tetra	Amazonia
Leporinus	fasciatus	banded leporinus	Amazonia
Megalamphodus	megalopterus	black phantom tetra	Amazonia
Megalamphodus	sweglesi	red phantom tetra	Amazonia
Paracheirodon	axelrodi	cardinal tetra	Amazonia
Pristella	maxillarus	X-ray tetra	Amazonia
Pterophyllum	scalare	angelfish	Amazonia
Sorubim	lima	shovel-nose catfish	Amazonia
Symphysodon	aequifasciatus	discus	Amazonia
Thayeria	obliqua	penguin tetra	Amazonia
Xiphophorus	maculatus	platy, moonfish	Atlantic coast of Mexico and Guatemala, northern Honduras
Melanotaenia	exquisitus	exquisite rainbowfish	Australia
Melanotaenia	nigrans	black rainbowfish	Australia
Melanotaenia	splendida australis	splendid rainbowfish	Australia
Melanotaenia	trifasciata	rainbowfish	Australia
Corydoras	paleatus	common corydoras	Brazil
Corydoras	pygmaeus	pygmy corydoras	Brazil
Gymnocorymbus	ternetzi	black skirt tetra	Brazil
Hasemania	nana	silvertip tetra	Brazil
Hyphessobrycon	pulchripinnis	lemon tetra	Brazil

Genus	Species	Common Name(s)	Range
Hypostomus	punctatus	plecostomus cat	Brazil
Nannostomus	trifasciatus	three-lined pencilfish	Brazil
Otocinclus	arnoldi	Arnold's otocinclus	Brazil
Semaprochilodus	taeniurus	flag-tailed prochilodus	Brazil, Colombia
Exodon	paradoxus	bucktoothed tetra	Brazil, Guyanas
Gasteropelecus	sternicla	common hatchetfish	Brazil, Guyanas
Hemmigrammus	caudovittatus	Buenos Aires tetra	Brazil, Paraguay, Argentina
Brachydanio	nigrofasciatus	spotted danio	Burma
Telmatherina	ladigesi	Celebes rainbowfish	Celebes Islands
Archocentrus	nigrofasciatum	convict	Central America
Cichlasoma	octofasciatum	Jack Dempsey	Central America
Cichlasoma	salvini	yellow-belly cichlid	Central America
Poecilia	reticulata	guppy	Central America
Thorichthys	meeki	firemouth	Central America
Xiphophorus	helleri	swordtail	Central America
Aequidens	pulcher	blue acara	Central and South America
Corydoras	metae	skunk corydoras	Colombia
Nematobrycon	palmeri	emperor tetra	Colombia
Campostoma	anomalum	central stoneroller	Eastern and Central U.S.
Cottus	bairdi	mottled sculpin	Eastern and Central U.S.
Macropodus	opercularis	paradisefish	Eastern Asia
Hyphessobrycon	flammeus	flame tetra	Eastern Brazil
Fundulus	notatus	black-spotted topminnow	Eastern U.S.
Fundulus	olivaceus	olive topminnow	Eastern U.S.
Lepomis	sp.	sunfish	Eastern U.S.
Noturus	miurus	brindled madtom	Eastern U.S.
Percina	caprodes	logperch	Eastern U.S.
Jordanella	floridae	flagfish	Florida
Copenia	arnoldi	splashing tetra	Guyana
Hemmigrammus	erythrozonus	glowlight tetra	Guyana

continued

List 1: Cross Reference of Fish Species by Locality (continued)

Genus	Species	Common Name(s)	Range
Hemmigrammus	ocellifer	head-and-taillight tetra	Guyana, Bolivia
Serrasalmus	nattereri	red piranha	Guyana, Brazil
Brachydanio	rerio	zebra danio	India
Barbus	conchonius	rosy barb	India, Bengal
Aplocheilus	blockii	panchax	India, Southeast Asia
Botia	morleti	Hora's loach	India, Thailand
Barbus	oligolepus	checkered barb	Indonesia
Barbus	tetrazona	tiger barb	Indonesia
Cyrtocara	moorii	Moor's African cichlid	Lake Malawi
Labeotropheus	trewavasae	Trewavas' African cichlid	Lake Malawi
Labidochromis	lividus	African cichlid	Lake Malawi
Melanochromis	johanni	Johann's African cichlid	Lake Malawi
Pseudotropheus	zebra	zebra African cichlid	Lake Malawi
Julidochromis	dickfeldi	Dickfeld's julie	Lake Tanganyika
Julidochromis	marlieri	Marlier's julie	Lake Tanganyika
Julidochromis	ornatus	ornate julie	Lake Tanganyika
Neolamprologus	brichardi	Brichard's African cichlid	Lake Tanganyika
Neolamprologus	leleupi	lemon cichlid	Lake Tanganyika
Neolamprologus	multifasciatus	shell-dwelling African cichlid	Lake Tanganyika
Tropheus	duboisi	Dubois's tropheus	Lake Tanganyika
Tropheus	moorii	Moor's tropheus	Lake Tanganyika
Bedotia	geayi	Madagascar rainbowfish	Madagascar
Trichogaster	leeri	pearl gourami	Malaysia, Sumatra, Borneo
Poecilia	velifera	sailfin molly	Mexico
Poecilia	sphenops	black molly	Mexico to South America
Astayanax	mexicanus	blind cave tetra	Mexico, SW U.S.
Iriatherina	werneri	threadfin rainbowfish	New Guinea
Melanotaenia	bosemani	Boseman's rainbowfish	New Guinea
Pelvicachromis	pulcher	kribensis	Nigeria
Phoxinus	eos	northern redbelly dace	Northeastern U.S.

Genus	Species	Common Name(s)	Range
Carnegiella	*strigata*	marbled hatchetfish	Peru
Corydoras	*agassizii*	Agassiz's corydoras	Peru
Hyphessobrycon	*bentosi*	Roberts' tetra	Peru
Monocirrhus	*polyacanthus*	leaf fish	Peru
Paracheirodon	*innesi*	neon tetra	Peru
Carnegiella	*marthae*	black-winged hatchetfish	Rio Negro
Hemmigrammus	*bleheri*	rummynose tetra	Rio Negro
Hyphessobrycon	*herbertaxelrodi*	black neon tetra	Rio Paraguay
Aphyocharax	*anisitsi*	bloodfin	South America
Cynolebias	*bellotti*	Argentine pearlfish	South America
Moenkhausia	*sanctaefilomenae*	yellow-banded moenkhausia	South America
Barbus	*everetti*	clown barb	Southeast Asia
Barbus	*schwanfeldi*	tinfoil barb	Southeast Asia
Brachydanio	*albolineatus*	pearl danio	Southeast Asia
Chanda	*ranga*	glassfish	Southeast Asia
Colisa	*laelia*	dwarf gourami	Southeast Asia
Kryptopterus	*minor*	glass catfish	Southeast Asia
Mastacembelus	*erythrotaenia*	fire eel	Southeast Asia
Pangio	*kuhlii*	coolie loach	Southeast Asia
Rasbora	*borapetensis*	red-tailed rasbora	Southeast Asia
Rasbora	*heteromorpha*	harlequin rasbora	Southeast Asia
Rasbora	*kalochroma*	clown rasbora	Southeast Asia
Toxotes	*jaculatrix*	archer fish	Southeast Asia
Trichogaster	*trichopterus*	blue gourami	Southeast Asia
Amia	*calva*	bowfin	Southeastern U.S.
Elassoma	*evergladei*	Everglades pygmy sunfish	Southeastern U.S.
Elassoma	*zonatum*	banded pygmy sunfish	Southeastern U.S.
Enneacanthus	*chaetodon*	black-banded sunfish	Southeastern U.S.
Enneacanthus	*gloriosus*	blue-spotted sunfish	Southeastern U.S.
Etheostoma	*blennioides*	greenside darter	Southeastern U.S.

continued

List 1: Cross Reference of Fish Species by Locality *(continued)*

Genus	Species	Common Name(s)	Range
Etheostoma	*flabellare*	fantail darter	Southeastern U.S.
Etheostoma	*rufilineatum*	redline darter	Southeastern U.S.
Fundulus	*chrysotus*	golden topminnow	Southeastern U.S.
Lepisosteus	*oculatus*	spotted gar	Southeastern U.S.
Lucania	*goodei*	bluefin topminnow	Southeastern U.S.
Luxilus	*coccogenis*	warpaint shiner	Southeastern U.S.
Poecilia	*latipinna*	green sailfin molly	Southeastern U.S.
Pteronotropis	*welaka*	bluenosed shiner	Southeastern U.S.
Xiphophorus	*variatus*	variegated platy, variatus platy	Southern Mexico
Cichlasoma	*cyanoguttatum*	Texas cichlid	Southern U.S.
Phoxinus	*erythrogaster*	southern redbelly dace	Southern U.S.
Barbus	*nigrofasciatus*	black ruby barb	Sri Lanka
Barbus	*titteya*	cherry barb	Sri Lanka
Danio	*aequipinnatus*	giant danio	Sri Lanka
Chromobotia	*macracanthus*	clown loach	Sumatra, Borneo
Nannostomus	*marginatus*	dwarf pencilfish	Surinam, Guyana
Phoxinus	*tennesseensis*	Tennessee dace	Tennessee
Betta	*splendens*	Siamese fighting fish	Thailand
Epalzeorhyncos	*bicolor*	red-tailed shark	Thailand
Epalzeorhyncos	*erythurus*	red-finned shark	Thailand
Trichopsis	*pumila*	dwarf croaking gourami	Thailand, Vietnam
Microgeophagus	*ramirezi*	butterfly cichlid	Venezuela, Colombia
Barbus	*callipterus*	clipper barb	West Africa
Barbus	*holotaenia*	blackstripe barb	West Africa
Pantodon	*buchholzi*	African butterflyfish	West Africa
Gnathonemus	*petersii*	Peters' elephantnose	West and central Africa
Tanichthys	*albonubes*	White Cloud Mountain minnow	White Cloud Mountain, China
Barbus	*hulstaerti*	African clown barb	Zaire River
Epiplatys	*chevalieri*	killifish	Zaire River
Hemichromis	*bimaculatus*	jewel cichlid	Zaire River

Genus	Species	Common Name(s)	Range
Nannochromis	*parilus*	none	Zaire River
Phenacogrammus	*interruptus*	Congo tetra	Zaire River
Protopterus	*dolloi*	African lungfish	Zaire River
Synodontis	*nigriventris*	upside-down catfish	Zaire River

Temperature

Next in importance for fish in captivity is temperature. Water temperature affects the amount of oxygen available, the metabolism of the fish, and a host of other important processes. Sudden temperature changes can have detrimental effects on both fish and plants.

List 2: Cross Reference of Fish by Minimum Temperature

Genus	Species	Common Name(s)	min T (°F)
Amia	*calva*	bowfin	39
Campostoma	*anomalum*	central stoneroller	39
Cottus	*bairdi*	mottled sculpin	39
Elassoma	*evergladei*	Everglades pygmy sunfish	39
Elassoma	*zonatum*	banded pygmy sunfish	39
Enneacanthus	*chaetodon*	black-banded sunfish	39
Enneacanthus	*gloriosus*	blue-spotted sunfish	39
Etheostoma	*blennioides*	greenside darter	39
Etheostoma	*flabellare*	fantail darter	39
Etheostoma	*rufilineatum*	redline darter	39
Fundulus	*chrysotus*	golden topminnow	39
Fundulus	*notatus*	black-spotted topminnow	39
Fundulus	*olivaceus*	olive topminnow	39
Lepisosteus	*oculatus*	spotted gar	39
Lepomis	*sp.*	sunfish	39
Luxilus	*coccogenis*	warpaint shiner	39
Noturus	*miurus*	brindled madtom	39

continued

List 2: Cross Reference of Fish by Minimum Temperature *(continued)*

Genus	Species	Common Name(s)	min T (°F)
Percina	caprodes	logperch	39
Phoxinus	eos	northern redbelly dace	39
Phoxinus	erythrogaster	southern redbelly dace	39
Phoxinus	tennesseensis	Tennessee dace	39
Poecilia	latipinna	green sailfin molly	39
Pteronotropis	welaka	bluenosed shiner	39
Lucania	goodei	bluefin topminnow	54
Xiphophorus	variatus	variegated platy, variatus platy	59
Macropodus	opercularis	paradisefish	61
Aequidens	pulcher	blue acara	64
Aphyocharax	anisitsi	bloodfin	64
Barbus	conchonius	rosy barb	64
Brachydanio	rerio	zebra danio	64
Cynolebias	bellotti	Argentine pearlfish	64
Hemmigrammus	caudovittatus	Buenos Aires tetra	64
Poecilia	reticulata	guppy	64
Tanichthys	albonubes	White Cloud Mountain minnow	64
Xiphophorus	helleri	swordtail	64
Xiphophorus	maculatus	platy, moonfish	64
Jordanella	floridae	flagfish	65
Barbus	callipterus	clipper barb	66
Archocentrus	nigrofasciatum	convict	68
Astayanax	mexicanus	blind cave tetra	68
Barbus	nigrofasciatus	black ruby barb	68
Barbus	oligolepus	checkered barb	68
Barbus	tetrazona	tiger barb	68
Bedotia	geayi	Madagascar rainbowfish	68
Brachydanio	albolineatus	pearl danio	68
Chanda	ranga	glassfish	68
Cichlasoma	cyanoguttatum	Texas cichlid	68

Genus	Species	Common Name(s)	min T (°F)
Gymnocorymbus	ternetzi	black skirt tetra	68
Megalamphodus	sweglesi	red phantom tetra	68
Nothobranchius	rachovii	annual killifish	68
Otocinclus	arnoldi	Arnold's otocinclus	68
Paracheirodon	innesi	neon tetra	68
Aphyosemion	australe	African killifish	70
Hemichromis	bimaculatus	jewel cichlid	70
Kryptopterus	minor	glass catfish	70
Thorichthys	meeki	firemouth	70
Ancistrus	dolichopterus	bristle-nosed plecostomus	72
Anostomus	anostomus	striped headstander	72
Apistogramma	agassizii	dwarf cichlid	72
Barbus	hulstaerti	African clown barb	72
Barbus	schwanfeldi	tinfoil barb	72
Cichlasoma	octofasciatum	Jack Dempsey	72
Cichlasoma	salvini	yellow-belly cichlid	72
Colisa	laelia	dwarf gourami	72
Corydoras	agassizii	Agassiz's corydoras	72
Corydoras	metae	skunk corydoras	72
Corydoras	paleatus	common corydoras	72
Corydoras	pygmaeus	pygmy corydoras	72
Cyrtocara	moorii	Moor's African cichlid	72
Danio	aequipinnatus	giant danio	72
Epalzeorhyncos	bicolor	red-tailed shark	72
Epalzeorhyncos	erythurus	red-finned shark	72
Gnathonemus	petersii	Peters' elephantnose	72
Hasemania	nana	silvertip tetra	72
Hemmigrammus	ocellifer	head-and-taillight tetra	72
Hyphessobrycon	bentosi	Roberts' tetra	72
Hyphessobrycon	callistus	none	72

continued

List 2: Cross Reference of Fish by Minimum Temperature *(continued)*

Genus	Species	Common Name(s)	min T (°F)
Hyphessobrycon	*erythrostigma*	bleeding heart tetra	72
Hyphessobrycon	*flammeus*	flame tetra	72
Hyphessobrycon	*herbertaxelrodi*	black neon tetra	72
Hyphessobrycon	*heterorhabdus*	flag tetra	72
Hyphessobrycon	*loretoensis*	loreto tetra	72
Hypostomus	*punctatus*	plecostomus cat	72
Julidochromis	*dickfeldi*	Dickfeld's julie	72
Julidochromis	*marlieri*	Marlier's julie	72
Julidochromis	*ornatus*	ornate julie	72
Labeotropheus	*trewavasae*	Trewavas' African cichlid	72
Labidochromis	*lividus*	African cichlid	72
Leporinus	*fasciatus*	banded leporinus	72
Megalamphodus	*megalopterus*	black phantom tetra	72
Melanochromis	*johanni*	Johann's African cichlid	72
Microgeophagus	*ramirezi*	butterfly cichlid	72
Moenkhausia	*sanctaefilomenae*	yellow-banded moenkhausia	72
Monocirrhus	*polyacanthus*	leaf fish	72
Nannochromis	*parilus*	none	72
Neolamprologus	*brichardi*	Brichard's African cichlid	72
Neolamprologus	*leleupi*	lemon cichlid	72
Neolamprologus	*multifasciatus*	shell-dwelling African cichlid	72
Pseudotropheus	*zebra*	zebra African cichlid	72
Rasbora	*borapetensis*	red-tailed rasbora	72
Semaprochilodus	*taeniurus*	flag-tailed prochilodus	72
Synodontis	*nigriventris*	upside-down catfish	72
Telmatherina	*ladigesi*	Celebes rainbowfish	72
Thayeria	*obliqua*	penguin tetra	72
Trichogaster	*trichopterus*	blue gourami	72
Tropheus	*duboisi*	Dubois's tropheus	72
Tropheus	*moorii*	Moor's tropheus	72

Genus	Species	Common Name(s)	min T (°F)
Barbus	titteya	cherry barb	73
Carnegiella	strigata	marbled hatchetfish	73
Chalceus	macrolepidotus	pink-tailed chalceus	73
Exodon	paradoxus	bucktoothed tetra	73
Gasteropelecus	sternicla	common hatchetfish	73
Hemmigrammus	bleheri	rummynose tetra	73
Hyphessobrycon	pulchripinnis	lemon tetra	73
Nematobrycon	palmeri	emperor tetra	73
Pantodon	buchholzi	African butterflyfish	73
Paracheirodon	axelrodi	cardinal tetra	73
Rasbora	heteromorpha	harlequin rasbora	73
Serrasalmus	nattereri	red piranha	73
Sorubim	lima	shovel-nose catfish	73
Brachydanio	nigrofasciatus	spotted danio	74
Epiplatys	chevalieri	killifish	74
Hemmigrammus	erythrozonus	glowlight tetra	74
Pristella	maxillarus	X-ray tetra	74
Trichogaster	leeri	pearl gourami	74
Barbus	everetti	clown barb	75
Barbus	holotaenia	blackstripe barb	75
Betta	splendens	Siamese fighting fish	75
Carnegiella	marthae	black-winged hatchetfish	75
Farlowella	gracilis	whiptail catfish	75
Iriatherina	werneri	threadfin rainbowfish	75
Mastacembelus	erythrotaenia	fire eel	75
Nannostomus	marginatus	dwarf pencilfish	75
Nannostomus	trifasciatus	three-lined pencilfish	75
Pangio	kuhlii	coolie loach	75
Pelvicachromis	pulcher	kribensis	75
Phenacogrammus	interruptus	Congo tetra	75

continued

List 2: Cross Reference of Fish by Minimum Temperature (continued)

Genus	Species	Common Name(s)	min T (°F)
Poecilia	sphenops	black molly	75
Poecilia	velifera	sailfin molly	75
Protopterus	dolloi	African lungfish	75
Pterophyllum	scalare	angelfish	75
Aplocheilus	blockii	panchax	77
Chromobotia	macracanthus	clown loach	77
Copenia	arnoldi	splashing tetra	77
Rasbora	kalochroma	clown rasbora	77
Toxotes	jaculatrix	archer fish	77
Trichopsis	pumila	dwarf croaking gourami	77
Botia	morleti	Hora's loach	79
Symphysodon	aequifasciatus	discus	79
Melanotaenia	bosemani	Boseman's rainbowfish	81
Melanotaenia	exquisitus	exquisite rainbowfish	81
Melanotaenia	nigrans	black rainbowfish	81
Melanotaenia	splendida australis	splendid rainbowfish	81
Melanotaenia	trifasciata	rainbowfish	81

Water Hardness

Water hardness can be an important factor in successful captive husbandry of fish. Several generalizations may be made regarding the relationship between water hardness and fish health:

- Moving a fish from soft water to hard water is often easier than the opposite.

- Severe bloating and death can occur when fish are forced to live in water with too many dissolved ions.

- Fish adapted to very soft water—some tetras, for example—develop a condition known as *calcium block* when kept in water that is too hard.

- It is easier to choose fish that will accept the water hardness you have to offer, rather than to amend your water to meet the needs of a specific fish.

- Fish, like all creatures, must contend with less-than-ideal conditions in their natural habitat, as well as seasonal changes; within reason, many will adapt to your water.

List 3: Cross Reference of Fish Species by Hardness Range

Genus	Species	Common Name(s)	min dKH	min ppm CaCO$_3$	max KH	max ppm CaCO$_3$
Hemmigrammus	bleheri	rummynose tetra	0	0	5	89
Hyphessobrycon	bentosi	Roberts' tetra	0	0	5	89
Hyphessobrycon	heterorhabdus	flag tetra	0	0	5	89
Hyphessobrycon	loretoensis	loreto tetra	0	0	5	89
Hypostomus	punctatus	plecostomus cat	0	0	25	446
Megalamphodus	sweglesi	red phantom tetra	0	0	15	268
Microgeophagus	ramirezi	butterfly cichlid	0	0	10	179
Monocirrhus	polyacanthus	leaf fish	0	0	5	89
Nannostomus	trifasciatus	three-lined pencilfish	0	0	5	89
Nothobranchius	rachovii	annual killifish	0	0	10	179
Paracheirodon	axelrodi	cardinal tetra	0	0	5	89
Paracheirodon	innesi	neon tetra	0	0	10	179
Symphysodon	aequifasciatus	discus	0	0	5	89
Anostomus	anostomus	striped headstander	2	36	20	357
Aphyocharax	anisitsi	bloodfin	2	36	30	536
Aphyosemion	australe	African killifish	2	36	10	179
Aplocheilus	blockii	panchax	2	36	12	214
Barbus	conchonius	rosy barb	2	36	10	179
Barbus	everetti	clown barb	2	36	10	179
Barbus	holotaenia	blackstripe barb	2	36	8	143
Barbus	hulstaerti	African clown barb	2	36	5	89
Barbus	nigrofasciatus	black ruby barb	2	36	12	214
Barbus	oligolepus	checkered barb	2	36	15	268
Barbus	tetrazona	tiger barb	2	36	10	179
Barbus	titteya	cherry barb	2	36	12	214
Botia	morleti	Hora's loach	2	36	5	89
Carnegiella	marthae	black-winged hatchetfish	2	36	5	89
Carnegiella	strigata	marbled hatchetfish	2	36	20	357

continued

List 3: Cross Reference of Fish Species by Hardness Range *(continued)*

Genus	Species	Common Name(s)	min dKH	min ppm CaCO$_3$	max KH	max ppm CaCO$_3$
Chalceus	macrolepidotus	pink-tailed chalceus	2	36	20	357
Colisa	laelia	dwarf gourami	2	36	10	179
Copenia	arnoldi	splashing tetra	2	36	12	214
Corydoras	agassizii	Agassiz's corydoras	2	36	25	446
Corydoras	metae	skunk corydoras	2	36	25	446
Corydoras	paleatus	common corydoras	2	36	25	446
Corydoras	pygmaeus	pygmy corydoras	2	36	25	446
Cynolebias	bellotti	Argentine pearlfish	2	36	5	89
Epiplatys	chevalieri	killifish	2	36	10	179
Exodon	paradoxus	bucktoothed tetra	2	36	20	357
Farlowella	gracilis	whiptail catfish	2	36	10	179
Gasteropelecus	sternicla	common hatchetfish	2	36	15	268
Gnathonemus	petersii	Peters' elephantnose	2	36	10	179
Hasemania	nana	silvertip tetra	2	36	10	179
Hemichromis	bimaculatus	jewel cichlid	2	36	10	179
Hyphessobrycon	callistus	none	2	36	15	268
Hyphessobrycon	erythrostigma	bleeding heart tetra	2	36	12	214
Hyphessobrycon	flammeus	flame tetra	2	36	12	214
Hyphessobrycon	herbertaxelrodi	black neon tetra	2	36	12	214
Otocinclus	arnoldi	Arnold's otocinclus	2	36	15	268
Trichopsis	pumila	dwarf croaking gourami	2	36	10	179
Aequidens	pulcher	blue acara	3	54	10	179
Ancistrus	dolichopterus	bristle-nosed plecostomus	4	71	10	179
Cichlasoma	octofasciatum	Jack Dempsey	4	71	10	179
Protopterus	dolloi	African lungfish	4	71	15	268
Apistogramma	agassizii	dwarf cichlid	5	89	10	179
Astayanax	mexicanus	blind cave tetra	5	89	30	536
Barbus	callipterus	clipper barb	5	89	20	357
Barbus	schwanfeldi	tinfoil barb	5	89	20	357
Brachydanio	albolineatus	pearl danio	5	89	10	179

Genus	Species	Common Name(s)	min dKH	min ppm CaCO$_3$	max KH	max ppm CaCO$_3$
Brachydanio	nigrofasciatus	spotted danio	5	89	10	179
Brachydanio	rerio	zebra danio	5	89	15	268
Cichlasoma	cyanoguttatum	Texas cichlid	5	89	12	214
Danio	aequipinnatus	giant danio	5	89	10	179
Epalzeorhyncos	bicolor	red-tailed shark	5	89	15	268
Epalzeorhyncos	erythurus	red-finned shark	5	89	15	268
Gymnocorymbus	ternetzi	black skirt tetra	5	89	30	536
Hemmigrammus	erythrozonus	glowlight tetra	5	89	15	268
Hemmigrammus	ocellifer	head-and-taillight tetra	5	89	15	268
Hyphessobrycon	pulchripinnis	lemon tetra	5	89	25	446
Kryptopterus	minor	glass catfish	5	89	12	214
Leporinus	fasciatus	banded leporinus	5	89	20	357
Mastacembelus	erythrotaenia	fire eel	5	89	15	268
Megalamphodus	megalopterus	black phantom tetra	5	89	20	357
Melanotaenia	bosemani	Boseman's rainbowfish	5	89	15	268
Melanotaenia	exquisitus	exquisite rainbowfish	5	89	15	268
Melanotaenia	nigrans	black rainbowfish	5	89	15	268
Melanotaenia	splendida australis	splendid rainbowfish	5	89	15	268
Melanotaenia	trifasciata	rainbowfish	5	89	15	268
Moenkhausia	sanctaefilomenae	yellow-banded moenkhausia	5	89	30	536
Nannostomus	marginatus	dwarf pencilfish	5	89	15	268
Nematobrycon	palmeri	emperor tetra	5	89	20	357
Pangio	kuhlii	coolie loach	5	89	15	268
Pantodon	buchholzi	African butterflyfish	5	89	10	179
Pelvicachromis	pulcher	kribensis	5	89	15	268
Phenacogrammus	interruptus	Congo tetra	5	89	20	357
Poecilia	reticulata	guppy	5	89	30	536
Pristella	maxillarus	X-ray tetra	5	89	35	625
Pterophyllum	scalare	angelfish	5	89	20	357

continued

Genus	Species	Common Name(s)	min dKH	min ppm CaCO$_3$	max KH	max ppm CaCO$_3$
Rasbora	borapetensis	red-tailed rasbora	5	89	10	179
Rasbora	heteromorpha	harlequin rasbora	5	89	20	357
Rasbora	kalochroma	clown rasbora	5	89	10	179
Semaprochilodus	taeniurus	flag-tailed prochilodus	5	89	20	357
Serrasalmus	nattereri	red piranha	5	89	20	357
Sorubim	lima	shovel-nose catfish	5	89	20	357
Synodontis	nigriventris	upside-down catfish	5	89	15	268
Tanichthys	albonubes	White Cloud Mountain minnow	5	89	20	357
Trichogaster	leeri	pearl gourami	5	89	30	536
Trichogaster	trichopterus	blue gourami	5	89	35	625
Amia	calva	bowfin	10	179	20	357
Bedotia	geayi	Madagascar rainbowfish	10	179	25	446
Betta	splendens	Siamese fighting fish	10	179	25	446
Campostoma	anomalum	central stoneroller	10	179	20	357
Cottus	bairdi	mottled sculpin	10	179	20	357
Elassoma	evergladei	Everglades pygmy sunfish	10	179	20	357
Elassoma	zonatum	banded pygmy sunfish	10	179	20	357
Enneacanthus	chaetodon	black-banded sunfish	10	179	20	357
Enneacanthus	gloriosus	blue-spotted sunfish	10	179	20	357
Etheostoma	blennioides	greenside darter	10	179	20	357
Etheostoma	flabellare	fantail darter	10	179	20	357
Etheostoma	rufilineatum	redline darter	10	179	20	357
Fundulus	chrysotus	golden topminnow	10	179	20	357
Fundulus	notatus	black-spotted topminnow	10	179	20	357
Fundulus	olivaceus	olive topminnow	10	179	20	357
Hemmigrammus	caudovittatus	Buenos Aires tetra	10	179	35	625
Iriatherina	werneri	threadfin rainbowfish	10	179	20	357
Lepisosteus	oculatus	spotted gar	10	179	20	357
Lepomis	sp.	sunfish	10	179	20	357

Genus	Species	Common Name(s)	min dKH	min ppm CaCO$_3$	max KH	max ppm CaCO$_3$
Lucania	goodei	bluefin topminnow	10	179	15	268
Luxilus	coccogenis	warpaint shiner	10	179	20	357
Macropodus	opercularis	paradisefish	10	179	30	536
Nannochromis	parilus	none	10	179	20	357
Noturus	miurus	brindled madtom	10	179	20	357
Percina	caprodes	logperch	10	179	20	357
Phoxinus	eos	northern redbelly dace	10	179	20	357
Phoxinus	erythrogaster	southern redbelly dace	10	179	20	357
Phoxinus	tennesseensis	Tennessee dace	10	179	20	357
Poecilia	latipinna	green sailfin molly	10	179	20	357
Pteronotropis	welaka	bluenosed shiner	10	179	20	357
Thayeria	obliqua	penguin tetra	10	179	20	357
Thorichthys	meeki	firemouth	10	179	10	179
Toxotes	jaculatrix	archer fish	10	179	20	357
Xiphophorus	maculatus	platy, moonfish	10	179	25	446
Cyrtocara	moorii	Moor's African cichlid	12	214	15	268
Julidochromis	dickfeldi	Dickfeld's julie	12	214	15	268
Julidochromis	marlieri	Marlier's julie	12	214	15	268
Julidochromis	ornatus	ornate julie	12	214	15	268
Labeotropheus	trewavasae	Trewavas' African cichlid	12	214	15	268
Labidochromis	lividus	African cichlid	12	214	15	268
Melanochromis	johanni	Johann's African cichlid	12	214	15	268
Neolamprologus	brichardi	Brichard's African cichlid	12	214	15	268
Neolamprologus	leleupi	lemon cichlid	12	214	15	268
Neolamprologus	multifasciatus	shell-dwelling African cichlid	12	214	15	268
Pseudotropheus	zebra	zebra African cichlid	12	214	15	268
Tropheus	duboisi	Dubois's tropheus	12	214	15	268
Tropheus	moorii	Moor's tropheus	12	214	15	268
Xiphophorus	helleri	swordtail	12	214	30	536

continued

List 3: Cross Reference of Fish Species by Hardness Range (*continued*)

Genus	Species	Common Name(s)	min dKH	min ppm CaCO$_3$	max KH	max ppm CaCO$_3$
Archocentrus	nigrofasciatum	convict	15	268	20	357
Chanda	ranga	glassfish	15	268	30	536
Chromobotia	macracanthus	clown loach	15	268	30	536
Cichlasoma	salvini	yellow-belly cichlid	15	268	20	357
Telmatherina	ladigesi	Celebes rainbowfish	15	268	30	536
Xiphophorus	variatus	variegated platy, variatus platy	15	268	30	536
Jordanella	floridae	flagfish	20	357	50	893
Poecilia	sphenops	black molly	25	446	35	625
Poecilia	velifera	sailfin molly	25	446	35	625

pH

Aquarium water tends to become more acidic with time. This may or may not be desirable for your fish. The water's pH can affect all sorts of vital processes.

List 4: Cross Reference of Fish Species by pH Range

Genus	Species	Common Name(s)	pH min	pH max
Hypostomus	punctatus	plecostomus cat	5.0	8.0
Nematobrycon	palmeri	emperor tetra	5.0	7.5
Otocinclus	arnoldi	Arnold's otocinclus	5.0	7.5
Paracheirodon	axelrodi	cardinal tetra	5.0	6.5
Paracheirodon	innesi	neon tetra	5.0	7.0
Aphyosemion	australe	African killifish	5.5	6.5
Carnegiella	marthae	black-winged hatchetfish	5.5	6.5
Carnegiella	strigata	marbled hatchetfish	5.5	6.5
Chalceus	macrolepidotus	pink-tailed chalceus	5.5	7.5
Colisa	laelia	dwarf gourami	5.5	6.0
Exodon	paradoxus	bucktoothed tetra	5.5	7.5

Genus	Species	Common Name(s)	pH min	pH max
Hasemania	nana	silvertip tetra	5.5	6.0
Hyphessobrycon	bentosi	Roberts' tetra	5.5	7.0
Hyphessobrycon	herbertaxelrodi	black neon tetra	5.5	7.5
Hyphessobrycon	pulchripinnis	lemon tetra	5.5	8.0
Leporinus	fasciatus	banded leporinus	5.5	7.5
Megalamphodus	sweglesi	red phantom tetra	5.5	7.5
Moenkhausia	sanctaefilomenae	yellow-banded moenkhausia	5.5	8.5
Nannostomus	trifasciatus	three-lined pencilfish	5.5	6.5
Poecilia	reticulata	guppy	5.5	8.5
Rasbora	heteromorpha	harlequin rasbora	5.5	7.5
Semaprochilodus	taeniurus	flag-tailed prochilodus	5.5	7.5
Serrasalmus	nattereri	red piranha	5.5	7.5
Anostomus	anostomus	striped headstander	5.8	7.5
Nannostomus	marginatus	dwarf pencilfish	5.8	7.5
Aphyocharax	anisitsi	bloodfin	6.0	8.0
Apistogramma	agassizii	dwarf cichlid	6.0	6.5
Aplocheilus	blockii	panchax	6.0	6.8
Astayanax	mexicanus	blind cave tetra	6.0	7.0
Barbus	conchonius	rosy barb	6.0	6.5
Barbus	everetti	clown barb	6.0	6.5
Barbus	holotaenia	blackstripe barb	6.0	6.5
Barbus	hulstaerti	African clown barb	6.0	6.5
Barbus	nigrofasciatus	black ruby barb	6.0	6.5
Barbus	oligolepus	checkered barb	6.0	7.0
Barbus	schwanfeldi	tinfoil barb	6.0	7.5
Barbus	tetrazona	tiger barb	6.0	6.5
Barbus	titteya	cherry barb	6.0	6.5
Betta	splendens	Siamese fighting fish	6.0	8.0
Botia	morleti	Hora's loach	6.0	6.5
Brachydanio	albolineatus	pearl danio	6.0	6.5

continued

Genus	Species	Common Name(s)	pH min	pH max
Brachydanio	*nigrofasciatus*	spotted danio	6.0	6.5
Brachydanio	*rerio*	zebra danio	6.0	7.5
Corydoras	*agassizii*	Agassiz's corydoras	6.0	8.0
Corydoras	*metae*	skunk corydoras	6.0	8.0
Corydoras	*paleatus*	common corydoras	6.0	8.0
Corydoras	*pygmaeus*	pygmy corydoras	6.0	8.0
Cynolebias	*bellotti*	Argentine pearlfish	6.0	6.5
Danio	*aequipinnatus*	giant danio	6.0	6.5
Epiplatys	*chevalieri*	killifish	6.0	6.5
Farlowella	*gracilis*	whiptail catfish	6.0	7.0
Gasteropelecus	*sternicla*	common hatchetfish	6.0	7.0
Gymnocorymbus	*ternetzi*	black skirt tetra	6.0	8.5
Hemichromis	*bimaculatus*	jewel cichlid	6.0	7.0
Hemmigrammus	*bleheri*	rummynose tetra	6.0	6.5
Hemmigrammus	*caudovittatus*	Buenos Aires tetra	6.0	8.5
Hemmigrammus	*erythrozonus*	glowlight tetra	6.0	7.5
Hemmigrammus	*ocellifer*	head-and-taillight tetra	6.0	7.5
Hyphessobrycon	*callistus*	none	6.0	7.5
Hyphessobrycon	*erythrostigma*	bleeding heart tetra	6.0	7.5
Hyphessobrycon	*flammeus*	flame tetra	6.0	7.5
Hyphessobrycon	*heterorhabdus*	flag tetra	6.0	6.5
Hyphessobrycon	*loretoensis*	loreto tetra	6.0	6.5
Macropodus	*opercularis*	paradisefish	6.0	8.0
Megalamphodus	*megalopterus*	black phantom tetra	6.0	7.5
Monocirrhus	*polyacanthus*	leaf fish	6.0	6.5
Nothobranchius	*rachovii*	annual killifish	6.0	6.5
Pangio	*kuhlii*	coolie loach	6.0	7.0
Pantodon	*buchholzi*	African butterflyfish	6.0	7.0
Pelvicachromis	*pulcher*	kribensis	6.0	7.0
Phenacogrammus	*interruptus*	Congo tetra	6.0	6.5

Genus	Species	Common Name(s)	pH min	pH max
Pristella	maxillarus	X-ray tetra	6.0	8.0
Protopterus	dolloi	African lungfish	6.0	7.0
Pterophyllum	scalare	angelfish	6.0	8.0
Symphysodon	aequifasciatus	discus	6.0	7.0
Thayeria	obliqua	penguin tetra	6.0	7.5
Trichogaster	trichopterus	blue gourami	6.0	9.0
Trichopsis	pumila	dwarf croaking gourami	6.0	7.0
Aequidens	pulcher	blue acara	6.5	7.0
Amia	calva	bowfin	6.5	7.5
Ancistrus	dolichopterus	bristle-nosed plecostomus	6.5	7.0
Barbus	callipterus	clipper barb	6.5	7.5
Campostoma	anomalum	central stoneroller	6.5	7.5
Cichlasoma	cyanoguttatum	Texas cichlid	6.5	7.5
Cichlasoma	octofasciatum	Jack Dempsey	6.5	7.0
Copenia	arnoldi	splashing tetra	6.5	7.5
Cottus	bairdi	mottled sculpin	6.5	7.5
Elassoma	evergladei	Everglades pygmy sunfish	6.5	7.5
Elassoma	zonatum	banded pygmy sunfish	6.5	7.5
Enneacanthus	chaetodon	black-banded sunfish	6.5	7.5
Enneacanthus	gloriosus	blue-spotted sunfish	6.5	7.5
Epalzeorhyncos	bicolor	red-tailed shark	6.5	7.5
Epalzeorhyncos	erythurus	red-finned shark	6.5	7.5
Etheostoma	blennioides	greenside darter	6.5	7.5
Etheostoma	flabellare	fantail darter	6.5	7.5
Etheostoma	rufilineatum	redline darter	6.5	7.5
Fundulus	chrysotus	golden topminnow	6.5	7.5
Fundulus	notatus	black-spotted topminnow	6.5	7.5
Fundulus	olivaceus	olive topminnow	6.5	7.5
Gnathonemus	petersii	Peters' elephantnose	6.5	7.5
Jordanella	floridae	flagfish	6.5	8.0

continued

List 4: Cross Reference of Fish Species by pH Range (continued)

Genus	Species	Common Name(s)	pH min	pH max
Kryptopterus	minor	glass catfish	6.5	7.0
Lepisosteus	oculatus	spotted gar	6.5	7.0
Lepomis	sp.	sunfish	6.5	7.0
Lucania	goodei	bluefin topminnow	6.5	6.8
Luxilus	coccogenis	warpaint shiner	6.5	7.5
Microgeophagus	ramirezi	butterfly cichlid	6.5	7.0
Noturus	miurus	brindled madtom	6.5	7.5
Percina	caprodes	logperch	6.5	7.5
Phoxinus	eos	northern redbelly dace	6.5	7.5
Phoxinus	erythrogaster	southern redbelly dace	6.5	7.5
Phoxinus	tennesseensis	Tennessee dace	6.5	7.5
Poecilia	latipinna	green sailfin molly	6.5	7.5
Pteronotropis	welaka	bluenosed shiner	6.5	7.5
Rasbora	borapetensis	red-tailed rasbora	6.5	7.0
Sorubim	lima	shovel-nose catfish	6.5	7.5
Synodontis	nigriventris	upside-down catfish	6.5	7.5
Tanichthys	albonubes	White Cloud Mountain minnow	6.5	7.5
Trichogaster	leeri	pearl gourami	6.5	8.5
Archocentrus	nigrofasciatum	convict	7.0	8.0
Bedotia	geayi	Madagascar rainbowfish	7.0	7.0
Chanda	ranga	glassfish	7.0	8.0
Chromobotia	macracanthus	clown loach	7.0	8.0
Cichlasoma	salvini	yellow-belly cichlid	7.0	8.0
Iriatherina	werneri	threadfin rainbowfish	7.0	7.5
Mastacembelus	erythrotaenia	fire eel	7.0	7.5
Melanotaenia	bosemani	Boseman's rainbowfish	7.0	8.0
Melanotaenia	exquisitus	exquisite rainbowfish	7.0	8.0
Melanotaenia	nigrans	black rainbowfish	7.0	8.0
Melanotaenia	splendida australis	splendid rainbowfish	7.0	8.0
Melanotaenia	trifasciata	rainbowfish	7.0	8.0

Genus	Species	Common Name(s)	pH min	pH max
Rasbora	kalochroma	clown rasbora	7.0	7.5
Telmatherina	ladigesi	Celebes rainbowfish	7.0	7.0
Thorichthys	meeki	firemouth	7.0	7.0
Toxotes	jaculatrix	archer fish	7.0	7.5
Xiphophorus	helleri	swordtail	7.0	8.3
Xiphophorus	maculatus	platy, moonfish	7.0	8.2
Xiphophorus	variatus	variegated platy, variatus platy	7.0	8.3
Cyrtocara	moorii	Moor's African cichlid	7.5	8.5
Julidochromis	dickfeldi	Dickfeld's julie	7.5	9.0
Julidochromis	marlieri	Marlier's julie	7.5	9.0
Julidochromis	ornatus	ornate julie	7.5	9.0
Labeotropheus	trewavasae	Trewavas' African cichlid	7.5	8.5
Labidochromis	lividus	African cichlid	7.5	8.5
Melanochromis	johanni	Johann's African cichlid	7.5	8.5
Nannochromis	parilus	none	7.5	8.0
Neolamprologus	brichardi	Brichard's African cichlid	7.5	9.0
Neolamprologus	leleupi	lemon cichlid	7.5	9.0
Neolamprologus	multifasciatus	shell-dwelling African cichlid	7.5	9.0
Poecilia	sphenops	black molly	7.5	8.5
Poecilia	velifera	sailfin molly	7.5	8.5
Pseudotropheus	zebra	zebra African cichlid	7.5	8.5
Tropheus	duboisi	Dubois's tropheus	7.5	9.0
Tropheus	moorii	Moor's tropheus	7.5	9.0

Other Lists

Two additional ways of sorting may prove helpful. First, an alphabetic list by genus and species, cross referenced to the common name, and then the list alphabetized by common name, cross referenced to the genus and species.

List 5: Alphabetic Cross Reference of Genus Names

Genus	Species	Common Name(s)
Aequidens	*pulcher*	blue acara
Amia	*calva*	bowfin
Ancistrus	*dolichopterus*	bristle-nosed plecostomus
Anostomus	*anostomus*	striped headstander
Aphyocharax	*anisitsi*	bloodfin
Aphyosemion	*australe*	African killifish
Apistogramma	*agassizii*	dwarf cichlid
Aplocheilus	*blockii*	panchax
Archocentrus	*nigrofasciatum*	convict
Astayanax	*mexicanus*	blind cave tetra
Barbus	*callipterus*	clipper barb
Barbus	*conchonius*	rosy barb
Barbus	*everetti*	clown barb
Barbus	*holotaenia*	blackstripe barb
Barbus	*hulstaerti*	African clown barb
Barbus	*nigrofasciatus*	black ruby barb
Barbus	*oligolepus*	checkered barb
Barbus	*schwanfeldi*	tinfoil barb
Barbus	*tetrazona*	tiger barb
Barbus	*titteya*	cherry barb
Bedotia	*geayi*	Madagascar rainbowfish
Betta	*splendens*	Siamese fighting fish
Botia	*morleti*	Hora's loach
Brachydanio	*albolineatus*	pearl danio
Brachydanio	*nigrofasciatus*	spotted danio
Brachydanio	*rerio*	zebra danio
Campostoma	*anomalum*	central stoneroller
Carnegiella	*marthae*	black-winged hatchetfish
Carnegiella	*strigata*	marbled hatchetfish
Chalceus	*macrolepidotus*	pink-tailed chalceus
Chanda	*ranga*	glassfish

Genus	Species	Common Name(s)
Chromobotia	macracanthus	clown loach
Cichlasoma	cyanoguttatum	Texas cichlid
Cichlasoma	octofasciatum	Jack Dempsey
Cichlasoma	salvini	yellow-belly cichlid
Colisa	laelia	dwarf gourami
Copenia	arnoldi	splashing tetra
Corydoras	agassizii	Agassiz's corydoras
Corydoras	metae	skunk corydoras
Corydoras	paleatus	common corydoras
Corydoras	pygmaeus	pygmy corydoras
Cottus	bairdi	mottled sculpin
Cynolebias	bellotti	Argentine pearlfish
Cyrtocara	moorii	Moor's African cichlid
Danio	aequipinnatus	giant danio
Elassoma	evergladei	Everglades pygmy sunfish
Elassoma	zonatum	banded pygmy sunfish
Enneacanthus	chaetodon	black-banded sunfish
Enneacanthus	gloriosus	blue-spotted sunfish
Epalzeorhyncos	bicolor	red-tailed shark
Epalzeorhyncos	erythurus	red-finned shark
Epiplatys	chevalieri	killifish
Etheostoma	blennioides	greenside darter
Etheostoma	flabellare	fantail darter
Etheostoma	rufilineatum	redline darter
Exodon	paradoxus	bucktoothed tetra
Farlowella	gracilis	whiptail catfish
Fundulus	chrysotus	golden topminnow
Fundulus	notatus	black-spotted topminnow
Fundulus	olivaceus	olive topminnow
Gasteropelecus	sternicla	common hatchetfish

continued

List 5: Alphabetic Cross Reference of Genus Names *(continued)*

Genus	Species	Common Name(s)
Gnathonemus	*petersii*	Peters' elephantnose
Gymnocorymbus	*ternetzi*	black skirt tetra
Hasemania	*nana*	silvertip tetra
Hemichromis	*bimaculatus*	jewel cichlid
Hemmigrammus	*bleheri*	rummynose tetra
Hemmigrammus	*caudovittatus*	Buenos Aires tetra
Hemmigrammus	*erythrozonus*	glowlight tetra
Hemmigrammus	*ocellifer*	head-and-taillight tetra
Hyphessobrycon	*bentosi*	Roberts' tetra
Hyphessobrycon	*callistus*	none
Hyphessobrycon	*erythrostigma*	bleeding heart tetra
Hyphessobrycon	*flammeus*	flame tetra
Hyphessobrycon	*herbertaxelrodi*	black neon tetra
Hyphessobrycon	*heterorhabdus*	flag tetra
Hyphessobrycon	*loretoensis*	loreto tetra
Hyphessobrycon	*pulchripinnis*	lemon tetra
Hypostomus	*punctatus*	plecostomus cat
Iriatherina	*werneri*	threadfin rainbowfish
Jordanella	*floridae*	flagfish
Julidochromis	*dickfeldi*	Dickfeld's julie
Julidochromis	*marlieri*	Marlier's julie
Julidochromis	*ornatus*	ornate julie
Kryptopterus	*minor*	glass catfish
Labeotropheus	*trewavasae*	Trewavas' African cichlid
Labidochromis	*lividus*	African cichlid
Lepisosteus	*oculatus*	spotted gar
Lepomis	*sp.*	sunfish
Leporinus	*fasciatus*	banded leporinus
Lucania	*goodei*	bluefin topminnow
Luxilus	*coccogenis*	warpaint shiner
Macropodus	*opercularis*	paradisefish

Genus	Species	Common Name(s)
Mastacembelus	erythrotaenia	fire eel
Megalamphodus	megalopterus	black phantom tetra
Megalamphodus	sweglesi	red phantom tetra
Melanochromis	johanni	Johann's African cichlid
Melanotaenia	bosemani	Boseman's rainbowfish
Melanotaenia	exquisitus	exquisite rainbowfish
Melanotaenia	nigrans	black rainbowfish
Melanotaenia	splendida australis	splendid rainbowfish
Melanotaenia	trifasciata	rainbowfish
Microgeophagus	ramirezi	butterfly cichlid
Moenkhausia	sanctaefilomenae	yellow-banded moenkhausia
Monocirrhus	polyacanthus	leaf fish
Nannochromis	parilus	none
Nannostomus	marginatus	dwarf pencilfish
Nannostomus	trifasciatus	three-lined pencilfish
Nematobrycon	palmeri	emperor tetra
Neolamprologus	brichardi	Brichard's African cichlid
Neolamprologus	leleupi	lemon cichlid
Neolamprologus	multifasciatus	shell-dwelling African cichlid
Nothobranchius	rachovii	annual killifish
Noturus	miurus	brindled madtom
Otocinclus	arnoldi	Arnold's otocinclus
Pangio	kuhlii	coolie loach
Pantodon	buchholzi	African butterflyfish
Paracheirodon	axelrodi	cardinal tetra
Paracheirodon	innesi	neon tetra
Pelvicachromis	pulcher	kribensis
Percina	caprodes	logperch
Phenacogrammus	interruptus	Congo tetra
Phoxinus	eos	northern redbelly dace
Phoxinus	erythrogaster	southern redbelly dace

continued

List 5: Alphabetic Cross Reference of Genus Names *(continued)*

Genus	Species	Common Name(s)
Phoxinus	tennesseensis	Tennessee dace
Poecilia	latipinna	green sailfin molly
Poecilia	reticulata	guppy
Poecilia	sphenops	black molly
Poecilia	velifera	sailfin molly
Pristella	maxillarus	X-ray tetra
Protopterus	dolloi	African lungfish
Pseudotropheus	zebra	zebra African cichlid
Pteronotropis	welaka	bluenosed shiner
Pterophyllum	scalare	angelfish
Rasbora	borapetensis	red-tailed rasbora
Rasbora	heteromorpha	harlequin rasbora
Rasbora	kalochroma	clown rasbora
Semaprochilodus	taeniurus	flag-tailed prochilodus
Serrasalmus	nattereri	red piranha
Sorubim	lima	shovel-nose catfish
Symphysodon	aequifasciatus	discus
Synodontis	nigriventris	upside-down catfish
Tanichthys	albonubes	White Cloud Mountain minnow
Telmatherina	ladigesi	Celebes rainbowfish
Thayeria	obliqua	penguin tetra
Thorichthys	meeki	firemouth
Toxotes	jaculatrix	archer fish
Trichogaster	leeri	pearl gourami
Trichogaster	trichopterus	blue gourami
Trichopsis	pumila	dwarf croaking gourami
Tropheus	duboisi	Dubois's tropheus
Tropheus	moorii	Moor's tropheus
Xiphophorus	helleri	swordtail
Xiphophorus	maculatus	platy, moonfish
Xiphophorus	variatus	variegated platy, variatus platy

Plants

Plants, together with the various kinds of algae, provide the basis for all other organisms living in freshwater and terrestrial habitats. Photosynthesis, the process by which the sun's energy is captured in sugar molecules, feeds us all.

As is the case with fish, thousands of aquatic and bog plants have been cultivated in aquariums. All major plant groups are represented, including mosses, ferns, and flowering plants. The only ones missing are the gymnosperms (conifers, cycads, and a few others).

Location

The first plant list is arranged geographically, to facilitate its use in designing habitat tanks.

List 6: Freshwater Plants by Locality

Genus	Species	Variety	Common Name(s)	Range
Ansellia	africana		leopard orchid	Africa
Bolbitis	heudelotii		African water fern	Africa
Ceratopteris	cornuta		floating fern	Africa
Nymphaea	lotus		tiger lily	Africa, Southeast Asia
Echinodorus	horizontalis		Honduran sword plant	Amazonia
Limnophila	sessiliflora		dwarf ambulia	Asia
Marsilea	drummondi		Australian water clover	Australia
Marsilea	exarata		four leaf water clover	Australia
Echinodorus	amazonicus		Amazon sword plant	Brazil
Echinodorus	martii		ruffled sword plant	Brazil
Echinodorus	osiris		red sword plant	Brazil
Echinodorus	quadricostatus		dwarf sword plant	Brazil
Alternanthera		"reineckii"	Reineck's alternanthera	Brazil, Paraguay
Cabomba	caroliniana		green cabomba	Central America
Echinodorus	cordifolius		radicans sword plant	Central America
Echinodorus	latifolius		narrow-leaved sword plant	Central America
Chara	species		crystalwort	Eastern U.S.

continued

List 6: Freshwater Plants by Locality *(continued)*

Genus	Species	Variety	Common Name(s)	Range
Fontinalis	species		water moss	Eastern U.S.
Sagittaria	australis		southern arrowhead	Eastern U.S.
Sagittaria	latifolia		narrow-leaved arrowhead	Eastern U.S.
Hygrophila	polysperma		dwarf hygro	India
Rotala	macrandra		giant red rotala	India
Hygrophila	corymbosa		giant hygro	India, Southeast Asia
Hygrophila	difformis		water wisteria	India, Southeast Asia
Limnophila	aquatica		giant ambulia	India, Sri Lanka
Vallisneria	americana	biwaensis	corkscrew val	Japan
Aponegeton	boivinianus		none	Madagascar
Aponegeton	madagascarensis		Madagascar lace plant	Madagascar
Aponegeton	ulvaceus		none	Madagascar
Cryptocoryne	affinis		none	Malaysia
Cabomba	aquatica		yellow cabomba	New World tropics
Anubias	barteri	glabra	smooth anubias	Nigeria, Cameroon
Anubias	barteri	nana	dwarf anubias	Nigeria, Cameroon
Ludwigia	repens		creeping ludwigia	North and Central America
Echinodorus	parviflorus		Peruvian sword plant	Peru, Brazil, Bolivia
Lagarosiphon	major		African water pest	South Africa
Cabomba	furcata		red cabomba	South America
Echinodorus	bleheri		broadleaf sword plant	South America
Echinodorus	tenellus		pygmy chain sword plant	South America
Egeria	densa		water pest	South America
Heteranthera	zosterifolia		stargrass	South America
Hygrophila	guianensis		Thai hygro	South America
Limnobium	laevigatum		frogsbit	South America
Barclaya	longifolia		orchid lily	Southeast Asia
Microsorium	pteropus		Java fern	Southeast Asia

Genus	Species	Variety	Common Name(s)	Range
Rotala	rotundifolia		dwarf rotala	Southeast Asia
Vesicularia	dubyana		Java moss	Southeast Asia
Limnobium	spongia		American frogsbit	Southeastern U.S.
Nitella	species		crystalwort	Southeastern U.S.
Nymphoides	aquatica		banana plant	Southeastern U.S.
Potomageton	species		pondweed	Southeastern U.S.
Sagittaria	graminea		dwarf arrowhead	Southeastern U.S.
Aponegeton	crispus		ruffled aponegeton	Sri Lanka
Cryptocoryne	beckettii		Beckett's crypt	Sri Lanka
Cryptocoryne	wendtii		Wendt's crypt	Sri Lanka
Cryptocoryne	willisii		common crypt	Sri Lanka
Cryptocoryne	balansae	crispatula	Thai crypt	Thailand
Cryptocoryne	cordata		none	Thailand
Bacopa	caroliniana		giant bacopa	United States
Azolla	filiculoides		azolla	Worldwide
Bacopa	monnieri		dwarf bacopa	Worldwide
Ceratophyllum	demersum		hornwort	Worldwide
Ceratopteris	thalictroides		water sprite	Worldwide
Eichornia	crassipes		water hyacinth	Worldwide
Lemna	minor		duckweed	Worldwide
Salvinia	auriculata		salvinia	Worldwide
Vallisneria	spiralis	spiralis	spiral eelgrass	Worldwide

Temperature

Sorting plants according to their minimum temperature requirements has been standard horticultural practice for a long time. Temperature influences the rate of photosynthesis, along with many other important cellular functions. Matching the aquarium environment to the plant's preferred temperature avoids various maladies. Pale, stringy growth, and loss of leaves occur, for example, in plants kept too warm.

List 7: Freshwater Plants by Minimum Temperature

Genus	Species	Variety	Common Name(s)	min T (°F)
Chara	species		crystalwort	39
Eichornia	crassipes		water hyacinth	39
Fontinalis	species		water moss	39
Potomageton	species		pondweed	39
Sagittaria	australis		southern arrowhead	39
Sagittaria	latifolia		narrow-leaved arrowhead	39
Nitella	species		crystalwort	45
Lemna	minor		duckweed	50
Limnobium	spongia		American frogsbit	55
Vallisneria	spiralis	spiralis	spiral eelgrass	59
Ceratophyllum	demersum		hornwort	64
Ceratopteris	cornuta		floating fern	64
Lagarosiphon	major		African water pest	64
Vesicularia	dubyana		Java moss	64
Ansellia	africana		leopard orchid	65
Aponegeton	boivinianus		none	68
Aponegeton	madagascarensis		Madagascar lace plant	68
Azolla	filiculoides		azolla	68
Egeria	densa		water pest	68
Hygrophila	polysperma		dwarf hygro	68
Ludwigia	repens		creeping ludwigia	68
Microsorium	pteropus		Java fern	68
Nymphoides	aquatica		banana plant	68
Rotala	rotundifolia		dwarf rotala	68
Salvinia	auriculata		salvinia	68
Bacopa	monnieri		dwarf bacopa	71
Alternanthera		"reineckii"	Reineck's alternanthera	72
Anubias	barteri	glabra	smooth anubias	72
Anubias	barteri	nana	dwarf anubias	72
Aponegeton	crispus		ruffled aponegeton	72

Genus	Species	Variety	Common Name(s)	min T (°F)
Aponegeton	ulvaceus		none	72
Bacopa	caroliniana		giant bacopa	72
Barclaya	longifolia		orchid lily	72
Cabomba	caroliniana		green cabomba	72
Cryptocoryne	affinis		none	72
Cryptocoryne	willisii		common crypt	72
Echinodorus	cordifolius		radicans sword plant	72
Echinodorus	horizontalis		Honduran sword plant	72
Echinodorus	latifolius		narrow-leaved sword plant	72
Echinodorus	osiris		red sword plant	72
Echinodorus	parviflorus		Peruvian sword plant	72
Echinodorus	quadricostatus		dwarf sword plant	72
Echinodorus	tenellus		pygmy chain sword plant	72
Hygrophila	corymbosa		giant hygro	72
Limnobium	laevigatum		frogsbit	72
Limnophila	sessiliflora		dwarf ambulia	72
Marsilea	drummondi		Australian water clover	72
Marsilea	exarata		four leaf water clover	72
Nymphaea	lotus		tiger lily	72
Sagittaria	graminea		dwarf arrowhead	72
Echinodorus	amazonicus		Amazon sword plant	74
Bolbitis	heudelotii		African water fern	75
Cabomba	aquatica		yellow cabomba	75
Cabomba	furcata		red cabomba	75
Ceratopteris	thalictroides		water sprite	75
Cryptocoryne	beckettii		Beckett's crypt	75
Cryptocoryne	wendtii		Wendt's crypt	75
Echinodorus	bleheri		broadleaf sword plant	75
Echinodorus	martii		ruffled sword plant	75
Heteranthera	zosterifolia		stargrass	75

continued

List 7: Freshwater Plants by Minimum Temperature *(continued)*

Genus	Species	Variety	Common Name(s)	min T (°F)
Hygrophila	difformis		water wisteria	75
Hygrophila	guianensis		Thai hygro	75
Limnophila	aquatica		giant ambulia	75
Vallisneria	americana	biwaensis	corkscrew val	75
Cryptocoryne	balansae	crispatula	Thai crypt	77
Cryptocoryne	cordata		none	77
Rotala	macrandra		giant red rotala	77

Plants and Water Hardness

The dissolved mineral content of the water affects plant metabolism as much as it does fish metabolism, although in different ways. The balance between calcium and carbon dioxide, which is affected by hardness, affects how plants obtain their carbon for use in photosynthesis.

List 8: Freshwater Plants by Minimum Hardness Preference

Genus	Species	Variety	Common Name(s)	min ppm $CaCO_3$	max ppm $CaCO_3$
Chara	species		crystalwort	35	250
Eichornia	crassipes		water hyacinth	35	250
Fontinalis	species		water moss	35	250
Nitella	species		crystalwort	35	250
Potomageton	species		pondweed	35	250
Sagittaria	australis		southern arrowhead	35	250
Sagittaria	latifolia		narrow-leaved arrowhead	35	250
Aponegeton	madagascarensis		Madagascar lace plant	36	54
Alternanthera		"reineckii"	Reineck's alternanthera	36	143
Cabomba	furcata		red cabomba	36	143
Cryptocoryne	cordata		none	36	143
Azolla	filiculoides		azolla	36	179
Cabomba	aquatica		yellow cabomba	36	179
Marsilea	exarata		four leaf water clover	36	179

Genus	Species	Variety	Common Name(s)	min ppm CaCO$_3$	max ppm CaCO$_3$
Aponegeton	boivinianus		none	36	214
Barclaya	longifolia		orchid lily	36	214
Bolbitis	heudelotii		African water fern	36	214
Cabomba	caroliniana		green cabomba	36	214
Cryptocoryne	balansae	crispatula	Thai crypt	36	214
Echinodorus	amazonicus		Amazon sword plant	36	214
Echinodorus	martii		ruffled sword plant	36	214
Echinodorus	quadricostatus		dwarf sword plant	36	214
Limnobium	laevigatum		frogsbit	36	214
Microsorium	pteropus		Java fern	36	214
Nymphaea	lotus		tiger lily	36	214
Rotala	macrandra		giant red rotala	36	214
Anubias	barteri	glabra	smooth anubias	36	268
Anubias	barteri	nana	dwarf anubias	36	268
Aponegeton	crispus		ruffled aponegeton	36	268
Aponegeton	ulvaceus		none	36	268
Bacopa	monnieri		dwarf bacopa	36	268
Cryptocoryne	beckettii		Beckett's crypt	36	268
Cryptocoryne	willisii		common crypt	36	268
Echinodorus	bleheri		broadleaf sword plant	36	268
Echinodorus	latifolius		narrow-leaved sword plant	36	268
Echinodorus	parviflorus		Peruvian sword plant	36	268
Echinodorus	tenellus		pygmy chain sword plant	36	268
Hygrophila	corymbosa		giant hygro	36	268
Hygrophila	difformis		water wisteria	36	268
Hygrophila	guianensis		Thai hygro	36	268
Hygrophila	polysperma		dwarf hygro	36	268
Lemna	minor		duckweed	36	268
Ludwigia	repens		creeping ludwigia	36	268

continued

List 8: Freshwater Plants by Minimum Hardness Preference (*continued*)

Genus	Species	Variety	Common Name(s)	min ppm CaCO₃	max ppm CaCO₃
Marsilea	drummondi		Australian water clover	36	268
Rotala	rotundifolia		dwarf rotala	36	268
Vesicularia	dubyana		Java moss	36	268
Limnobium	spongia		American frogsbit	36	214
Cryptocoryne	affinis		none	54	268
Heteranthera	zosterifolia		stargrass	54	268
Limnophila	sessiliflora		dwarf ambulia	54	268
Nymphoides	aquatica		banana plant	89	179
Ceratopteris	thalictroides		water sprite	89	214
Echinodorus	horizontalis		Honduran sword plant	89	214
Lagarosiphon	major		African water pest	89	214
Limnophila	aquatica		giant ambulia	89	214
Salvinia	auriculata		salvinia	89	214
Vallisneria	americana	biwaensis	corkscrew val	89	214
Vallisneria	spiralis	spiralis	spiral eelgrass	89	214
Bacopa	caroliniana		giant bacopa	89	268
Ceratophyllum	demersum		hornwort	89	268
Ceratopteris	cornuta		floating fern	89	268
Cryptocoryne	wendtii		Wendt's crypt	89	268
Echinodorus	cordifolius		radicans sword plant	89	268
Echinodorus	osiris		red sword plant	89	268
Sagittaria	graminea		dwarf arrowhead	89	268
Egeria	densa		water pest	143	268
Ansellia	africana		leopard orchid	N/A	N/A

Plants and pH

The pH of the water plays a major role in the balance between the various forms in which carbon dioxide is present and available to plants. Like fish, many plants adapt to pH values outside their optimum range.

List 9: Freshwater Plants by pH Preference

Genus	Species	Variety	Common Name(s)	pH min	pH max
Eichornia	crassipes		water hyacinth	5.0	8.0
Aponegeton	madagascarensis		Madagascar lace plant	5.5	6.5
Alternanthera		"reineckii"	Reineck's alternanthera	5.5	7.0
Aponegeton	ulvaceus		none	5.5	7.0
Microsorium	pteropus		Java fern	5.5	7.0
Rotala	rotundifolia		dwarf rotala	5.5	7.2
Ceratopteris	cornuta		floating fern	5.5	7.5
Lemna	minor		duckweed	5.5	7.5
Ludwigia	repens		creeping ludwigia	5.5	7.5
Bolbitis	heudelotii		African water fern	5.8	7.0
Vesicularia	dubyana		Java moss	5.8	7.5
Cabomba	aquatica		yellow cabomba	6.0	6.8
Cabomba	furcata		red cabomba	6.0	6.8
Barclaya	longifolia		orchid lily	6.0	7.0
Cryptocoryne	cordata		none	6.0	7.0
Marsilea	exarata		four leaf water clover	6.0	7.0
Rotala	macrandra		giant red rotala	6.0	7.0
Salvinia	auriculata		salvinia	6.0	7.0
Azolla	filiculoides		azolla	6.0	7.2
Nymphaea	lotus		tiger lily	6.0	7.2
Vallisneria	americana	biwaensis	corkscrew val	6.0	7.2
Anubias	barteri	glabra	smooth anubias	6.0	7.5
Anubias	barteri	nana	dwarf anubias	6.0	7.5
Bacopa	caroliniana		giant bacopa	6.0	7.5
Bacopa	monnieri		dwarf bacopa	6.0	7.5
Ceratophyllum	demersum		hornwort	6.0	7.5
Heteranthera	zosterifolia		stargrass	6.0	7.5
Limnophila	sessiliflora		dwarf ambulia	6.0	7.5

continued

List 9: Freshwater Plants by pH Preference (*continued*)

Genus	Species	Variety	Common Name(s)	pH min	pH max
Cryptocoryne	affinis		none	6.0	7.8
Echinodorus	parviflorus		Peruvian sword plant	6.0	7.8
Limnophila	aquatica		giant ambulia	6.5	7.0
Aponegeton	crispus		ruffled aponegeton	6.5	7.2
Cabomba	caroliniana		green cabomba	6.5	7.2
Ceratopteris	thalictroides		water sprite	6.5	7.2
Cryptocoryne	balansae	crispatula	Thai crypt	6.5	7.2
Cryptocoryne	willisii		common crypt	6.5	7.2
Echinodorus	amazonicus		Amazon sword plant	6.5	7.2
Echinodorus	horizontalis		Honduran sword plant	6.5	7.2
Echinodorus	martii		ruffled sword plant	6.5	7.2
Echinodorus	tenellus		pygmy chain sword plant	6.5	7.2
Hygrophila	guianensis		Thai hygro	6.5	7.2
Nymphoides	aquatica		banana plant	6.5	7.2
Aponegeton	boivinianus		none	6.5	7.5
Cryptocoryne	beckettii		Beckett's crypt	6.5	7.5
Cryptocoryne	wendtii		Wendt's crypt	6.5	7.5
Echinodorus	bleheri		broadleaf sword plant	6.5	7.5
Echinodorus	cordifolius		radicans sword plant	6.5	7.5
Echinodorus	latifolius		narrow-leaved sword plant	6.5	7.5
Echinodorus	osiris		red sword plant	6.5	7.5
Echinodorus	quadricostatus		dwarf sword plant	6.5	7.5
Egeria	densa		water pest	6.5	7.5
Hygrophila	corymbosa		giant hygro	6.5	7.5
Hygrophila	difformis		water wisteria	6.5	7.5
Limnobium	laevigatum		frogsbit	6.5	7.5
Limnobium	spongia		American frogsbit	6.5	7.5
Marsilea	drummondi		Australian water clover	6.5	7.5
Potomageton	species		pondweed	6.5	7.5
Sagittaria	australis		southern arrowhead	6.5	7.5

Genus	Species	Variety	Common Name(s)	pH min	pH max
Sagittaria	*graminea*		dwarf arrowhead	6.5	7.5
Sagittaria	*latifolia*		narrow-leaved arrowhead	6.5	7.5
Vallisneria	*spiralis*	*spiralis*	spiral eelgrass	6.5	7.5
Hygrophila	*polysperma*		dwarf hygro	6.5	7.8
Fontinalis	species		water moss	6.5	8.0
Lagarosiphon	*major*		African water pest	6.8	8.0
Chara	species		crystalwort	7.0	8.0
Nitella	species		crystalwort	7.0	8.0
Ansellia	*africana*		leopard orchid	N/A	N/A

Other Helpful Plant Lists

Following are plants listed alphabetically by scientific name and common name.

List 10: Alphabetic Cross Reference of Plants by Common Name

Common Name(s)	Genus	Species	Variety
African water fern	*Bolbitis*	*heudelotii*	
African water pest	*Lagarosiphon*	*major*	
Amazon sword plant	*Echinodorus*	*amazonicus*	
American frogsbit	*Limnobium*	*spongia*	
Australian water clover	*Marsilea*	*drummondi*	
banana plant	*Nymphoides*	*aquatica*	
Beckett's crypt	*Cryptocoryne*	*beckettii*	
broadleaf sword plant	*Echinodorus*	*bleheri*	
common crypt	*Cryptocoryne*	*willisii*	
corkscrew eelgrass	*Vallisneria*	*americana*	*biwaensis*
creeping ludwigia	*Ludwigia*	*repens*	
crystalwort	*Chara*	species	
crystalwort	*Nitella*	species	
duckweed	*Lemna*	*minor*	
dwarf ambulia	*Limnophila*	*sessiliflora*	

continued

List 10: Alphabetic Cross Reference of Plants by Common Name *(continued)*

Common Name(s)	Genus	Species	Variety
dwarf anubias	*Anubias*	*barteri*	*nana*
dwarf arrowhead	*Sagittaria*	*graminea*	
dwarf bacopa	*Bacopa*	*monnieri*	
dwarf hygro	*Hygrophila*	*polysperma*	
dwarf rotala	*Rotala*	*rotundifolia*	
dwarf sword plant	*Echinodorus*	*quadricostatus*	
floating fern	*Ceratopteris*	*cornuta*	
floating fern	*Salvinia*	*auriculata*	
four leaf water clover	*Marsilea*	*exarata*	
frogsbit	*Limnobium*	*laevigatum*	
giant ambulia	*Limnophila*	*aquatica*	
giant bacopa	*Bacopa*	*caroliniana*	
giant hygro	*Hygrophila*	*corymbosa*	
giant red rotala	*Rotala*	*macrandra*	
green cabomba	*Cabomba*	*caroliniana*	
Honduran sword plant	*Echinodorus*	*horizontalis*	
hornwort	*Ceratophyllum*	*demersum*	
Java fern	*Microsorium*	*pteropus*	
Java moss	*Vesicularia*	*dubyana*	
leopard orchid	*Ansellia*	*africana*	
Madagascar lace plant	*Aponegeton*	*madagascarensis*	
narrow-leaved arrowhead	*Sagittaria*	*latifolia*	
narrow-leaved sword plant	*Echinodorus*	*latifolius*	
none	*Aponegeton*	*boivinianus*	
none	*Aponegeton*	*ulvaceus*	
none	*Cryptocoryne*	*affinis*	
none	*Cryptocoryne*	*cordata*	
orchid lily	*Barclaya*	*longifolia*	
Peruvian sword plant	*Echinodorus*	*parviflorus*	
pondweed	*Potomageton*	*species*	

Common Name(s)	Genus	Species	Variety
pygmy chain sword plant	*Echinodorus*	*tenellus*	
radicans sword plant	*Echinodorus*	*cordifolius*	
red cabomba	*Cabomba*	*furcata*	
red floating fern	*Azolla*	*filiculoides*	
red sword plant	*Echinodorus*	*osiris*	
Reineck's alternanthera	*Alternanthera*		*"reineckii"*
ruffled aponegeton	*Aponegeton*	*crispus*	
ruffled sword plant	*Echinodorus*	*martii*	
smooth anubias	*Anubias*	*barteri*	*glabra*
southern arrowhead	*Sagittaria*	*australis*	
spiral eelgrass	*Vallisneria*	*spiralis*	*spiralis*
stargrass	*Heteranthera*	*zosterifolia*	
Thai crypt	*Cryptocoryne*	*balansae*	*crispatula*
Thai hygro	*Hygrophila*	*guianensis*	
tiger lily	*Nymphaea*	*lotus*	
water hyacinth	*Eichornia*	*crassipes*	
water moss	*Fontinalis*	species	
water pest	*Egeria*	*densa*	
water sprite	*Ceratopteris*	*thalictroides*	
water wisteria	*Hygrophila*	*difformis*	
Wendt's crypt	*Cryptocoryne*	*wendtii*	
yellow cabomba	*Cabomba*	*aquatica*	

TANK SPECIFICATIONS

Table 1: Standard Aquarium Tank Dimensions, Floor Loads, and Lighting Requirements

(ß=Breeder, H=High, L=Long, X=Extra High, HX=Hex)

Tank Capacity	Nominal Dimensions L × D × H (in.)	Floor Load (lbs/ft²)	Fluorescent Lighting (watts)	Metal Halide Lighting (watts)
30X	24x12x24	120	40	NA
110X	48x18x30	147	160	200
20H	24x12x16	80	40	NA
20L	30x12x12	64	40	NA
25	24x12x20	100	40	NA
29	30x12x18	93	40	NA
30	36x12x16	80	60	NA
30B	36x18x12	53	120	100
33L	48x13x12	66	80	200
37	30x12x22	118	40	100
38	36x12x20	101	60	100
40B	36x18x16	71	120	150

continued

Table 1: Standard Aquarium Tank Dimensions, Floor Loads, and Lighting Requirements *(continued)*

(ß=ßreeder, H=High, L=Long, X=Extra High, HX=Hex)

Tank Capacity	Nominal Dimensions L × D × H (in.)	Floor Load (lbs/ft²)	Fluorescent Lighting (watts)	Metal Halide Lighting (watts)
40L	48x13x16	80	80	200
45	36x12x24	120	120	150
50	36x18x18	89	120	150
55	48x13x20	110	80	200
65	36x18x24	116	120	300
75	48x18x20	100	160	200
90	48x18x24	120	240	300
120	48x24x24	120	320	300
77	60x13x24	154	160	300
125	72x18x22	111	NA	450
150	72x18x28	133	NA	450
180	72x24x24	120	NA	450
210	72x24x29	140	NA	600
35HX	23x20x24	128	90	100
60HX	27x24x28	130	160	150

MEASUREMENTS AND CONVERSIONS

Water

1 gallon of water weighs 8 pounds (lb) or 3.6 kilograms (kg)

1 cubic foot of water contains 7.5 gallons (gal) or 28.5 liters (L)

Liquid Measure

1 gal = 3.8 L = 4 quarts (qt) = 8 pints (pt) = 128 fluid ounces (fl oz) = 231 cubic inches (in^3)

1 L = 1000 milliliters (ml) = 1000 cubic centimeters (cc) = 1 kg = 2.2 lb

1 tablespoon = 3 teaspoons = 0.5 fl oz = 15 ml = 300 drops

1 cup (C) = 8 fl oz = 236.8 ml

Light Intensity

1 foot-candle (fc) = 1 lumen

1 lux = 1 lumen per square meter = 1 foot-candle per 10.76 square feet

Temperature Conversions

° Centigrade = (° Fahrenheit − 32) ÷1.8

° Fahrenheit = (° Centigrade × 1.8) + 32

Alkalinity Conversions

50 ppm $CaCO_3$ = 2.92 gr/gal $CaCO_3$ = 2.8 dKH = 1 meq/L

Abbreviations

ppm = parts per million

gr/gal = grains per gallon

dKH = degrees of German hardness

meq/L = milli-equivalents per liter

Water Hardness Designations

very soft = < 75 ppm $CaCO_3$

soft = 75–150 ppm $CaCO_3$

moderately hard = 150–225 ppm $CaCO_3$

hard = 225–350 ppm $CaCO_3$

very hard = > 350 ppm $CaCO_3$

RIVER MAPS

T his appendix shows you the river regions from which the aquarium designs originated.

Brazil

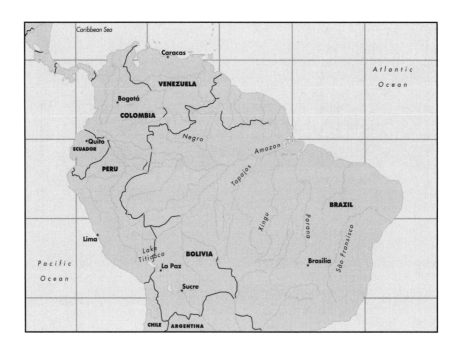

Cameroon

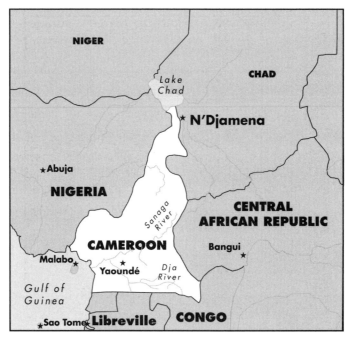

Central America

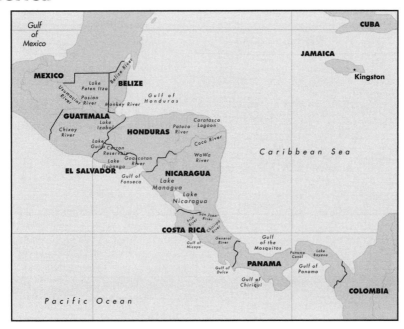

Democratic Republic of the Congo

Indonesia

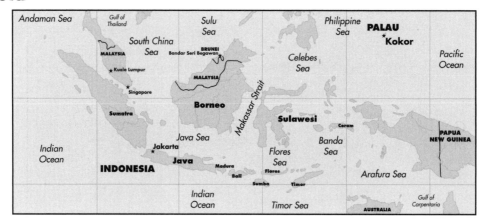

Mexico

Sri Lanka

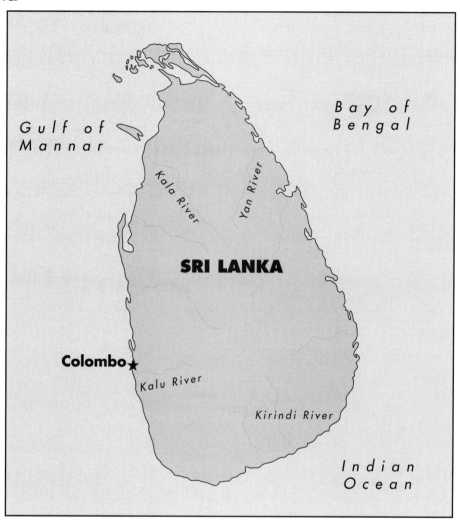

Tanzania

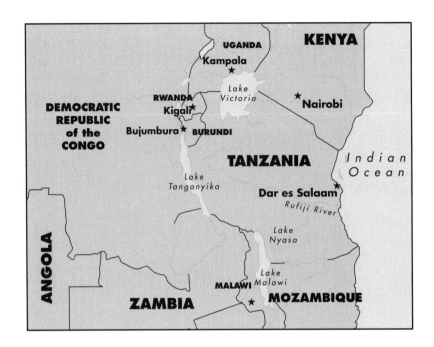

Thailand

United States

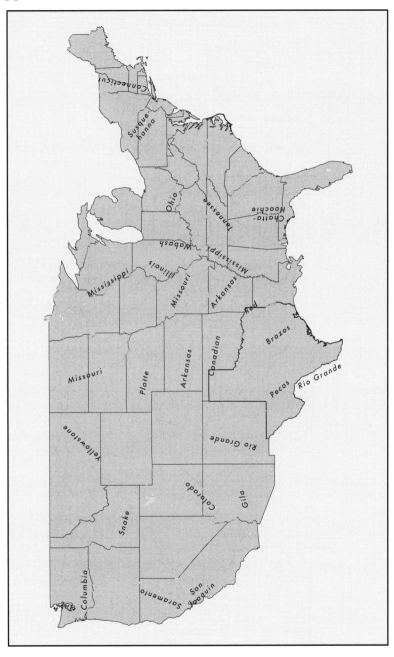

INDEX

D

daphnia (water fleas), 20–21
dead tree roots, aquascaping, 52
dealers
    background products, 47–49
    desirable traits, 33–35
    plant presentation, 34–35
    pricing considerations, 33
dechlorinators, water treatment, 9
deionization tank, 8
digital photography, backgrounds, 47–48
dioramas, background uses, 49
discus, soft/acidic water, 7
distilled water, hardness, 8
do-it-yourselfers, 5
driftwood, aquascaping, 51–52
dropsy, 70
dyed gravel, 51

E

earthworms, live food use, 19
Echinodorus tenellus, forced perspective, 55
ecological space, carrying capacity element, 11
electricity
    built-in aquariums, 58
    free-standing aquariums, 62
    GFCI (ground-fault circuit interrupters), 58, 62
Epsom salt, water hardness, 9
estuaries, model designs, 87–90
estuarine habitats, synthetic seawater mix, 9
Ethylenediaminetetraacetate (EDTA), chelated iron supplement, 15
euthanasia, debilitated fish, 70

F

farm ponds, southeast United States, 188–189
feces (stringy), 32
feeder goldfish, live foods, 18
feeder guppies, live foods, 18–19
fertilizer, aquatic plants, 15–17
fiber media, filters, 64
filters.
    built-in aquariums, 59–61
    canister, 63
    free-standing aquariums, 63–64
    hang-on, 63
    media changing guidelines, 22
    media types, 64
    throughput rates, 12
    undergravel, 64
    waste removal role, 10–11
    wet-dry systems, 59–61
filtration systems, recirculating pumps, 10–11
finishes
    built-in aquariums, 61
    free-standing aquariums, 65
fins, health indicators, 32–33
fish. *See* fish species lists; species
fish foods. *See also* foods
    feeder goldfish, 18
    feeder guppies, 18–19
    live foods, 18–21
    overfeeding cautions, 18
    selection guidelines, 17–21
    single ingredient versus compounds, 17
fish species lists
    genus names, 244–248
    locality, 222–227
    pH range, 238–243
    temperature, 227–232
    water hardness range, 232–238
floor loads
    built-in aquariums, 58–59
    free-standing aquariums, 63

Florida peninsula, flagfish, 192–193
fluidized beds, biofiltration, 11
fluorescent lighting, aquarium design, 13–14, 43–46
foods. *See also* fish foods
    diet-related problems, 71
    live foods, 18–21
    lungfish, 104
    selection guidelines, 17–21
    twice-daily feedings, 18
forced perspective, aquarium design technique, 54–55
free-standing aquariums
    cost estimates, 65
    electricity/water supply, 62
    filtration systems, 63–64
    finished surfaces, 65
    floor loads, 63
    lighting, 63
    maintenance, 64–65
fungal diseases, 70

G

gas exchange, design, 12–13
German degrees (dGH, or KH), 8
gills, health indicators, 32–33
glass tanks, cleaning, 22
grains per gallon (gr/gal $CaCO_3$), water hardness, 8
gravel, substrate use, 51
ground-fault circuit interrupters (GFCI), 58, 62
guppies, live food use, 18–19

H

habitat types, aquarium design, 28–29
hang-on filters, free-standing aquariums, 63